Fatherhood Politics in

the United States

Fatherhood Politics in the United States

MASCULINITY, SEXUALITY, RACE, AND MARRIAGE

Anna Gavanas

UNIVERSITY OF ILLINOIS PRESS

URBANA AND CHICAGO

Library of Congress Cataloging-in-Publication Data
Gavanas, Anna, 1971–
Fatherhood politics in the United States : masculinity, sexuality, race, and marriage / Anna Gavanas.
p. cm.
Includes bibliographical references and index.
ISBN 0-252-02884-8 (cloth : alk. paper)
1. Fatherhood—Social aspects—United States. 2. Masculinity—
United States. 3. Sex role—United States. 4. Marriage—United States.
5. Fatherhood Responsibility Movement. I. Title.
HQ756.G355   2004
306.874′2′0973—dc21   2003009667

I dedicate this book to the memory of my brother,
Christos Gavanas (1976–2001),
and to my partner in life,
Tan Nguyen

CONTENTS

PREFACE

Marriage and fatherhood are crucial in the current debates over welfare reform and family policy. Parenthood and "child well-being" are the ultimate holy grounds within these contestations, which revolve mainly around issues of masculinity and fatherhood. But why is the gendering of parenting activities, particularly the maleness of fatherhood, considered so important at this juncture of U.S. family politics?

In this book I explore the ways gender, race, and sexuality, as social and historical constructions, are strategically challenged and reproduced by those who have a stake in American family politics. During two years of fieldwork behind the scenes of the powerful fatherhood responsibility movement, I talked to national and local representatives and participated in fatherhood conferences, men's workshops, and the Promise Keepers' mass meetings (see the appendix for details on the interviewees and the methodology of the study). During this time, I spent a lot of time observing all-male group discussions. As I listened to the program participants talking about their everyday problems with such issues as unemployment, drug abuse, and relationships *as men,* I kept thinking of my own brother and father in Sweden, who struggled with similar issues. I am certainly aware that deconstructing notions of masculinity and fatherhood as defined by, for instance, work, marriage, and heterosexuality may not alleviate the very real structural and global problems of unemployment or racial, gendered, and sexual inequalities. However, by tracing and analyzing some of the processes, internal contestations, myths, and dilemmas of U.S. fatherhood politics, I hope to contribute to a more informed and productive approach to the current debate on marriage and the issues that family members face in contemporary societies.

By widening the discussion and analyzing the competing voices in fatherhood politics, I hope to benefit the often polarized and antagonistic discussions of gendered, sexual, and racial politics. I also seek to communicate with groups concerned with family policy, including representatives of the fatherhood responsibility movement. My aim is not only to understand and fairly portray participants' points of view but also to challenge the ideas expressed in fatherhood politics by putting them in historical and theoretical perspective. Whereas some readers might think that I am not sufficiently critical of various aspects of the fatherhood responsibility movement, some of its representatives may think that I am being too critical merely by situating their politics in certain contexts. For instance, by connecting marriage-oriented organizations to discussions on whiteness, I might situate pro-marriage representatives in discussions with which they do not wish to associate. Similarly, representatives of poor, low-income, and minority men may wish to disassociate themselves from debates over masculinist aspects within the civil rights movement, because they consider themselves gender egalitarian. Finally, representatives throughout the fatherhood responsibility movement may find sexual dimensions of fatherhood politics to be irrelevant and may object to any attempt to pin them down in terms of sexual perspectives. Even analyzing the fatherhood responsibility movement in terms of gender politics might cause some of its representatives to protest. Nevertheless, I sincerely hope that my discussions open up challenging and mutually fruitful dialogues and that my representations reflect the respect, complexity, and friendliness of the people I met in the field.

In this book I demonstrate some of the numerous ways in which fatherhood programs address issues of uttermost importance to biological men and families and help heterosexual fathers deal with daily struggles as breadwinners and nurturers. I also discuss the ways some of the notions of gendered, sexual, social, and moral order in U.S. fatherhood politics may reinforce oppressive relations among men, as well as between men and women. I do so by illuminating problems involved when participants in local fatherhood programs construct masculinity, fatherhood, and brotherhood as biologically "male" institutions, primarily to differentiate themselves from women and gay men. I thereby seek to demonstrate the widespread need for alternative masculinities and fatherhoods, highlighting the ways the "masculinization" of fatherhood builds on potentially oppressive patterns and contradictions in century-long political traditions. For example, in fatherhood programs, certain sports provide particularly popular metaphors and practices for constituting "male" versions of parenthood in terms of "coaching" or playing ball in exclusively male settings. One of the things I am trying to come to grips with in this book is how "male bonding" over "guy things" works in U.S. masculinity politics. For instance, sport, religion, "womanizing," and work are longstanding and overlapping "male" arenas for the contestation and mobilization of U.S. masculinity politics. In these arenas, as I demonstrate in chapter 4, men reshape and reconfirm "manhood" by competing and bonding with other men. In tracing the histories of such masculinizing arenas and the stakes involved, I discuss the contemporary gendering, racialization, and heterosexualization of parenthood and family.

My ethnographic study of contemporary fatherhood and marriage politics might be a particularly useful contribution to political, public, and academic debates. For instance, as I demonstrate in the concluding chapter, being a young female in the heterosexually oriented field of fatherhood politics provoked some revealing disclosures. Moreover, having grown up in Sweden has allowed me to discern aspects that might be hidden from view for many people who are more caught up in U.S. family politics. For instance, the prevalence of religion and sport in political rhetoric may be taken for granted by many people who grew up in the United States. To me, the legacy of religious and sport rhetoric combined with the symbolism of "family," marriage, and "child well-being" to make the fatherhood politics under study particularly "American." Since the founding of the nation, notions of "the family" and contestations over its definition have been at the heart of U.S. politics.

ACKNOWLEDGMENTS

First, I would like to express my deepest gratitude to Professor Don Kulick, whose brilliant advice and enduring support were crucial throughout the years of writing this book. My research is also greatly indebted to Professor Barbara Hobson, whose wonderful mentorship and friendship have enabled me develop ideas in a vibrant scholarly community.

I am also indebted to Professor Michael Kimmel, whose work on men and masculinities has been a great inspiration for my research. In addition, I am grateful for the helpful comments, outstanding work, and friendly support of Fanny Ambjörnsson, Mary Frances Berry, Melinda Chateauvert, Ulrika Dahl, Lena Gemzöe, John Gillis, Mark Graham, Anna Hasselström, Jeff Hearn, Sigrun Helmfrid, Tova Höjdestrand, Thais Machado-Borges, Lissa Nordin, Ann Orloff, and Lena Sawyer. At the early stages of this project, three anthropologists were wonderfully supportive, and I am forever grateful to them: Gunilla Bjeren, Jan Lindström, and George Saunders.

I would like to thank my editor, Joan Catapano, at the University of Illinois Press for her experienced support. I am also indebted to Jane Mohraz for her editorial work and to Professor Ralph LaRossa and a second anonymous reviewer for their insightful comments. I thank the Swedish Foundation for International Cooperation in Research and Higher Education (STINT) for the postdoctoral grant that enabled me to finalize this book.

I also thank the people I met in the fatherhood responsibility movement, who were generous and helpful in sharing their ideas and contacts with me. I particularly appreciate the friendship of the persons I call Bill, Bob, Joe, and Michael in the book.

I am deeply grateful to my close friends and family. My mother, Eva Pettersson, has always supported me in all kinds of crazy projects. My sister and closest friend, Elin Gavanas, has always been my ally. My father, Manolis Gavanas, is a great source of inspiration. My DJ mentor and friend Anna Öström is my ultimate kompis and coconspirator. Finally, I thank my dear childhood friends, who have always been there for me: Marion Jernråda, Liv Landell, and Sara Ljung.

Fatherhood Politics in

the United States

Fatherhood at the Nexus of U.S. Politics

One of today's most successful political movements claims to be situated "beyond" politics, particularly beyond gendered and sexual politics. Crucial actors in shaping and reframing U.S. debates on families belong to the fatherhood responsibility movement[1] (Mincy and Pouncy 1999, 83). This movement emerged in the 1990s as U.S. policy debates on single motherhood, "family breakdown," and "family values" shifted into a debate on fatherlessness, masculinities, and marriage. Under the banners of fatherhood and "child well-being," the fatherhood responsibility movement has developed bipartisan federal initiatives that foreground fatherlessness as "one of the greatest social evils of our generation" and "an engine driving our worst social problems" (Horn, Blankenhorn, and Pearlstein 1999, 169). The fatherhood responsibility movement contends that fathers have been marginalized in families and that parenting has been feminized by becoming synonymous with motherhood (Blankenhorn 1995, 13; Gore 1996). By carving out particularly "male" versions of parenting, the movement masculinizes fatherhood in response to social and economic changes that have affected men's positions in families. Based on two years of participant observation and interviews between 1996 and 1998 (see the appendix for details), this study looks behind the scenes of this powerful movement and analyzes its implications for racial, sexual, and gender relations. It also examines the political stakes, contestations, and strategies masked by "nonpolitical" rhetoric on "the family" and "child well-being."

There has been a surge of attention to fatherhood in the United States, and programs, research, and policy on fatherhood are growing and evolving rapidly. The fatherhood responsibility movement is a principal force behind this growth. It featured Vice President Al Gore's "Father to Father Initiative" in

1994; national, congressional, mayoral, and presidential task forces since 1997; and the Fathers Count Act of 1999 (H.R. 3073) and the Responsible Fatherhood Act of 2000 (H.R. 4671). These bills, which are still pending, would provide a tremendous boost to the fatherhood responsibility movement by awarding yearly sums of $25 million for media campaigns, $50 million for state and local organizations, and $35 million for the promotion of fatherhood (Hawkins 2000). The budget proposal for 2002 included $364 million in grants to promote marriage and responsible fatherhood (Leonard 2001). The fatherhood responsibility movement claims to have established a national consensus that the key to attacking most social ills—including the federal deficit—is fatherhood responsibility (Horn, Blankenhorn, and Pearlstein 1999). The movement has achieved such positive responses from politicians, funders, and the public that some of its leaders sometimes worry that they have become *too* popular and, as one of them put it, "as politically safe as apple pie."

Wade Horn, the former president of the National Fatherhood Initiative and one of the most prominent leaders in the fatherhood responsibility movement, was appointed the assistant secretary for children and families in the Department of Health and Human Services in 2001. Horn's appointment, recent fatherhood bills, and President George W. Bush's marriage initiative have met strong protests from feminist and civil rights groups, which fear that marriage-centered messages on fatherhood will further dismantle governmental assistance for poor, low-income, and unmarried fathers and mothers. For instance, the National Organization for Women (NOW) strongly opposed the Fathers Count Act of 1999, labeling the act "dangerous legislation" and claiming that it would undermine support for custodial parents, who in most cases are women. NOW fears that the act's pro-marriage message might endanger the financial possibilities for women to opt out of bad marriages, which indirectly may result in an increase of domestic violence rates (Rhodes 2000). NOW also claims that the Fathers Count Act might benefit fathers' rights groups seeking increased control over property, ex-wives, and children, which might undermine mothers' legal rights and protection in terms of custody, visitation, and financial assistance (Conolly 1999). Despite the alleged consensus around the importance of fathers, there are conflicting opinions about what constitutes the well-being of children and which policies would best benefit "the family." In this book I investigate the claims at stake in U.S. family politics.

Current contestations over fatherhood are conditioned by feminist politics, lesbian and gay civil rights claims, (white) women's increased labor force participation, as well as the related issue of the gendered division of household labor. Today's fatherhood politics constitutes a range of responses to changes in family formation, employment patterns, and the nature of work. The contemporary context for fatherhood politics is also affected by recent debates over marriage, sexual politics, child well-being, welfare, and single parent households (Marsiglio 1995; Donovan 1998; Stacey 1998). When groups in the fatherhood responsibility movement approach all these changes and issues, they reflect the asymmetric positions and stakes of different groups of men. In other words, the fatherhood responsibility movement displays a wide range of responses to the changing social, economic, and political conditions for fathers. Explicitly or implicitly, actors in fatherhood politics emphasize the perspectives of competing constituencies of men in asymmetric positions relative to one another, the state, and the labor market. To map out the different perspectives represented, I have clustered these groups into two wings of the fatherhood responsibility movement according to their racial, socioeconomic, and ideological approaches. I call one wing the *fragile-families wing,* representing low-income, poor, and minority men[2] and emphasizing equal opportunities for education and breadwinning. The term *fragile families* was coined by Ronald Mincy at the Ford Foundation's Strengthening Fragile Family Initiative, who defined it as "a family formed by out-of-wedlock birth(s) to disadvantaged parents" (Mincy and Pouncy 1999, 83). The other wing I call the *pro-marriage wing,* which promotes marriage as key to fatherhood responsibility for all types of men.

Clearly, there are serious rifts beneath the mobilization around "fatherhood responsibility." In public demonstrations, however, the fatherhood responsibility movement tries to avoid displaying divergences and strives to overcome barriers of income, race, and politics. In their "manifesto," *The Fatherhood Movement: A Call to Action,* leaders present an all-encompassing image by including men's organizations as diverse as fathers' rights groups, pro-marriage groups, therapeutic men's groups, and fatherhood programs for low-income minorities, as well as such faith-based grass-roots manifestations as the Promise Keepers and the Million Man March (Horn, Blankenhorn, and Pearlstein 1999). However, neither pro-feminist men's organizations nor gay men's organizations are generally considered part of the fatherhood responsibility movement. In the concluding chapter, I explain why many of the foundational ideas of the fatherhood responsibility movement run counter to the politics of pro-feminist and gay male activism.

One of my main purposes in this study is to investigate the gender politics of the fatherhood responsibility movement. I approach the fatherhood responsibility movement from the point of view of "masculinity politics," defined by the sociologist Robert Connell as "those mobilizations and struggles where the meaning of masculine gender is at issue, and, with it, men's position in gender relations. In such politics masculinity is made a principal theme, not taken for granted as background" (1995, 205). The meanings of fatherhoods and masculinities are contested by and within the fatherhood responsibility movement. However, there are also difficulties in defining the fatherhood responsibility movement in terms of masculinity politics, because most representatives[3] say that their goals and concerns are not specific to men but will benefit the interests of women and children as well. Representatives of the fatherhood responsibility movement seek to avoid controversy and achieve a wide political appeal by *not* positioning themselves in terms of gender politics. Most point out that they are primarily concerned with children. For strategic reasons, the fatherhood responsibility movement attempts to design and situate itself "beyond" politics, under the banner of child and family well-being. Nevertheless, the *pro-marriage* groups emphasize and promote gender difference in parenting, often according to sociobiological, biblical, or pop-Freudian notions. Marriage proponents often talk about the ways men and women are "wired" differently and have different innate "natures" and "behaviors" as parents. However, when asked to elaborate on these notions, they also acknowledge the impact of culture and change and thus demonstrate a "looser" essentialist approach. The sociologist Michael Schwalbe defines "loose essentialism" as "an assumption of an essential, internal difference, yet it is nonspecific or 'loose,' with regard to claims about how this difference will be manifested in personality and behavior" (1996, 64). In contrast to the pro-marriage groups that focus on gender difference, *fragile-families* groups, in their notions of gender and parental roles, tend to emphasize flexibility and similarities, although fragile-families representatives also often express loose essentialist ideas, especially when it comes to male sexuality. In fatherhood politics, intersecting gendered and sexual ideas are rhetorical tools in complex responses to feminist claims. For instance, pro-marriage representatives are opposed to what they see as a "radical" feminism designed to eradicate gendered parental difference and marginalize men. In contrast, fragile-families representatives sometimes claim to engage in "strategic dialogue" with what they call "women's groups."

The issue of marriage is key to U.S. debates on family formation and gender relations (Daniels 1998; Popenoe 1988, 1996; Stacey 1996). Gendered ideas of marriage and "marriageability" are central to the contestations between men who are in different structural positions to achieve the ideals of married fatherhood. Constructions of male-female relations also inform negotiations over whether men should be positioned as leaders or "team partners" of women in their families. As I demonstrate throughout this study, sexual dimensions are hidden but crucial to U.S. conflicts over marriage and gender relations. This study investigates the ways in which the competing gendered, racialized, and sexual politics of the fatherhood responsibility movement are mutually reinforcing and inseparable. Sexual politics in the fatherhood responsibility movement rarely refers to sexual orientations other than heterosexual. The movement articulates itself within the bounds of a firm heteronormativity, defined as constructions of normality, maturity, and naturalness that necessitate a heterosexual, monogamous, family-oriented lifestyle based on more or less essentialist notions of gendered and sexual difference and complementarity. When representatives of the fatherhood responsibility movement speak of the importance of marriage or "the two-parent family" to social order and child well-being, their point of reference and their goal are heterosexual families. It is thus not the legitimacy of marriage as a heterosexual institution that is discussed in the fatherhood responsibility movement. Rather, the fatherhood responsibility movement discusses how and to what extent marriage is still viable as a social norm. What is interesting here are the ways heteronormative perspectives are constituted and their implications for the legitimacy and legal, social, and economic conditions of a wide set of family forms and social groups. In this book, one of the things I argue is that the pro-marriage and fragile-families wings implicitly converge over heteronormative notions of masculinity. They do so by positing the control of perceived innate male heterosexuality at the center of fatherhood politics. Such sexual notions are connected with racialized notions in multiple ways in the fatherhood responsibility movement.

Participants in fatherhood politics have somewhat diverse perspectives on parenting and gender relations, but this study suggests that those in the fatherhood responsibility movement face the same dilemma when promoting the indispensability of fatherhood as a particularly "male" institution. In arguing that fathers are needed because of the specific and irreplaceable contribution of (biological) men to parenting, the fatherhood responsibility movement reinforces more or less essentialist notions of gender difference. Such loose essentialist notions of masculinity are tied to conceptions of male heterosexuality, which provide a common foundation to notions of parental difference in the movement. In other words, the binary notions of gender in fatherhood politics are inextricably linked to notions of heterosexuality and complementarity, which are reproduced in settings where "responsible fatherhood" is promoted. According to such gendered and sexualized notions of male parenting, men are defined by their difference from women based on conceptions of male sexual "promiscuity." However, men are ideally harnessed into "responsible fatherhood," heterosexual monogamy, and specifically "male" parental ideals. In mostly all-male settings, fatherhood organizations teach men how to assume and manage "male" familial responsibilities, such as role modeling and being a provider, disciplinarian, playmate, and nurturer to children. Fatherhood programs frequently encourage such notions of male family involvement by using "masculine" metaphors and practices as tools for fathers to bond over domestic matters. In an attempt at strategic alliance between different constituencies of men, the fatherhood responsibility movement uses unifying homosocial grounds, such as sport and religion, to masculinize fatherhood. Representatives feel that fatherhood needs to be masculinized because notions of parenting have become too feminized by policy and public discourse that equates parenthood with motherhood. Here, the fatherhood responsibility movement runs into a century-old paradox within U.S. fatherhood politics: *how do you masculinize domesticity and simultaneously domesticate masculinity?*

The Long History of the "New Father"

> [W]hile it may be gratifying for men in the late twentieth century to believe
> that they are the first generation to change a diaper or give the baby a bath,
> the simple truth is that they are not.
> —Ralph LaRossa, *The Modernization of Fatherhood*

The fatherhood responsibility movement uses a mixture of conceptions to define "responsible fatherhood," drawing on negotiations throughout U.S. history. For instance, notions of the modern "New Father," who, unlike the distant patriarch of the past, is involved in everyday parenting, draw on century-old white and middle-class conceptions of parenthood. Although recent notions of involved fatherhood might be marketed as "new," the defining characteristics and dilemmas of responsible fatherhood promotion can be traced back to the end of the nineteenth century. Religious conceptions of fathers as moral leaders, still represented by, for example, the Promise Keepers, a Christian men's organization, may be traced to colonial times. From the end of the nineteenth century, childrearing "experts" and policymakers have called for father involvement in response to shifting political, social, and economic conditions. Constructions of fatherhood have changed throughout U.S. history, but certain themes keep reemerging. The fatherhood responsibility movement's framings of fatherhood as an indispensably *male* parenting contribution echo late-nineteenth-century fatherhood discussions. At the end of the nineteenth century, "experts" and reformers, urged on by notions of domesticity as "feminine," sought to "masculinize" fatherhood.

Domesticity has not always been considered feminine. Prior to the twentieth century, family involvement was not necessarily considered contrary to "maleness"—quite the opposite. In the seventeenth and eighteenth centuries, fathers had important childrearing tasks: they were the primary custodians of children, and they were mainly responsible for their instruction and moral guidance (LaRossa 1997, 24; Gillis 1996, 186; Griswold 1993). According to the historian John Gillis (1996), fathers' relationships with their children were not only close but full-time in the seventeenth and eighteenth centuries. Protestant treatises at the time defined fatherhood as work (Gillis 1996, 186). Constructions of fatherhood in the seventeenth and eighteenth centuries were heavily influenced by Christian ideas that framed men as moral leaders of the family (LaRossa 1997, 25; Frank 1998, 9; Rotundo 1993). There were, however, denominational differences among Protestants, Puritans, Quakers, and Anglicans regarding ideal fathering styles (Frank 1998, 9). The biblical dominance in colonial fatherhood discourses increasingly competed and coexisted with naturalistic and "scientific" ones in the nineteenth century (Frank 1998, 6). However, the public presence and promotion of Christian framings of fatherhood ideals never disappeared from U.S. family politics despite the secularization of family and childrearing discourses (Frank 1998, 24). As I show in chapter 4, notions of fathers as moral leaders have recently reappeared in U.S. fatherhood politics. The Promise Keepers' promotion of male "servant leadership" in the 1990s is part of a long-standing religious rhetoric that occupies a significant position in contemporary fatherhood politics.

Domesticity and family involvement became associated with femininity in the nineteenth-century market economy. Industrial society demanded that middle-class fathering revolve around workplace schedules instead of preindustrial, home-based economic conditions, where fatherhood was part of everyday work (Frank 1998, 12; Griswold 1993, 2). "Marketplace masculinity" entailed defining fathers first and foremost as breadwinners. In the 1800s, when fathers' responsibilities became defined mainly by paid work, mothers became increasingly central to family life. They came to be viewed as the primary custodians of children (Griswold 1993, 30; Gillis 1996, 190; LaRossa 1997, 28). Everyday childrearing gradually became more a mother's responsibility than a father's (Frank 1998, 15; Rotundo 1993). To middle-class fathers, the home became a refuge from the cruel marketplace rather than their everyday work environment. In the 1800s, middle-class fathers were described as "Sunday fathers" and "fireside fathers," since fathering became part of men's recreation upon returning from their paid jobs and was defined in contrast to the everyday unpaid care-work of mothers (Frank 1998; Gillis 1996, 196).

In this context of early-nineteenth-century shifts in fatherhood politics, one can discern the roots of the contradictions at the heart of "new" involved fatherhood, where domesticity has female connotations and men are primarily defined as breadwinners in the family. The historian Stephen Frank (1998) describes the nineteenth-century shifts in fatherhood discourse toward "new" fatherhood in terms of "opposing tendencies." On the one hand, fathers withdrew from their homes into the marketplace, and, on the other hand, fathers were increasingly encouraged by "experts" and reformers to get more involved with their children (Frank 1998, 115; Griswold 1993, 120). In this context, one can identify the roots of contemporary efforts to "masculinize" domesticity and cast fathers as "playmates" and "role models" in complementary relation to mothers as primary caretakers.

"New" fatherhood of the early 1900s thus basically entailed occasionally assisting mothers after work. Subsequently, the "fun dads" of the early 1900s, who saw their children in the evenings and on weekends and holidays, were somewhat distant figures (Gillis 1996, 193). Since women had come to symbolize the home, male domesticity became problematic according to early-twentieth-century binary notions of gender. As John Gillis put it, "[T]oo intimate a relationship with one's children had become unmanly, likely to call into question not only a fellow's masculinity but also his maturity" (1996, 193). Carving out specifically "male" modes of domesticity, such as after-work "fun dads," allowed fathers to be involved in their families while still maintaining their ground as "real men."

The "frolicsome dad" epitomized nineteenth-century modernization of fatherly authority, tied to leisure, play, and companionship rather than moral leadership (LaRossa 1997; Frank 1998, 114). "Modern" fatherhood entailed less authoritarian notions of childrearing, in contrast to the patriarchal notions of the seventeenth and eighteenth centuries. Moreover, "modern" nineteenth-century constructions of white and middle-class masculinity were connected to notions of marriage and maturity (Frank 1998). "Companionate marriage" at the beginning of the twentieth century was characterized by ideals of romance, mutual respect, and democratic family relations. Within the context of marriage, male responsibilities were framed in terms of *husbands'* roles—as opposed to fathers' roles (Frank 1998, 39)—and the role of husband became the measure of manhood (Gillis 2000, 230). While "playmate" ideals of husbandry called for (white) middle-class men's involvement in family life, they also threatened to make men dispensable, since anyone can play with children. The historical sociologist Ralph LaRossa (1997) frames 1920s middle-class notions of fathers as "family men" and "pals" within a "culture of daddyhood" that simultaneously legitimized and diminished fathers' importance to families.

However, the "family man" as a white middle-class standard defined by breadwinning and recreation needs to be contrasted with the working-class man in the nineteenth century, whose family continued to see itself as a work unit (Frank 1998, 4). The low salaries of working-class men had to be combined with the incomes of their wives and children, and long working hours were not conducive for working-class fathers to spend leisure time with their families (Griswold 1993, 42). The conditions for nineteenth-century African American fathers and families were even worse (Frank 1998, 5). Slavery, segregation, racism, and discrimination profoundly restricted the possibilities for African American fathers throughout U.S. history, and they continue to affect African American fatherhood politics to this day. As this book demonstrates (see chapters 1 and 3), the specific histories of African American and other minority fatherhoods provide a foundation for fragile-families challenges to white and middle-class hegemony in work, education, and family politics.

The defining characteristics of "masculine domesticity" shifted between emphasizing role modeling and play and generally moved away from moral leadership throughout the 1900s, whereas breadwinning was the constant hallmark of fatherhood. "Parenting experts" in the 1950s framed fathers' specific "sex roles" as necessary for the good of children, family, and society and warned that mother-dominated socialization might have potentially feminizing effects (Weiss 2000, 85, 88–89). Accordingly, mid-twentieth-century parenting experts carved out "masculine" parenting characteristics (Weiss 2000, 89). "Discipline," "play," "role modeling," and "protection" were considered particularly male parenting characteristics, in complementary relation to notions of motherhood and femininity. However, too much participation in childcare threatened to feminize men by likening them to mothers, who were seen as primary caretakers (Weiss 2000, 91–92). As married (white and middle-class) women increasingly entered the labor force in the 1950s, household economy and the gendered division of breadwinning and parenting were transformed. The incomes of wives who worked before they had children became necessary for making down payments for homes and for financing husbands' educations (Weiss 2000). By the 1960s, economic conditions for breadwinning and caregiving *necessitated* involved fatherhood as middle-class men faced their female partners' careers and demands as well as their own shifting conditions for breadwinning (Griswold 1993, 254).

The historian Robert Griswold argues that fatherhood has never been as politicized as in post-1960s renegotiations of work and care, urged by the reemergence of feminism (1993, 220–21). However, questions remain about the ways and extent men's movements of the 1990s differ from their predecessors in their conceptions of parenthood. For example, as this study demonstrates, the fatherhood responsibility movement partly reinforces recurring efforts to masculinize fatherhood. Emphases on fathers as playmates, role models, and moral leaders still partly define fatherhood politics, negotiating the shifting social and economic conditions for men in work and family.

Fatherhood Politics across Contemporary Men's Movements

In the wake of second-wave feminism of the 1960s, there was a surge of men's movements. Fatherhood issues cut across a wide range of post-1960s men's groups: men's liberation, men's and fathers' rights, pro-feminist men, gay men's liberation, and men's therapeutic groups, as well as the Million Man March and the Promise Keepers (Collier 1996, 13). When the fatherhood responsibility movement entered the stage in the mid-1990s, it sought to encompass post-1960s men's groups. The fatherhood responsibility movement tries to bridge religious concerns about men's moral responsibilities, therapeutic concerns about men's "father wounds," civil rights concerns about equal opportunities for minority men, as well as legal concerns about men's participation in childrearing. However, the fatherhood responsibility movement collaborates with neither pro-feminist nor gay men's groups.

From Men's Liberation, through Men's Rights, to Fathers' Rights

Contemporary men's movements constitute themselves in relation to second-wave feminism one way or another, usually echoing century-old concerns about "feminization." In the early 1970s, "men's liberation" groups formed to discuss the implications of feminism. These groups marked the beginnings of three major movement traditions that eventually diverged into different directions: rights, therapy, and pro-feminist groups. Although both men's rights and pro-feminist men's groups pondered the shifting meanings, privileges, and burdens of masculinity, they had opposite approaches to gender relations. Simply put, both pro-feminist and men's rights advocates consider themselves "antisexist," but men's rights advocates view sexism as a symmetrical relation, while pro-feminist men view it as a patriarchal relation (Lingard and Douglas 1999, 36). Pro-feminist analyses focus on patriarchal gender relations and men's violence, while men's rights advocates focus on men's individual *powerlessness*.

Men's rights advocates locate women's power mainly in interpersonal relations as mothers and heterosexual partners. For instance, the leading men's rights advocate Warren Farrell claims in *The Myth of Male Power* (1993) that male employers are disempowered by their secretaries' "miniskirt power, cleavage power, and flirtation power" (quoted in Messner 1997, 44). Another common grievance among men's rights advocates is the harsh legal sanctions against men (as compared with women) for domestic abuse and sexual assault. Men's rights advocates often lament the "costs of masculinity," such as the demands of breadwinning and men's hazardous working conditions. All these cases of perceived discrimination make up the men's rights view that men are considered, by government and society, to be more expendable than women. Men's rights advocates feel that men are marginalized as parents, workers, and citizens while still obligated as family providers (Messner 1997, 39).

Fathers' rights organizations share many of the concerns of men's rights groups but focus on discrimination against men in divorce, child support, visitation, and custody legislation. One of the main functions of fathers' rights organizations is to lobby and provide a "legitimizing context" and "vocabulary of motives" for (primarily white and middle-class) men with personal divorce and custody problems (Bertoia and Drakich 1993). Most fathers' rights advocates are personally involved in postdivorce battles, making angry cases about the injustices suffered by men who are victimized by biased court systems and vindictive ex-wives. Some fathers' rights advocates even describe governmental collection of child support as robbery and rape (Bertoia and Drakich 1993, 606–7; Clatterbaugh 1997, 70).

In other words, fathers' and men's rights organizations assert that men are victims of legal, social, and psychological injustices (Clatterbaugh 1997, 69, Messner 1997, 44). There are, however, multiple approaches *within* these movements. For instance, there are men's rights groups promoting "gender reconciliation" (Clatterbaugh 1997), and fathers' rights advocates range from liberal to conservative (Williams and Williams 1995). Liberal fathers' rights advocates express support for most liberal feminist principles of shared carework and flexible parental relations. In contrast, conservative fathers' rights advocates approach "radical" feminism as the enemy and promote patriarchal notions of gender difference in parenting.

Appropriating feminist and civil rights rhetoric, men's and fathers' rights organizations frame their claims in terms of equality and rights. Despite their claims for victimhood, men's and fathers' rights advocates are usually white, middle-class, heterosexual men who tend to overlook their institutional and socioeconomic advantages in work and the family—both before and after divorce (Messner 1997, 47). Although they criticize fathers' obligations as economic providers, fathers' rights organizations rarely discuss the nonmonetary obligations of parenting. Fathers' rights organizations seek not sole custody but liberal access to children, but mothers are still expected to assume primary responsibility for everyday childcare (Bertoia and Drakich 1993, 600–601). Promoting joint custody in the name of gender equality does not necessarily entail equal division of caregiving (Messner 1997, 45).

The Mythopoetic Men's Movement and the Politics of the "Deep Masculine"

Like men's rights and pro-feminist groups, so called masculinity therapy or mythopoetic groups emerged out of men's liberation. The "mythopoetic men's movement" refers to spiritual and therapeutic groups that were popular among mainly white, middle-class, heterosexual, and middle-aged men in the 1980s and 1990s. Mythopoetic groups focus on men's "inner lives," partly in response to second-wave feminism (Lingard and Douglas 1999, 41). Not unlike those in the fatherhood responsibility movement, mythopoetic men maintain that a "father void" or a "father wound" is one of the most serious social problems of the day (Kimmel and Kaufman 1995, 23). Mythopoetic men frequently discuss their own fathers in terms of physical or emotional absence (Schwalbe 1996, 78) and seek to better themselves as men or fathers. Using Jungian methods, mythopoetics develop "positive masculine traits" by "activating" certain "masculine archetypes" and searching for their "deep masculine" selves (Schwalbe 1996, 55).

Unlike the organizations oriented to fathers' rights and fatherhood responsibility, the mythopoetic men's movement does not seek to impact public policy directly. Mythopoetics deploy a "nonpolitical" stance through a strategically anti-intellectualist focus on individual men's pain, anger, and emotional problems (Schwalbe 1996, 32). They do, however, engage in gender politics by promoting more or less essentialist notions of masculinity (Schwalbe 1996). The "gender angle" makes mythopoetic activity especially appealing to its participants, who get a chance to bond, legitimize, and redefine manhood while ignoring gendered and socioeconomic structure (Schwalbe 1996, 30; Clatterbaugh 1995, 59).

According to the sociologist Michael Schwalbe, mythopoetics remake "man" as a moral identity in response to what they see as feminist critiques of men as innately violent, competitive, aggressive, and emotionally inept (1996, 102). Feminist critics, mythopoetic leaders say, have made men feel ashamed of their innate "masculine energies" (Schwalbe 1996, 51). Feeling that their very being is attacked, mythopoetics interpret feminist critique as being aimed at the "natural" state of things instead of social and economic structures and institutions. Although mythopoetic leaders and participants commonly express support for liberal principles of gender equality, mythopoetic all-male gatherings partly reconfirm masculinist notions of manhood by appropriating historical and ethnic images of men as "warriors," "kings," and "conquerors" (Clatterbaugh 1995, 47; Kimmel, ed., 1995). For instance, drawing on such heroic images of the "deep masculine," mythopoetics may claim that it is okay for men to be a bit rough, tough, fierce, and assertive (Schwalbe 1996, 111). However, mythopoetic men also make a point of allowing themselves to be emotional, noncompetitive, and nurturing, which are traits they associate with nontraditionalist manhood (Schwalbe 1996, 25). Mythopoetics also question the traditional centrality of work in men's lives, which is another way in which these groups may appear to redefine traditional notions of manhood, although it is difficult to estimate the practical implications of these discussions.

The Promise Keepers and the Million Man March

The mythopoetic men's movement overlaps with the Promise Keepers on grounds of "spirituality." Bill McCartney, a former college football coach, founded the Promise Keepers in 1990. Since then, the organization has gone national (and even seeks to go global), operating through an elaborate leadership structure that stretches from local churches to the national level. Throughout the 1990s, local and regional Promise Keepers gatherings grew rapidly, and around 600,000 participants gathered in approximately twenty football stadium rallies per year (Longwood 1999, 3). The Promise Keepers' "Stand in the Gap" demonstration in Washington, D.C., on October 4, 1997, drew from half a million to a million men (Donovan 1998, 823). Since 1997, however, the Promise Keepers has faced economic setbacks, and meeting participation has waned (Longwood 1999, 3).

In all-male gatherings at football stadiums and in local churches, the Promise Keepers promotes "spiritual renewal" and "masculine leadership" as the moral (not political, social, or economic) antidote to a moral crisis it identifies as manifested in abortion, out-of-wedlock births, drugs, crime, and pornography (Clatterbaugh 1997, 184). The Promise Keepers often emphasizes that the social problems it identifies should be dealt with at a cultural/moral level instead of an economic/structural one. On moral, not secular political, grounds (but with gendered, sexual, social, and economic implications), the Promise Keepers seeks to reassert a hierarchy of authority that, in the words of the sociologist Michael Messner, "stretches from God the Father, to His Son, to the father of a family and finally, down to his wife and children" (1997, 32). The Promise Keepers construes this patriarchal rationale as nonpolitical. Since it does not directly address policy change and avoids confrontation with feminist critics, the Promise Keepers claims to be concerned with spiritual, not governmental, issues.

There is a significant discursive and collaborative overlap between the fatherhood responsibility movement and the Promise Keepers. In both movements, Christian ideas serve as a unifying rhetorical foundation across a wide range of constituencies involved in fatherhood politics, reflecting traditions that are a century old in men's movements (see chapter 4). The Promise Keepers' "struggle for men's souls" intersects with the "spiritual" aspects of the mythopoetics and the fatherhood responsibility movement (Kimmel 1998a). In addition, the discourse and practice of the Promise Keepers partly intersect with that of the African American religious men's mobilization in the Million Man March.

Lead by the Nation of Islam's Louis Farrakhan,[4] the Million Man March gathered over 800,000 African American men in Washington, D.C., on October 16, 1995. The Million Man March was supported by a broad African American religious foundation, including the Muslim community as well as different Christian organizations. There was, however, opposition from some African American Christian churches and leaders concerning Farrakhan's leadership (W. Nelson 1998, 252). Not unlike the Promise Keepers, the Million Man March crystallized contestations over gendered and sexual order. In his mission statement explaining the purpose of the march, Farrakhan urged African American men to become "responsible heads" of their families, just as the Promise Keepers had (quoted in Walton 1995, 19). However, the Million Man March framed notions of male responsibilities within a wider focus on racial, economic, and social justice and concentrated on African American communities.

Unlike the other "spiritual" men's movements (such as the Promise Keepers and the mythopoetics), the Million Man March *combines* spiritual and socioeconomic grievances in urging male financial and familial responsibilities. The march set out to disprove negative stereotypes about African American men and to encourage brotherhood, male responsibility, and economic empowerment in African American communities. Other minority-oriented groups in the fatherhood responsibility movement also draw on civil rights traditions, which were often framed in religious terms. However, abolitionist and civil rights movements were not mobilized as merely men's movements, although their claims were often framed in terms of "manhood." As this book demonstrates, the civil rights movement was a forerunner to the fragile-families wing of the fatherhood responsibility movement. Fragile-families organizations continue civil rights struggles for the equal opportunities of minority men. They sometimes do so in cooperation with women's organizations concerned with child support and domestic violence, partly challenging hegemonic models of manhood.

Pro-Feminist Men's Movement

Also challenging dominant notions of manhood, the contemporary pro-feminist men's movement emerged out of early 1970s men's liberation groups. Unlike men's and fathers' rights organizations, mythopoetic groups, and other largely white, middle-class, and heterosexual men's mobilizations, pro-feminist groups focus on gendered stratification. Pro-feminist men have mobilized in support of feminist politics since first-wave feminism (Kimmel 1992), mostly in academic and activist settings connected through loosely organized networks rather than a centralized movement (Collier 1995, 9). Pro-feminist men's organizations mobilize around such issues as rape, men's violence, and pornography, although the scale of the organizations and projects is small compared with, for instance, that of feminist or gay and lesbian movements (Connell 1995, 221).

By merely examining the power dimensions of masculinity *as men,* pro-feminist activists have had their manhood questioned. Pro-feminist men have been asked whether they are "real men," as opposed to "pussy-whipped wimps," or whether they are heterosexual, as opposed to homosexual (Kimmel 1998b, 66). Pro-feminist men resist masculinist ideas, practices, and structures and try to transgress certain gender binaries in their own lives and politics. In the words of the pro-feminist philosopher Tom Digby, "[T]o the extent that men as a group are to be dominant over women as a group, every (or almost every) person will have to be overdetermined as a member of one and only one of those groups, and the two groups will have to be understood as fundamentally oppositional to each other. . . . Within such a context, male feminists are both a problem and a puzzle. By opposing male dominance, they disrupt gender oppositionality, but also . . . in both their writings and their lives they have the potential to blur and muddle the gender binary itself" (1998, 2–3).

In critical dialogue with the other men's movements, pro-feminist scholars like Digby envision an alternative politics of gender and parenting in which masculinity and domesticity are not mutually exclusive. However, in aligning themselves with feminist struggles, pro-feminist men face dilemmas regarding *which* type of feminism to support. Some strands of pro-feminist thought have been critiqued for mirroring essentialist versions of feminist thought. By integrating feminist visions into daily life, pro-feminist activists also face difficulties combining macropolitical perspectives with individualist ones (Lingard and Douglas 1999, 40). Moreover, some pro-feminist activists have been criticized for expressing political pessimism by engaging in guilt-ridden discussions of the evils of white, heterosexual, and middle-class masculinity (Collier 1995, 20). Other pro-feminist groups (as well as radical feminist thought) are critiqued from lesbian and gay perspectives for a reductionist "privileging of gender," at the expense of focusing on sexual oppression (Messner 1997, 84). While pro-feminist groups do protest homophobia and appeal to the concerns of gay and bisexual constituencies, their politics differ from gay men's politics.

Gay Male Liberation

On Friday, June 27, 1969, the patrons of a Manhattan gay bar called Stonewall Inn resisted a police raid, which grew into a weekend of riots by homosexuals proclaiming gay power in the streets of Greenwich Village. The New York Stonewall riots set off the gay liberation movement (Clatterbaugh 1997, 137). On the one hand, gay liberation came out of the "homophile movement" of the 1940s and the early 1960s, and, on the other hand, gay and lesbian liberation movements were influenced by radical civil rights and feminist movements (Messner 1997, 80). Gay liberation was partly a response to attacks on gay and lesbian groups by the religious Right (Messner 1997, 82) and partly overlapped with radical feminist (as well as pro-feminist) struggles to end gendered and sexual oppression (Clatterbaugh 1997, 140). Early gay liberation consisted of mainly white and middle-class men concerned with decriminalizing and depathologizing homosexuality, fighting homophobia, and protesting violence, discrimination, and oppression in, for instance, the workplace and family law. Like feminists, gay liberationists named heterosexual men, patriarchy, the nuclear family, and heterosexism as sources of oppression (Connell 1995, 217). Gay liberation thus mobilized around some of the same concerns of pro-feminist men: violence, male privilege, fatherhood, and homophobia. By integrating the struggle against sexual oppression and the struggles against gendered oppression, gay liberation both challenged and reinforced feminist perspectives.

As gay politics has reconfigured into various coalitions and institutions since the 1970s, alliances with feminists weakened. For instance, tensions between gay male liberationists and (radical and lesbian) feminists crystallized during the 1980s pornography debates. In the 1980s "sex wars," gay male liberationists tended to view pornography in terms of sexual liberation, whereas radical feminists tended to view it in terms of gendered oppression and violence against women (Messner 1997, 84). On the one hand, as Kenneth Clatterbaugh points out, gay male liberationists challenged the radical feminist and pro-feminist "assumption that *all* masculinity is created and maintained by male sexual power over women" (1997, 143). On the other hand, gay male liberation has been framed as masculinist by feminist critics because it deemphasized the gendered dimensions of sexual politics. For instance, in the words of Michael Messner, "despite the potential of gay liberation to strip off the masks of masculinity, it appears that the dominant tendency in gay culture eventually became an attempt to claim, eroticize, and display the dominant symbols of hegemonic masculinity" (1997, 83). In this view, struggles for gay male liberation may be reduced to sexual liberation while ignoring gendered and racial struggles, just as the struggles for the liberation of African American men may be reduced to racial liberation while ignoring gendered and sexual stratification (Messner 1997).

Reshaping Masculinity Politics

Early-twentieth-century authors feared that woman suffrage might turn men into effeminate housewives while women gained more political and economic power. Just as the "new" involved fatherhood of the early 1900s was ridiculed as "maternal fatherhood" (LaRossa 1997, 86–87), "Mr. Moms" are ridiculed in the fatherhood responsibility movement almost a century later. Since male domesticity was not always considered feminine, male family involvement did not become a contradiction or a "problem" until the end of the nineteenth century. In conjunction with industrialization, white middle-class fatherhood became defined by breadwinning in the marketplace, in binary opposition to the everyday unpaid care-work of mothers. At the end of the 1900s, the fatherhood responsibility movement reinvigorated the century-old dilemmas of masculine domesticity by calling for specifically male notions of father involvement in the face of the perceived feminization of the family brought about by women's increasing centrality to childrearing. In encompassing post-1960s men's movements' competing concerns for the legal, religious, and therapeutic aspects of fatherhood, as well as minority men's concerns for civil rights and equal labor market opportunities, the fatherhood responsibility movement reshapes the terrain of masculinity politics.

There are competing and contradictory tendencies within post-1960s legal and therapeutic movements as they reframe their claims in response to the shifting political terrains of gender and family politics. On the one hand, the fathers' rights and mythopoetic men's movements mobilize around men's individual feelings of powerlessness, anxiety, and anger (Collier 1996, 41). On the other hand, those in men's rights groups and mythopoetic men perceive their "discriminated" status *relative* to their own previous positions, instead of comparing themselves with more disadvantaged groups.

The gendered marginalization, discrimination, and feminization of men seem to be the most common rallying calls for post-1960s men's movements.

However, there are also alternative men's mobilizations, such as pro-feminist and gay men's movements as well as minority men who mobilize against racial discrimination. When the fatherhood responsibility movement emerged at the end of the 1900s, it strategically absorbed a wide range of earlier men's movements' concerns and reframed these in politically centrist terms of family- and child well-being. By the end of the 1990s, all the men's movements except the fatherhood responsibility movement had declined sharply in activity and attendance levels (Clatterbaugh 2000, 890). According to Kenneth Clatterbaugh, the pro-feminist movement has been weakened by the institutionalization of feminism itself and by sectarian battles. Likewise, the alliances between gay politics and feminist politics have weakened since the 1970s and reconfigured into various coalitions and institutions ranging from assimilationist to queer.[5] Men's and fathers' rights groups have been weakened by different organizations' diverging agendas. The mythopoetics, Clatterbaugh says, "had no place to go," because they had no larger visions beyond occasional gatherings, which goes for the Promise Keepers as well (2000, 890–91). In sum, according to Clatterbaugh, "none of the men's movements has been successful in addressing the wide spectrum of men in U.S. society" (2000, 892). In contrast, the fatherhood responsibility movement has become exceptionally successful by constituting a wide strategic alliance of diverging constituencies of men. By successfully framing itself in terms of "nonpolitical" concerns for child well-being and avoiding civil rights, gay/lesbian, and feminist critique, the fatherhood responsibility movement gained increasing political resonance at the beginning of the twenty-first century.

Notes

1. The fatherhood responsibility movement is sometimes just called the fatherhood movement or "the field of fatherhood promotion." I use the label *fatherhood responsibility movement* to make clear that my study focuses on fatherhood responsibility, not the concerns of other contemporary men's movements, such as the fathers' rights movement.

2. African American men were the primary focus in the fragile-families organizations in my study. During my fieldwork, African American men were the most frequently discussed specific group of men among fragile-families interviewees, and almost all of the interviewees and participants I encountered in the fragile-families wing were African American, except at the conferences I attended in Los Angeles and San Francisco, which were more racially mixed and discussed a wider range of racial/ethnic issues.

3. I use the word *representative* (rather than *interviewee* or *informant*) to refer to the people I interview and quote from the fatherhood responsibility movement.

4. In their issue on the Nation of Islam (Fall–Winter 1996), the editors of the *Black Scholar* describe the organization as follows: "Founded in 1930, the Nation of Islam

(NOI) at the outset seemed little different from any number of small, African American religious organizations. . . . However, by the 1960s the Nation, with its tens of thousands of members, had become a force to be reckoned with in African American life. Offering an alternative vision to that presented by established civil rights organizations, the NOI called for separation instead of integration, militant self-defense in contrast to passive resistance, and the embrace of Islam as opposed to Christianity" ("The Nation of Islam" 1996, n.p.).

5. Queer activism, which emerged out of feminism as well as gay, lesbian, bisexual, and transgendered activism in the 1990s, rejects essentialist gendered and sexual identifications as foundations for its opposition to heteronormative assimilation.

The Contested Terrain
of U.S. Fatherhood Politics

Mapping Out the Field of Fatherhood Politics

Uniting around "the family" and child well-being fits into mainstream values that any U.S. citizen could support. Who could say that responsible fatherhood is a bad idea? Who is going to disagree if someone says that everybody should love his or her children? On the surface, the fatherhood responsibility movement appears to unite around and resonate with a national political consensus. However, the internal divisions in the fatherhood responsibility movement illustrate how the banner of children and family masks opposing claims, grievances, and stakes. Fatherhood politics and family policy can be compared to a minefield where political agents divided by race and socioeconomic class are setting off highly charged social, economic, and moral bombshells.

The fatherhood responsibility movement constitutes a strategic alliance of competing constituencies of men that build on diverging social movement traditions. Nevertheless, the fatherhood responsibility movement fits into most criteria for what sociologists call a social movement: it is centrally coordinated, has official leaders, proselytizes for new members (although there is no official status for "membership" except for organizational affiliations), and is aimed at changing public policy (Schwalbe 1996, 5). However, it lacks two common criteria: the participants do not share a common identity (other than as biological and heterosexual men), and they do not share a common enemy, although Wade Horn, who was then the president of the National Fatherhood Initiative, named "family relativism" as a common enemy (1999, 13). For sim-

plicity's sake, since this study is not primarily concerned with social movement theory, I label the fatherhood responsibility movement a *movement* (for
discussion, see Mincy and Pouncy 2002). Whether the fatherhood politics I
investigate fits neatly into a movement label is less interesting in this context.
In this book, I am more interested in the ways the actors of the fatherhood responsibility movement represent themselves, what they seek to accomplish,
and the ideas, practices, and strategies they employ to these ends.

To conceive of the fatherhood responsibility movement is a very complex
task. First, one is talking about different levels (local, state, federal) and organizations dealing with different aspects (coordination, training, policymaking, research, "hands on" work with fathers) and different societal sectors
(employment, faith communities, health care, education, recreation, the juridical system). Second, even though the organizations in the fatherhood responsibility movement have several common interests, they often deal with
separate issues. There are injustices and concerns that some organizations
bring up and others do not, because the men or fathers they represent simply
do not face the same problems in their lives. Despite these problems and com-
plexities, this study approaches the fatherhood responsibility movement in
terms of a movement within the field (which is another term that representatives frequently use to conceive of themselves) of strategic alliances mainly between pro-marriage and fragile-families groups. These fatherhood organizations have a mutual interest in the growth of the field of fatherhood politics
through increased political and public attention, a competing interest in public and private funding, and a common interest in increasing local activity
around fatherhood responsibility issues. Because of these common interests,
fatherhood organizations come together and call themselves a movement in
different political and public campaigns.

Unlike earlier studies (Coltrane 2001; Daniels 1998; Silverstein and Auerbach 1999; Stacey 1996), which focus mostly on the vocal and politically visible marriage proponents in the fatherhood responsibility movement,[1] this
study examines both fragile-families and pro-marriage groups in the fatherhood responsibility movement. Within the fragile-families wing, I focus on
the significant national groups, such as the National Center for Strategic
Nonprofit Planning and Community Leadership, the National Practitioners
Network for Fathers and Families, and the Center on Fathers, Families, and
Public Policy. I also talked with representatives from other well-known fragile-families organizations, such as the Fatherhood Project,[2] and numerous
local programs, such as the Baltimore City Healthy Start Men's Services. Within the pro-marriage wing, I have talked with members of the highly influential National Fatherhood Initiative, the Institute for Responsible Fatherhood

and Family Revitalization, the National Center for Fathering, and the Institute for American Values. These fragile-families and pro-marriage organizations compete for funding from governmental and private foundations.

The National Center for Strategic Nonprofit Planning and Community Leadership (NPCL) was founded in 1996 to help low-income (single) fathers and fragile families. Headed by Dr. Jeffrey Johnson, the organization is funded by the U.S. Department of Labor, the Department of Health and Human Services (DHHS), as well as such private foundations as the Ford Foundation, the Mott Foundation, the Lilly Endowment, and the Hewlett Foundation. The NPCL is part of the Ford Foundation's Strengthening Fragile Families Initiative, headed by Dr. Ronald Mincy, and also coordinates government funds. According to its annual report, the NPCL disbursed over $2 million in grants to community-based organizations and child support enforcement agencies in 1998. In 2000, the NPCL had a budget of $5,148,939. The NPCL runs local demonstration programs and provides training for nonprofit organizations and practitioners working with fragile families. For instance, together with the Ford Foundation, the NPCL has worked with the demonstration project Partners for Fragile Families (PFF) since 1996. One of the objectives of the PFF is to encourage collaboration between community-based organizations and child support enforcement agencies at the federal, state, and local levels to help "dead broke" fathers (Mincy and Pouncy 2002, 567). In collaboration with the Department of Labor, the Department of Health and Human Services, the Mott Foundation, and several other foundations, the PFF had a $20 million budget in 1996 to encourage parents to establish legal paternity and find jobs (Mincy and Pouncy 2002, 567).

The National Practitioners Network for Fathers and Families (NPNFF), founded in 1995, is a member-driven nonprofit organization that collaborates with the NPCL. The NPNFF provides support for fathers and fragile families, organizes conferences, and mobilizes practitioners, funders, researchers, and policymakers to advocate for policy reform. It is funded by the Funders Collaboration on Fathers and Families, which consists of the Ford, Casey, Mott, and Danforth foundations. The Casey Foundation was one of the most significant grant-givers for programs in the fatherhood responsibility movement at the time of my fieldwork. The NPNFF had a budget of $657,199 in 2001.

The Center on Fathers, Families, and Public Policy (CFFPP) was established in 1995 primarily to provide policy research and advocacy for fragile families. The CFFPP receives most of its funding from the Ford Foundation, but it also gets funds from the Mott, Hewlett, and public welfare foundations. The CFFPP had a budget of $250,262 in 2002.

The pro-marriage National Fatherhood Initiative (NFI), founded in 1994 by Dr. Wade Horn and Don Eberly, has been highly visible through its media and political campaigns and has been instrumental in forming fatherhood initiatives and propositions at all political levels as well as national conferences involving a wide range of social sectors. The NFI had roughly a $1 million budget in 1998 from such private foundations as Casey and Coca-Cola; only approximately $90,600 of this budget was government grants. In 2000, the NFI had a budget of $1,697,008 and in 2001, $2,735,805.

The pro-marriage Institute for Responsible Fatherhood and Family Revitalization (IRFFR) was founded by Charles Ballard in 1982 in Cleveland, Ohio, and moved to Washington, D.C., in 1994. The IRFFR is a unique pro-marriage organization in that it works with fragile families and sends married couples into low-income communities with the mission of living there as role models. Its 1998 annual report stated that it had a budget of roughly $2.4 million. It had grown to $4,327,190 by 2000 and $5,108,287 in 2001.

The National Center for Fathering (NCF), founded by Ken Canfield in 1990, develops research on fatherhood, provides resources and training for fathers, and publishes *Today's Father* magazine. The NCF works with corporations, schools, courts, and faith-based institutions to encourage father involvement. In 1998, the organization received about $1.3 million from the Casey Foundation, Bank of America, and other private foundations and corporations. The NCF has a budget of $1,600,757 in 2000 and $1,593,902 in 2001.

David Blankenhorn, who is also a cofounder of the NFI, founded the pro-marriage Institute for American Values in 1987. According to its mission statement, the organization is concerned with "the breakdown of family structure" and the "decline in child well-being" in the United States. Although the organization is not strictly concerned with fatherhood issues, it is the pro-marriage wing's major source of research. The organization received approximately $900,000 in 1998 from private foundations, corporations, and individuals. In 2002, its budget was $1,051.297.

The fragile-families groups are mainly concerned with low-income and poor unmarried African American and other minority fathers and their "fragile families." Fragile-families organizations focus on men who are unemployed or unskilled, low-paid workers and never- married, noncustodial social or biological fathers. Fragile-families organizations work closely with the Office of Child Support Enforcement and the Department of Health and Human Services. Many are funded by the Ford Foundation, which is generally considered liberal in the field of fatherhood politics. Unlike marriage proponents who focus on political and public campaigns, fragile-families representatives are more concerned with working directly with fathers. In the words of one leading fragile-families representative, "[W]e're kind of getting our hands dirty working with the guys."[3] In their work with noncustodial fathers, the fragile-families organizations promote "team parenting" so that children can have both biological parents in their lives, with marriage as an optional goal—not a priority. The team parenting concept was developed by the National Practitioners Network for Fathers and Families and refers to unmarried fragile families in which biological mothers and fathers raise and support their children regardless of whether the parents are "romantically involved" or living in the same household (Mincy and Pouncy 1999).

Fragile-families representatives approach the problems of fatherhood from the perspectives of low-income/poor African American men and other minorities, and they frequently highlight racism. Unlike marriage proponents, fragile-families representatives do not emphasize the gendered differences between men and women. Instead, fragile-families organizations construct masculinity politics in terms of the racial and socioeconomic differences among men. Most fragile-families representatives are African American or from other minorities and identify primarily with the men they represent. In other words, fragile-families organizations do not focus on the concerns of middle- and upper-class white men and fathers. In interviews, representatives often bring up problems they identify in low-income and poor minority communities, such as unemployment, poverty, out-of-wedlock births, disconnection, and "angry young men" driven to the streets and fathers "driven underground" by "the system." Some representatives also touch on a lack of recognition of, and understanding for, responsible but poor fathers, the constraints and concerns of "nontraditional" fragile families, and the negative impact of stereotypes about minority men and fathers. Like the marriage proponents, fragile-families representatives also point out that the government's view of men and fathers is restricted to the role of a breadwinner. The fragile-families representatives I interviewed also complained that men have not had access to public benefits and parenting programs because of the women-directedness of family policy.[4]

Pro-marriage groups concentrate on moral obligations and cultural values, promoting marriage as central to the "culture of fatherhood." These groups maintain that men need to be (good) husbands in order to be good fathers. Organizations in the pro-marriage wing approach men primarily as custodial and biological fathers and preferably as husbands. They explicitly talk about all kinds of fathers, but they do not usually focus on government programs for low-income, poor, or minority men and fathers. At the time of my fieldwork, most leading marriage proponents were white, although they rarely positioned themselves in terms of racial politics. Marriage proponents generally approach fatherhood politics from a general and nonstructural viewpoint and do not focus on the gendered, sexual, and racial power relations that traditionally have benefited white middle-class men in the United States (Schwalbe 1996). Marriage proponents try to involve all social sectors (education, business, civic, faith-based, private social service, public policy, media, and philanthropy) in a politically broad-based mass movement. The National Fatherhood Initiative started bipartisan congressional, gubernatorial, and mayoral task forces. It also helps run state-based initiatives and is closely connected with political leaders and legislators. In 2001, two of its leaders, Wade Horn and Don Eberly, obtained high positions in the Bush administration. National Fatherhood Initiative works closely with its cofounders David Blankenhorn from the Institute for American Values and David Popenoe at the Rutgers University–based National Marriage Project. Together with other pro-marriage leaders, these men are also instrumental in the self-proclaimed "marriage movement," which seeks to put marriage at the center of the national agenda as a "natural progression" of the fatherhood responsibility movement. Although individuals like Blankenhorn and Popenoe may prefer other labels, they and their organizations are generally considered conservative in the fatherhood responsibility movement. In addition, their organizations are funded mostly by foundations that are considered fairly conservative by feminist critics and fragile-families representatives.

A common grievance among representatives from pro-marriage groups is a lack of recognition of men's unique and irreplaceable contributions as fathers and of fathers' roles other than as breadwinners. Other common concerns are divorce, out-of-wedlock childbearing, and the "de-culturation" of marriage. Most pro-marriage groups link the "decline of fatherhood" to changing gender roles advocated by feminists and liberals. Marriage proponents often point to a current "confusion" about men's roles, which they consider extremely harmful to society because the blurring of roles feminizes men and makes fathers seem superfluous. To counter this, marriage proponents stress conceptions of gendered and sexual *difference* between women and men. Pro-marriage leaders translate such differences to complementary and indispensable differences in mothers' and fathers' roles and "natures."

Of central strategic significance to the fatherhood responsibility movement are the many churches and religious/spiritual organizations and leaders working with fathers, families, and communities. All-male religious grassroots manifestations, such as the Promise Keepers and the Million Man March, are an integral part of fatherhood politics. They are considered components of the fatherhood responsibility movement by its leading representatives (Horn, Blankenhorn, and Pearlstein 1999; Mincy and Pouncy 2002), and they are therefore approached as part of fatherhood politics in this study. As I demonstrate throughout this study, the fatherhood responsibility movement partially overlaps with the Million Man March and the Promise Keepers in their messages about male responsibility, leadership, and role modeling. Some fatherhood conferences, organized primarily by pro-marriage organizations, feature Promise Keepers speakers. Religious/spiritual leaders and organizations are often represented at workshops and conferences organized by both the pro-marriage and the fragile-families wings. Spiritual discourses and (in most cases Christian) rhetoric permeate the fatherhood responsibility movement at all levels—from national public manifestations to the everyday work of local programs. Working with "the faith-based community" is thought to be of particular importance to social and political mobilization in African American communities and key to affecting those communities (Hill 1993, 1997; Billingsley 1992). For the pro-marriage wing, churches are vital in promoting moral messages about responsibility and lifelong monogamous marriages. The biblical or "spiritual" foundations for masculinity are common grounds for the two wings of the fatherhood responsibility movement.

The fatherhood responsibility movement can be contrasted with fathers' rights groups. Fathers' rights organizations declare "radical feminists" to be the enemy more openly than do marriage proponents, and they speak against feminist, in the words of one of their representatives, "gender terrorism." To get an overview of fatherhood politics, I interviewed a few representatives from the national fathers' rights organizations, such as the American Fathers Coalition and Fathers United. However, although fathers' rights groups participate to some extent in conferences within the fatherhood responsibility movement, they are marginal to the public campaigns and social programs of the movement. At least at the time of my fieldwork, pro-marriage and fragile-families representatives alike differentiate themselves from the fathers' rights movement. Neither pro-marriage nor fragile-families groups explicitly express antifeminist agendas, and they therefore try to distinguish themselves from fathers' rights groups even though these groups are considered part of the movement. The fatherhood responsibility movement does share fathers' rights groups' desire to remove barriers to fathers' involvement in the child support system.[5]

The fatherhood responsibility movement can also be contrasted with the pro-feminist men's movement. Pro-feminist men's organizations seek to subvert essentialist, sexist, and homophobic notions of gender, sexuality, and parenting. I interviewed a few representatives from pro-feminist men's organizations to contextualize the fatherhood responsibility movement within a wider field of masculinity politics. One of these pro-feminist men's groups, the National Organization for Men against Sexism (NOMAS), born under the name Men and Masculinity in the 1970s, focuses on such issues as rape, sexism, and homophobia (Messner 1997). NOMAS constitutes the largest contemporary U.S. organization for pro-feminist men (Clatterbaugh 1997). In the conclusion, I elaborate on the differences between the fatherhood responsibility movement and the pro-feminist men's movement.

Commonalities and Lines of Controversy

There are a number of mainstream political concerns shared by the pro-marriage and the fragile-families wings of the fatherhood responsibility movement: (1) a concern with child well-being, (2) a view of the family as foundational to society, (3) an attribution of importance to fathers and a link between "father absence" and "social ills" (although the perceived causes, consequences, and fixedness of that link differ among representatives), (4) an agenda to redefine the role of fathers in family, labor market, and government policy from being solely financial providers to being emotionally involved, nurturing mentors as well. Furthermore, as I argue in the last three chapters of this book, the fatherhood responsibility movement unites around strategies to make fatherhood "male" in complementary and opposite relation to motherhood. To this end, fatherhood programs draw on century-old traditions and contestations in "male" arenas, such as sport.

The fatherhood responsibility movement constitutes a multidimensional response to changing patterns of family formation as well as gendered and sexual practices. As mentioned in the introduction, one of the most significant changes affecting the conditions of fatherhood is (white) women's increased participation in the labor force. In 1950, only 23 percent of married white women with children under six were employed; by the mid-1980s, 70 percent of this category of women were working for wages (Griswold 1993, 222). Nineteenth-century notions of fatherhood have been challenged by transformations in the industrial economy and employment, by women's earning power and economic autonomy, and by cohabitation, divorce, and same-sex family formation (Williams 1998). The fatherhood responsibility movement proclaims a "fatherhood crisis," but one should not forget that the "fatherhood crisis" and crises over marriage and the family are recurring themes in U.S. politics (Coltrane 2001, 391; Gillis 2000; Lasch 1977, 8; Schneider and Smith 1978).

Since the nineteenth century, "the family"—its definition and viability—has been a crucial concern in U.S. political and academic discourses (Schneider and Smith 1978). Crystallizing deeper contestations and power struggles along the lines of race, socioeconomic class, gender, and sexuality, the 1960s "family wars" (Berger and Berger 1983) focused on African American female-headed families (Rainwater and Yancey 1967), whereas the 1980s debates focused on the "illegitimacy" of "voluntary single motherhood" (Popenoe 1988). The family has become the point at which gender, sexuality, and racial stratification intersect and the point at which the state may legitimately move to influence phenomena framed as "social problems" (Berger and Berger 1983; Hunter 1991; Rainwater and Yancey 1967). Racial contestation has always played an integral part in U.S. family policymaking. Policymakers have a long history of associating African American men with family breakdown and absent fatherhood and perpetuating racist images of young African American men as "dangerous," "promiscuous," and unmarriageable (Collier 1996; Marsiglio 1995). "Family pathology" and "juvenile delinquency," especially among African Americans, were national public policy concerns in the 1950s and 1960s. Since the 1960s, there has been an ongoing academic discussion about African American men and families (Billingsley 1992; Hannerz 1969; Hill 1993, 1997). In 1965, Daniel Patrick Moynihan, then assistant secretary of the Department of Labor, published a report entitled *The Negro Family: The Case for National Action,* which became the focus of a highly charged national debate. The Moynihan Report, as it came to be known, warned of the disastrous consequences of "family breakdown" and the "tangle of pathology" Moynihan had found in African American communities. These consequences included notions that reemerge in today's discussions around fatherhood: father absence, "illegitimacy," female-headed families, welfare dependency, crime, low school performance, and violence (Rainwater and Yancey 1967). "Broken homes," working mothers, and "erratic" or "effeminate" fathers were assumed to accompany poverty among African Americans (Ehrenreich 1989: 23). Spokespersons for African American constituencies criticized the Moynihan Report for "blaming the victim" (Stacey 1996, 5; Majors and Gordon 1994). Ironically, the report was part of a governmental strategy to deal with the increasing civil rights demands for racial justice, which involved abolishing not only legal racism but also labor market discrimination (Rainwater and Yancey 1967). In the discussions that followed the report, African American men's unequal economic conditions were connected to their marginal positions in families (Hannerz 1969; E. Anderson 1978). Although the political context is different today, racial and socioeconomic injustices are still central issues to fragile-families representatives.

In public campaigns, representatives of the fatherhood responsibility movement present their concern for fatherhood responsibility, child well-being, and the family as politically neutral and "beyond ideology" (Horn, Blankenhorn, and Pearlstein 1999). When analyzing such rhetoric, one should keep in mind that U.S. politics has seen a variety of agendas under the banner of family and children (Gillis 1996; Stacey 1996). In the 1960s, concern about "family breakdown" masked a variety of political agendas. Symbolizing values of care, nurturance, and altruism in the 1970s and the 1980s, the family was conjured up as a fortress against cynicism, individualism, and the market (Bellah et al. 1985; Ginsburg 1989; Lasch 1977). In the mid-1990s, both Democrat and Republican politicians used pro-family rhetoric (Stacey 1996).

From the early 1800s until the 1960s, marriage was at the heart of the definition of family in the United States (Cott 2000; Rotundo 1993; Schneider 1968; Schneider and Smith 1978). Since then, marriage has become a focal point at which battles over the definition of *family values* are fought. Marriage seems to be the most divisive issue in the fatherhood responsibility movement. This is where the pro-marriage and fragile-families wings strongly disagree even though they share similar, sometimes contradictory, principles. Many pro-marriage representatives come out of a tradition that defends the institution of marriage and the "superiority" of the nuclear family in the face of changing patterns of family formation and perceived feminist and liberal "attacks" on "the family" (Popenoe 1988, 1996; Blankenhorn 1995; Whitehead 1993). As I demonstrate in chapters 2 and 5, many pro-marriage representatives look at the fatherhood responsibility movement as the first stage of a "marriage movement." Some marriage proponents even claim that they have been silenced by "politically correct" liberals and feminists and cannot even mention "the M-word," that is, marriage (Blankenhorn 1995; Whitehead 1993; Ooms 1998). The pro-marriage wing of the fatherhood responsibility movement overlaps with the already existing marriage movement, featuring the same leading figures (for example, Popenoe, Blankenhorn, and Horn) and quoting the same authors (for example, Barbara Whitehead, Maggie Gallagher, Popenoe, and Blankenhorn). The marriage movement, along with marriage proponents in the fatherhood responsibility movement, seeks to reestablish lifelong, monogamous, and heterosexual marriage as a norm in all societal sectors. Many marriage proponents in the fatherhood responsibility movement are also active marriage movement proponents and vice versa.

In contrast, most fragile-families representatives think that marriage is a good thing but point out that it does not guarantee positive outcomes for children. Their priority is to work on a range of socioeconomic and structural problems in families and communities and to increase the "marriageability" of low-income, poor, and minority men. Although marriage proponents regard marriage as an ideal, they do not say that less than ideal families necessarily result in negative outcomes for children. Nevertheless, they maintain that marriage is primarily about securing the well-being of children, with the bonus of making the parents "happier, healthier and wealthier" (Horn quoted in Committee of Ways and Means 1999). Although marriage proponents say that marriage might not solve everybody's problems, they believe that marriage can serve as an incentive to increase employability and father responsibility. These might seem like small differences in views, but divisive perspectives on marriage actually reflect fundamental ideological divisions and provoke fierce discussions in the fatherhood responsibility movement. According to the pro-marriage wing, "responsible fathers" marry before they have children, whereas the fragile-families wing points out that marriage is often unattainable for their low-income, poor, and minority constituencies. Fragile-families organizations seek recognition for unmarried "team parent" fathers as equally responsible fathers. Thus, for instance, Ronald Mincy, senior program officer for the Ford Foundation's Strengthening Fragile Families Initiative, wrote in a debate with marriage proponents that promoting marriage as a policy incentive in the fatherhood movement "makes second class citizens of a large and growing number of children who have unmarried fathers" (1999, 7).

Whereas *marriage* is a key issue for the pro-marriage wing, *work* is a key issue in the fragile-families wing of the fatherhood responsibility movement. Fragile-families organizations focus on African American/minority men's educational opportunities and access to careers in the labor market. In the fragile-families perspective, opportunity structures in the labor market affect men's standing in the marriage market. From this perspective, it makes more sense to focus on men's *financial* foundation for responsible fatherhood than on their *moral* commitment to marriage. Marriage proponents might acknowledge the relevance of employment for certain populations of fathers, but they do not bring this up as a primary issue. The relationship between work and fatherhood responsibility and their relative importance are thus contested within the fatherhood responsibility movement. Most representatives who are primarily concerned with low-income and poor African American fathers point out that a lack of jobs results in men turning away from family commitment. Fragile-families representatives consequently apply what they call a "money matters approach" and argue that economic and educational opportunity structures profoundly influence men's abilities to form and support a family, or, for that matter, to be "marriage material" (a term used in the fragile-families wing). Fragile-families organizations thus participate in policy debates by highlighting the ways the "failures" of low-income and poor African American men to get steady employment and to marry the mothers of their children are related to a lack of opportunities for education and professional socialization (Wilson 1996). Work then becomes a crucial issue in the fragile-families wing's constructions of masculinities and fatherhoods. In contrast, within the pro-marriage wing, work is often a given, almost a nonissue.

Marriage proponents neither position themselves nor primarily distinguish between men in terms of race/ethnicity or socioeconomic class. When discussing masculinities and fatherhoods, they generally assume "race-less" perspectives based on loose essentialist notions of male capacities, such as aggressiveness, "promiscuity," and competitiveness. They believe that men are prone to be career oriented, rule oriented, instrumental in their relations with others, and reluctant to show emotionality. These perspectives ignore the historical racial, sexual, and gendered relations that conditioned the emergence of these very notions. Marriage proponents promote such essentialist notions of gender difference through the unspoken privilege of assuming racial neutrality (Aanerud 1997, 36). By ignoring the ways their generalizing outlooks are situated in hierarchical relation to notions of women, gay men, and nonwhite men, marriage proponents resist positioning white middle-class masculinities (Aanerud 1997, 57; Robinson 2000). Gendered, sexualized, and racialized notions nevertheless implicitly inform pro-marriage distinctions between masculinities in terms of "constructive" versus "destructive" ones, which are devoid of structural or economic analysis. In other words, pro-marriage notions of responsible fatherhood as married, breadwinning fatherhood implicitly presume that all men have the same chance to become "constructive." "Constructive" masculinity entails harnessing the perceived innate male capacities mentioned above. Marriage proponents seek to "civilize" or contain "male" capacities within "productive" goals on behalf of family and society: heterosexual marriage, father involvement, monogamy, and law-abiding citizenship. As I demonstrate throughout this book, such notions have a long-standing racist history in the United States (Bederman 1995). According to pro-marriage notions of "destructive" masculinities, unless society/culture encourages a man to be constructive according to these goals, his "innate masculine energies" may transform into violence, homosexuality, "masculine excess," or "protest masculinity." Another pro-marriage notion of unproductive masculinity is androgynous, or "soft," masculinity because it supposedly erases masculine traits and feminizes men. Marriage proponents are therefore opposed to "androgyny advocacy" (Horn 1997, 25), which they associate with "radical" feminist and liberal politics.

Fatherhood Politics in Relation to Feminist Politics

The fatherhood responsibility movement reshapes U.S. public and policy debates on the positions, claims, and responsibilities of men in marriages and families. These discussions both challenge and reinforce postindustrial gendered notions of parenting (Gillis 1996; LaRossa 1997; Stacey 1996). Fatherhood organizations unite around agendas in response to the perceived "feminization of parenting," in other words, the perceived tendency of policy to equate "family" with "mother and child." The fatherhood responsibility movement consequently seeks to increase men's responsibilities and involvement as "nurturers," "playmates," and "role models," even though it is still debating its own conceptions of gendered relations and practices.

In interviews, representatives throughout the whole fatherhood responsibility movement often framed the redefinition of masculinity and fatherhood as a response to redefinitions of femininity and motherhood. However, both pro-marriage and fragile-families representatives almost always indicate that their responses are neither defenses against feminist gains nor antifeminist. On the contrary, they often point out that they are fighting for what feminists always have promoted: getting men to share responsibilities in caretaking and breadwinning. The women's studies scholar Judith Stacey analyzed the fatherhood movement, which she dismissively calls the "dada-ist movement," and came to a different conclusion. Analyzing the fatherhood movement in terms of a politics of displacement, Stacey maintains that "Dada-ism functions as a proxy rhetoric for antifeminist, antigay, xenophobic and anti-welfare sentiments . . ." (1998, 73). According to Stacey, "dada-ists" blame women, feminists, and their "liberal cultural allies" for rejecting paternal participation. In the "dada-ist" view, feminists and allies promote "emasculating" and "androgynous" visions of "The New Father" while seeking to reestablish 1950s "Ozzie and Harriet" authoritarian breadwinner dads (1996, 1998).

While the pro-marriage wing has received extensive feminist critique (Coltrane 2001; Gillis 2000; Silverstein and Auerbach 1999; Stacey 1996, 1998) and upon closer inspection do position themselves in opposition to what marriage proponents call "radical" feminist politics, critics often fail to highlight the more complex relation between the fragile-families wing and feminist politics. Fragile-families representatives sometimes claim to engage in collaborative dialogue with what they call "women's organizations." Fragile-families organizations' relations to African American feminisms seem particularly complex, since African American women's historical relations to the labor force as well as their families have been different from those of white middle-class feminists (Davis 1981), and their claims and demands may both converge with and diverge from African American men's specific issues (for further discussion, see Chateauvert 1998; Hill 1997; hooks 1992; and Staples and Johnson 1993). For example, African American women and men were equally oppressed by slavery (Davis 1981, 23), and the fight for black liberation emerged in conjunction with the fight for (white and African American) women's liberation in the early 1800s (Davis 1981). However, during civil rights discussions, African American women's participation in wage labor provided employers with an excuse to underpay African American male workers, and civil rights agendas partly diverged from feminist agendas in labor issues. In other words, African American women's demands as workers contradicted African American men's demands for "respectability" according to Eurocentric standards of male headship and gender complementary division of breadwinning and unpaid housework (Chateauvert 1998).

When describing historical processes affecting fatherhood in the United States, most pro-marriage and fragile-families representatives situate the fatherhood responsibility movement in response to feminist politics. They do so by naming the feminist movement as an important factor that has pushed fathers away from families, even though they accept "gender equity" as feminist accomplishments they have no intention of undoing. However, fragile-families and pro-marriage representatives' responses to gender relational processes differ. Marriage proponents want to reinforce more or less essentialist notions of gender and parental difference and cement those differences within the institution of marriage. Some leading marriage proponents also promote male leadership as part of their ideals of gendered division of labor and echo the "servant leadership" ideals of the Promise Keepers. One leading marriage proponent explained the servant-leader model more fully in an interview:[6]

> The term that's usually used is "*servant* leader," and people who don't like that model focus on the word *leader*. People who like that model focus on the word *servant*. So where you put the accent makes a great deal of difference. Servant leader means you lead by example, you lead by serving others. It comes from the Bible, and it comes from the reference that men should lead their families as Christ led the church. And ultimately, what Christ did for the church is he sacrificed his very life for the church, for God—allowed himself to be crucified for the sake of the rest of the world in biblical terms. And so what he—In his teachings is when he says, "You serve your fam—you lead your families like I lead the church." What he is really saying is "If need be your job is literally to die for your family, you know, if that's what it takes to keep your family safe." Now, I mean, is that a horrible idea? Is it a terrible idea? You know, that men ought to be so sacrificing for their family that they will literally, you know, put themselves *in arms* and die, if need be, to keep their families safe and secure. It's a much more self-sacrificial form style of leadership. Now there are clearly those people who believe in, you know, the man ruling . . . with an iron fist. . . . And I disagree with those people. I think that that is *not* what the biblical prescription of servant leaderhood is all about. I believe that servant leaderhood is "What can I do for you?"—not "You have to do what I say."

Pro-marriage representatives often combine such biblically inspired ideas of gender order with sociobiological, pop psychological, and pop anthropological discourses to underscore loose essentialist points. From a Christian perspective, many pro-marriage representatives compare the sacrifices of fathers with the sacrifices of Jesus in submitting himself to God. Such notions of the father's superior position in the family and his subordinate position in relation to God/Jesus constitute a Christian version of what I call "difference-based equality." Difference-based equality evokes a view of gendered relations where men and women are considered simultaneously equal and "different," which may still be hierarchical according to worldly standards. The religious studies scholar Mark Muesse describes a Christian (fundamentalist) view of the universe according to the following hierarchical order: God is on the top, followed by Christ, who is positioned above men. Women, who are at the bottom of this Christian (fundamentalist) hierarchy, follow men. Whereas women should "submit" to and "obey" their husbands, they are not "inferior"—just "different" (1996, 96). As many pro-marriage representatives argue, while positioned according to such hierarchy, men and women are equally indispensable for social and moral order. For example, in his final remarks recorded during the National Fatherhood Initiative's Second National Summit on Fatherhood in June 1998, one of the key speakers articulated the rationale behind the father as "chosen protector":

> I'm going to say one last thing. When I was a boy growing up in rural Mississippi, been raised in a good family and made to feel that I was quite smart. And one day I felt even smarter than usual. I made, I made an incredible discovery. God had made a mistake. I caught God in a mistake. And you can't imagine, you know, for a twelve year old, how important this was [laughter from audience], well, you're wondering what it was. I'd been fooling around, my buddies and I, with some honeybees. We made this discovery. That when a bee stings you, he dies. And I said, "What kind of designer and engineer would design an animal whose sole defense mechanism cost him his life?" You can only use it at the cost of your life. Now that's got to be a mistake. And I mentioned to my dad, I didn't know how I was going to correct it after all those millennia, but I mentioned to dad my discovery, and dad pointed out to me, he said, "Son, the bee doesn't sting you to protect himself, the bee stings you to defend the hive. For the bee the hive is the thing and the baby bees in the hive are the most important thing of all. So important that the bee that stings you is willing to give up his life in defense of the hive." Hah—that's how bees perpetuate themselves. And that's how it used to be in our neighborhoods where our children used to be our number one priority and that's how we need to make it again. How do we do it? Not by deposing the queens [laughter from audience] but by enlisting the contributions of the entire hive in the interest of the children.

This metaphor is intended to reveal a biblical/etiological rationale behind gendered, social, and moral order in assigning the father to be the protector of women (queens) and children (baby bees). It is simultaneously a defense against misunderstandings that the purpose of the bees is to depose the queen. What makes this funny for the audience is the presumption that there are "people" (read feminist critics?) who would claim that the self-sacrificing bees could possibly have such a self-serving agenda. Like Promise Keepers, marriage proponents sometimes imply that their notions of the father as the protector and the "servant leader" have been misunderstood—especially by feminists. In speeches and interviews, marriage proponents never fail to point out that they are driven by concern for child well-being rather than by male self-interest. This is also the defense the Promise Keepers use when explaining its biblical notion of servant leadership; it is about men assuming obligations for the sake of women and children.

In contrast, fragile-families representatives, well aware of the feminist critique of marriage proponents, claimed to be less "traditionalist" in their responses to changing gender relations and family forms. Their responses are conditioned by strategic concerns not to alienate decision makers in organizations on which they are financially dependent, such as the Ford Foundation and the Department of Health and Human Services. Fragile-families representatives at a national level therefore sometimes encourage local fatherhood programs to form strategic alliances with so-called women's groups to maximize their opportunities in agencies concerned with women, families, and children. One of the most prominent representatives of the fragile-families wing commented on the strategic reasons behind this message in an interview:

> On the one hand the responsible fatherhood programs haven't even gotten to a point to understand what their posture is to women's groups. But they know that they have to be sensitive to the issue. . . . They represent the interests of poor men, and public dollars is what they're going after. The middle and upper levels of DHHS [Department of Health and Human Services] are administered by women—it's just a question of having political common sense. . . . [Gives examples of women who are heads of different public programs and private foundations.] The women who are in high positions in private foundations are basically women who are spending the wealth that their husbands and fathers generated. Those women make decisions about who gets what money and the responsible fatherhood groups cannot have an adversary approach to them. However, fathers' rights groups [i.e. white middle- and upper-class men] don't need public money and as a consequence they will posture themselves in your face. The interests of these groups have yet to embrace the concerns of low-income men.

Therefore you hear responsible fatherhood groups talking to each other saying we have to be sensitive to issues of domestic violence, etc.

Regardless of whether this representative actually agrees with certain female decision makers, he needs to relate to them as part of a power structure upon which his organization depends. He therefore points out that representatives of poor men have to be "sensitive" to "women's issues" as a gesture to such female decision makers. He seems to assume that these decision makers have feminist agendas and implies that women in the private foundations do not deserve to make financial decisions because they are only "spending the wealth" generated by men. Ronald Mincy, a senior program officer of the Ford Foundation's Strengthening Fragile Families Initiative, made similar claims, arguing, together with Hillard Pouncy, that "female professionals dominate the maternal and child health, family support and income security systems on which fragile families depend" (1999, 87). According to Mincy and Pouncy, fragile-families representatives therefore have to "articulate a message about male-female roles and relationships that these professionals can hear" (1999, 87). Another leading fragile-families representative said in an interview that the "team parenting" concept was developed in the fragile-families wing in an effort to emphasize willingness to talk to what he, like the representative quoted above, called "women's groups." He added:

> How do we develop partnerships with other aspects of the fatherhood movement? But let me tell you something that I'm not going to [do] . . . ; I'm *not* going to give up on the importance in the role of women in this whole thing. And I'm going to actively engage women groups in our work in trying to expand the presence of dads. Now you know the further right [toward the marriage proponents] you go, you're not going to get that, you know what I mean, because you almost have like enemy camps with women. And so—to the extent to which we can develop strategic alliances so that we can kind of come up with a consistent message, I think we're going to have to do that because if we don't do that I just think that this whole movement will dissipate and not gain the real hold that it can without such linkages. And so I'm ready to talk.

Being "ready to talk" implies that fragile-families organizations, unlike pro-marriage groups, do not position themselves in adversarial relation to what they call "women's groups." Although the fragile-families organizations constitute themselves in strategic *dialogue* with women's organizations, they do not necessarily assume or integrate *feminist perspectives*. It is difficult to discern any general approach to gender relations at all in the fragile-families wing. Representatives seem to subscribe to various perspectives in primarily

African American family sociology and civil rights discourse, some of which have been criticized as masculinist (hooks 1992). Throughout the abolitionist and civil rights movements, African American struggles for rights and recognition were cast in terms of claims for "manhood," meaning the powers and privileges that allowed white middle-class men to count as men and citizens. Abolitionist and civil rights efforts to restore African American men to their "rightful place" as heads of their families were cast as "manhood rights" in the name of racial justice (Horton and Horton 1999; Griswold 1993, 214–15). African American feminists have long exposed the sexist presumptions that have informed gendered relations in the struggles for racial justice (Davis 1981; hooks 1992). While fragile-families organizations build on such masculinist struggles for racial justice (see chapter 3), they also participate in current contestations over the intersections and relative importance of racial and gender asymmetries.

The fragile-families wing's various approaches to gender relations may be contextualized within a wider field of African American masculinity politics. The sociologist Michael Messner identifies two dominant perspectives within U.S. "racialized masculinity politics."[7] *Conservative essentialists* promote mainly religious and biological, as well as antifeminist and antigay, notions of gender difference. Conservative essentialists, exemplified by leaders in the Million Man March, argue that blocked labor market and educational opportunities have "emasculated" African American men and that these men are therefore "not allowed to play their normal roles as family leaders and breadwinners" (Messner 1997, 73). *Radical reductionists* accord primary importance to struggles against racial and socioeconomic oppression at the expense of other forms of oppression. Thus, they reduce social justice struggles to a struggle against racial and socioeconomic oppression. Radical reductionists consider other social justice issues, such as sexism and heterosexism, to be of less importance or even in opposition to African American masculinity politics (Messner 1997, 72). While promoting principles of gender equality and seeking to be "sensitive to the issues of women's groups," fragile-families representatives may simultaneously draw on conservative essentialist and radical reductionist discourses in representing African American men. However, as I demonstrate in chapter 3, the fragile-families wing reflects a more diverse picture than the one Messner paints here.

Bridging Competing Historical Struggles

The discursive approaches of contemporary fatherhood politics emerged out of competing historical struggles. Despite the different perspectives and backgrounds of many representatives, the fatherhood responsibility movement is seen by its proponents as a means to "bridge the racial divide" (Blankenhorn 1999: xiv). The fatherhood responsibility movement seeks, in the words of its proponents, to overcome "barriers of income, race, and politics" through its conferences, campaigns, and initiatives (Horn, Blankenhorn, and Pearlstein 1999, 170). While presenting themselves as part of one social movement at national events, fragile-families and pro-marriage representatives paint two different pictures and draw on seemingly incompatible historical and ideological foundations for their masculinity politics. Simply put, the fragile-families wing focuses on equal opportunities, whereas the pro-marriage wing focuses on moral obligations. Hence, within the same "movement," there are contradictory claims for justice, as well as different perceived sources of fatherhood problems, despite the unified image presented in public contexts. African American masculinity politics, exemplified by the Million Man March and the civil rights movement, revolves mainly around rights and recognition in relation to other *men,* while primarily white middle-class contemporary men's movements, such as the Promise Keepers and the mythopoetic men's movement, defend notions of gender difference between men and *women.*

Despite its internal differences, the fatherhood responsibility movement is designed by representatives who have a political stake in presenting a unified and noncontroversial image of the movement. In speeches and texts, leading representatives (many of whom have doctorates) simultaneously invent and "analyze" their fatherhood politics by fitting themselves into various social movement definitions and movement histories (see, for example, Horn 1999; and Mincy and Pouncy 2002). Wade Horn actually uses the concept of "movement making" when discussing whether the fatherhood responsibility movement fits into his criteria for a social movement (1999, 11). At a pre–Father's Day press conference in Washington, D.C., in 1997, Horn claimed that fatherhood activists are increasingly willing to "put aside whatever philosophical, ideological or political differences may exist among them and come together and seek a common cause" (quoted in "National Fatherhood Initiative Leads 'A Call to Fatherhood'" 1997, 1). The resulting fatherhood politics is a strategic attempt to make one movement out of two seemingly divergent and asymmetric types of historical struggles. Whereas the pro-marriage wing is oriented toward individual and collective moral obligations of men as a generalized group, the fragile-families wing is primarily concerned with the equal opportunities, rights, and recognition of poor and minority men (and their families). When designing and situating their fatherhood politics, marriage proponents commonly draw on nineteenth-century social/moral reform movements, such as religious and voluntary associations and the temperance movement (Eberly 1999, 31–32; Horn 1999, 8). Drawing on such nineteenth-century movements, marriage proponents try to influence "cultural" processes as opposed to economic or structural processes. In contrast, fragile-families representatives draw on 1960s civil rights traditions and focus on racial oppression and socioeconomic injustices dating back to slavery. In an interview, Harry, a leading pro-marriage representative, contrasted his focus on moral obligations with the fragile-families wing's focus on equal opportunities:

> You see, most twentieth-century movements have been about rights, and they're rights based—not responsibility based. Think about the big movements in the twentieth century: civil rights is about rights for minorities, women's rights is about rights for women, the men's movement is about rights for men. The big movements in the twentieth century have primarily been rights based. Think back to the movements in the nineteenth century; what were they about? Responsibility. They were movements; for example—the temperance movement was about drinking responsibly. The religious movements were about coming to God, and you know sort of repenting and being better, changing yourself, being more responsible. Even the abolition movement I would argue was really about us, the slaveowners, the class of slaveowners being more responsible, and, you know, freeing the slaves. It wasn't so much about the rights of the slave, because Abraham Lincoln said; once we've freed them his plan was to ship them back to Africa. You know, he wasn't so much saying this is a movement about the rights of African Americans in America, it was about we as a white people, as a white nation, need to be more responsible and not own slaves, and once we've freed them all, we ship them all away. So the twentieth century was more about rights—*my* rights as a woman, *my* rights as a black, *my* rights as a—as a man. Where is the fatherhood movement? The fatherhood movement, at least the way *we* define it, is about responsibility. So it is a throwback to the . . . nineteenth century—it doesn't fit into twentieth century movements.

Despite marriage proponents' refusal to participate in fatherhood politics as a racialized group, Harry tellingly identifies with white slaveowners, a "white nation," and the "white people" when he describes the historical background for his version of the fatherhood movement. In stark contrast with Harry's perspective as a descendant of white *slaveowners* promoting "responsibility," the fragile-families representatives, most of whom were African American, generally approached fatherhood as descendants of *slaves*. Fragile-families representatives do so coming from a tradition of poor and minority men's struggles for civil rights and recognition of full citizenship, thereby of "manhood." Seen in this light, it is small wonder why the two wings of the fatherhood responsibility movement often seem incongruent in representing the diverging concerns and perspectives of, for instance, white middle-class and poor African American men.

Beneath the unified banners of "fatherhood responsibility" and "child well-being," the two wings not only draw on different historical struggles but also do not even seem to agree on the emergence of their history as a movement since the early 1990s. Representatives of the pro-marriage National Fatherhood Initiative think their own National Summit on Fatherhood in 1994 signified the actual birth of the fatherhood responsibility movement (see Horn 1999, 15n31). According to Wade Horn, who was president of the National Fatherhood Initiative at the time, the "galvanizing and defining moments" of the fatherhood movement were former vice president Dan Quayle's famous "Murphy Brown speech" and an article by the writer Barbara Dafoe Whitehead in the *Atlantic Monthly* (Horn 1999, 5–6). In the election year of 1992, Quayle critiqued the TV show *Murphy Brown* within a wider rhetoric against "illegitimate" childbearing (Griswold 1993, 236). In the article "Dan Quayle Was Right," Whitehead discussed the debate inspired by *Murphy Brown,* in which the female lead character decides to keep and rear an unplanned child on her own. In response to debates over single mothers and "family values," both Quayle and Whitehead argued that fathers are indispensable and central to children, families, and society. None of the fragile-families representatives I talked to mentioned these "moments" as particularly significant to the fatherhood responsibility movement. Instead, fragile-families representatives commonly identified then vice president Al Gore's fatherhood meetings in 1994 as the starting point of the fatherhood responsibility movement.

This disparity between pro-marriage and fragile-families representatives' constructions of the history and nature of fatherhood politics boils down to fundamental ideological differences. In an interview, Thomas, a leading fragile-families representative, framed the ideological incompatibilities within the fatherhood responsibility movement in terms of "racial diversity":

> I think that in the final analysis, the only way to properly understand the fatherhood movement is *as a* diversity discussion, all right? It is a predicament of American life. America has more than 161 different racial ethnic groups who all at any one time see themselves as the center of the universe, and that just like NFI [National Fatherhood Initiative] will probably *never* have a black spokesperson unless . . . he speaks to the issue of diversity in this country in terms of not only in political thought, but I think also in terms of racial makeup. For example, [the pro-marriage wing] will never be more than 20–30 percent of people of color. All right? Will never be, because of their philosophy. . . . Conversely, unless the individuals are poor, I don't see [the fragile-families wing] ever becoming more than 30 percent white . . . and as opposed to thinking of this as a movement that's going to

assimilate, where all the fatherhood messages are going to be one, I think to the *contrary*. What you're going to have, what this represents is a diversity—map of the different fatherhood groups in this country, and interesting enough, the diversity is both in philosophy *and in*—also in the politics, but also in its majority/minority, racial and ethnic makeup.... [A]nd so because we will not assimilate, you know and that is really why we won't assimilate; because the position is that we think that we can be whole individuals without buying into this philosophy, and that it does not mean that we can't strategically align ourselves, that we can't coexist.

Thomas did not specify the philosophical/political characteristics of the National Fatherhood Initiative, but his concerns clearly had something to do with its whiteness. Moreover, Thomas maintained during the same interview that the 1960s civil rights struggles, which the pro-marriage leader Harry considered unimportant to the fatherhood responsibility movement, enabled representatives of low-income and poor African American men to participate in today's fatherhood politics. As Thomas put it, the aim of the fragile-families wing is "to create a space" for representatives of poor and minority men to "be at the table" of fatherhood policymaking. Thomas and many of his fragile-families colleagues view the NFI and many other pro-marriage organizations as examples of the long-standing privileges of white middle- and upper-class men at this "table" of fatherhood politics. To participate in the making of fatherhood politics, fragile-families representatives feel that they have to "strategically align" themselves with the pro-marriage wing.

Notes

1. For instance, the women's studies scholar Judith Stacey uses statements by Wade Horn, David Popenoe, and David Blankenhorn, who are prominent leaders in the pro-marriage wing, to exemplify the rhetoric of the fatherhood responsibility movement (1996, 1998).

2. The Fatherhood Project, headed by James Levine, is a unique organization that focuses on nurturing and helps corporations and government agencies adopt father and family friendly practices (Mincy and Pouncy 2002, 570–71). The Fatherhood Project is also the only known organization in the field that promotes paternity leave (Mincy and Pouncy, 2002, 571).

3. The quotes from the representatives come from tape-recorded interviews and conference sessions or notes taken during interviews, conferences, or workshops.

4. However, this has recently started to change—partly as a result of the efforts of the fatherhood responsibility movement.

5. Fathers' rights organizations' ambiguous relationship with the fatherhood responsibility movement could be seen at a fragile-families conference I attended in Anaheim, California, June 10–14, 1998. During this conference, fathers' rights groups were represented inside but also protested outside the conference site.

6. Interviewees are anonymous and may sometimes be the same persons as the people quoted by name or by pseudonym in other parts of this book.

7. Messner uses the expression *racialized masculinity politics,* in which the fragile-families wing partly engages. However, I chose the label *fragile families* partly because it is used by representatives of poor and minority men in the fatherhood responsibility movement and partly because it refers to both constituencies of minority men and low-income/poor men of any race.

2   Pro-Marriage Fatherhood

The Straight Story on Married Men

The pro-marriage wing manifests the ways the politics of gender and sexuality in the fatherhood responsibility movement are mutually reinforcing and inseparable. Marriage proponents draw on a combination of biblical and sociobiological discourses that make up a loose essentialist approach to gender relations, one that conjures up both more and less specific notions of the "natures" of men and women (Schwalbe 1996). Their loose essentialist notions of gender difference perpetuate heteronormative duality as "the holy structure of sexuality" (Butler 1997, 276). That is, marriage proponents construct the monogamous, heterosexual, and married lifestyle as the hallmark of gendered normality, maturity, and morality, and they maintain that everyone who does not conform to this pattern is unfulfilled or deviant. On the basis of nature's or God's order, marriage proponents insist that for children and adults to be complete the marital union is necessary and must consist of a male and a female. It is common for marriage proponents to use such concepts as "complementary" and "parenting equation" to argue for the necessity of male-female and mother-father duality. In their campaigns, pro-marriage organizations frame their versions of social order as beyond politics and special interests (Horn, Blankenhorn, and Pearlstein 1999). In this view, child well-being and the necessity to "attach" men to a woman and children through marriage are simply unquestionable values and a "natural order" that everybody should strive for—regardless of political conviction. This chapter investigates the components of the pro-marriage "gender and parenting equation" and situates its rationale within the wider U.S. battleground of marriage and fatherhood politics.

Marriage proponents feel that married fatherhood is currently disintegrating in society because men and fathers are increasingly devalued and decentered as a result of wider cultural, social, and economic processes. The constraints on, practices of, and expectations for fathers and mothers are changing, as are family forms (Gillis 2000; Griswold 1995; Stacey 1996). Re-emerging in the 1960s, feminist movements have critiqued old models of fathers as authorities in the family and have promoted reproductive freedom, gender equality in families, rights and benefits on the basis of motherhood, and shared housework and care responsibilities. As mentioned earlier, the transition to a postindustrial society and changing government policies concerning families and education have been instrumental in the renegotiations of the gendered division of paid and unpaid labor. Marriage proponents believe that the importance of marriage and thereby the importance of fatherhood within marriage are diminishing as a result of these structural shifts, as well as increasing rates of divorce, cohabitation, and female-headed households. White middle- and upper-class men, as well as low-income, poor, and minority men, are struggling to come to grips with their changing positions in the family and their shifting conditions as breadwinners, husbands, and fathers. In discussing these shifts, marriage proponents tend to assume an all-encompassing and generic male perspective and claim to speak on behalf of all fathers and men.

Although marriage proponents rarely tie their notions of masculinity to sexuality, socioeconomic class, or race, their masculinity politics still has implications in these terms. This fact is highlighted for low-income, poor, and minority masculinities, as represented by the fragile-families wing. Pro-marriage cultural and moral strategies and gendered presumptions exclude the perspectives of certain masculinities and fatherhoods. A main symptom of this condition is that marriage proponents choose to focus on "culture" rather than socioeconomic structure when conceiving of changes that affect masculinity and fatherhood in the United States. Similarly, their masculinity politics ignores structural dimensions of the relations and negotiations between men and women in heterosexual families. With a culturalist approach, such pro-marriage organizations as the National Fatherhood Initiative, the Institute for Responsible Fatherhood and Family Revitalization, and the National Center for Fathering are working for a "culture" of married fatherhood.

As mentioned earlier, fragile-families representatives differentiate themselves primarily from other men, whereas marriage proponents differentiate themselves from women as a binary opposite to men within a "difference-based model of equality." In the same way that white middle-class men serve as a constant reference point for fragile-families representatives, generalized notions of "women" and "feminists" seem to be the reference point from which marriage proponents constantly distinguish or defend themselves. In the eyes of the pro-marriage representatives I interviewed, the big threat to pro-marriage masculinity and fatherhood is not other men but "androgyny advocates" (another word for feminists) who threaten to "androgynize" men in the family by denying their uniqueness and legitimacy as husbands and fathers. In this context, promoting fatherhood responsibility in an adversarial response to "androgyny advocacy" is a way for marriage proponents to reclaim loose essentialist notions of masculinity based on moral/cultural imperatives. The pro-marriage wing thus extends into a wider field of moral politics, such as Protestant biblical politics and the marriage movement. The marriage movement was partly launched and developed by key figures in the pro-marriage wing of the fatherhood responsibility movement, such as David Blankenhorn, David Popenoe, and Don Eberly.[1] Moreover, the marriage movement is modeled after the fatherhood responsibility movement and its strategies to achieve politically broad-based, "bipartisan" appeal. For instance, to this end, both movements emphasize a concern for child well-being above all else. In its statement of principles, the marriage movement laments a contemporary "marriage crisis," evident in increasing rates of divorce and unwed childbearing. It traces its roots not only to the fatherhood responsibility movement but also to initiatives in education, churches, research, law reform, and government.

The Male Force as Imperative for the Androcentric Trinity

At the nexus of the pro-marriage approach to fatherhood politics lies the distinction between men and women. The central belief is that men and women are totally different and that these two "different but equal" parts make a whole in marriage. This notion of gender relations is the basic ingredient that legitimizes and gives meaning to pro-marriage masculinity and fatherhood politics. Marriage proponents construe a certain sexualized version of manhood as the core of all men's being: aggressiveness, competitiveness, and promiscuous heterosexuality. They also think men are innately rational, rule oriented, instrumental in their relations to others, reluctant to showing emotionality, and career oriented. According to pro-marriage rationale, these "male traits" need to be contained and harnessed through external incentives. Unless male aggression and "promiscuity" are controlled by such social goals as married fatherhood, these same characteristics may turn into violent, destructive, and irresponsible behavior. With fathers, male traits "translate" into certain behaviors and parenting styles: physical "rough-and-tumble play," discipline, authority, risk taking, protection, and the like. These "male" parenting features partly correspond to century-old notions of men as playmates and role models, described in the introduction. According to the marriage proponents, recognition of gender differences and the value of married fatherhood are currently in decline. Marriage proponents therefore seek to reinforce and reinstitutionalize their deeply felt "truths" of gender difference in parenting and the importance of marriage to the well-being of children, adults, and society. Marriage proponents identify a cultural shift toward "androgyny" ideals as a major part of current "confusion" over masculinity. According to most pro-marriage representatives, "androgynizers" (i.e., feminists) in family policy, education, and therapy want "the New Fathers" to be more like mothers. The pro-marriage wing resists such ideas because they think they are socially and sexually destructive and "unnaturally" neutralize gender difference.

One major pro-marriage leader asserted in a keynote address to a regional conference, "This is the most controversial thing I'm going to say: men and women are different [audience laughs]. And sometimes this translates to differences between mothers and fathers." This statement exemplifies how important notions of gender difference are to the pro-marriage wing. Moreover, the statement suggests that there are people (i.e., feminists) who would consider this controversial. Echoing early-twentieth-century notions of "masculine" domesticity (LaRossa 1997), pro-marriage fatherhood politics seeks to reinforce loose essentialist notions of gender and parenting in the face of the perceived feminization of parenting ideals. Marriage proponents are reclaiming the husband and father as a moral and indispensable identity and are struggling for recognition of the "special endowments" of men and fathers. For instance, Harry, another leading pro-marriage representative, argued in an interview that men should be appreciated and recognized for just being men, without having to change or feel ashamed about their "manly ways":

> A lot of people say, there's nothing wrong with a guy being a father as long as he does it the way mothers do it. And I think that's not a very—I think inspirational message to men, I think what you have to do is say, "Hey, you can be a real guy, a man's man, and still be a great father." Being a real man doesn't mean beating your kid, or beating your wife, but you know, it doesn't mean you have to sort of check your trousers at the door. Ehhh— you know, you can be physical with your kid, in terms physical play wrestling with them on the floor. And that's a real contribution—not *superfluous*. You can encourage risk taking within reason, and that's good,

healthy, and reasonable for children. And then what kids really need in the end is both what mothers and fathers bring, not just mothers *or* fathers.

Harry's statement incorporates the connections marriage proponents draw between specific notions of male characteristics (such as "being physical") and "indispensable" father features (such as wrestling with their kids on the floor). Echoing nineteenth-century notions of the "frolicsome dad," marriage proponents constantly mention "rough-and-tumble play" as an important example of why fathers are irreplaceable. Fathers are considered particularly important to sons, who learn to control their "aggression" by wrestling with their fathers. The pro-marriage notion of gender difference thus extends to parental difference, which, in its turn, necessitates heterosexual duality, since fathers possess capabilities that mothers lack, and vice versa. In the words of a pro-marriage representative I interviewed, "culture" should honor and celebrate gender difference instead of "pretending that it doesn't exist."

One important gender difference according to many pro-marriage representatives is that motherhood is closer to biology, whereas culture ideally makes fathers out of men by convincing them to raise their offspring. Unless fathers are pressured by the legal and moral restrictions of marriage to invest their time, money, and effort in one family, marriage proponents believe they will follow their undomesticated "promiscuous" natures without assuming responsibility for their offspring. To pro-marriage representatives, this fundamental condition means that family policy must center on "attaching" men to their children. Marriage proponents sometimes use a combination of sociobiological and anthropological discourses to maintain the fundamental, universal "fact" that women have stronger "natural" ties to their children than do fathers. As Maggie Gallagher, who works with Blankenhorn at the Institute for American Values, puts it, "From an anthropological perspective, marriage is the institution by which societies have attached fathers to children. . . . Marriage is the institution that closes [the] shocking biological gap between a man's sexual and fathering capacities" (1999, 58). She goes on to say, "It is not biology, but law, custom and mores that make fathers out of men. . . . The tie between father and child is less 'natural,' more fragile, more a product of culture, than the tie between mother and child" (1999, 63). In the NFI newsletter, *Fatherhood Today,* Gallagher argues that the fundamental purpose of marriage is to create ties between sexually promiscuous men and their children. She maintains that marriage serves to "create a unity of interest between them and their children and a distinctly male role in the family" (1996, 7).

The keystone of pro-marriage fatherhood politics is what might be called an *androcentric trinity* foundational to all social and moral order and to civilization itself:[2] *men, marriage,* and *children.* Women are a necessary but marginal appendage *within* this male-centered trinity. While marriage proponents argue that marriage is good for men and children, they have little to say about what women get out of it, except perhaps protection and occasional assistance with tasks women are presumed to be biologically "called" for anyway. By extension, marriage proponents imply that unless all human societies are organized around heterosexual men and their power to uphold civilization, men may destroy society by unleashing their innate and irresponsible "promiscuity" or aggressions on one another or on women. Pro-marriage organizations therefore ultimately seek to recenter heterosexual men within the national agenda. They do so by defining "responsible fatherhood" according to ideals and notions of civilization that traditionally have been the prerogatives of white and middle-class heterosexual men (Bederman 1995; D. Nelson 1998). Simply put, according to pro-marriage thought, social order revolves around men's assumed lack of agency regarding their innate aggressions and heterosexual urges. Pro-marriage representatives commonly constructed this model of an androcentric trinity from a combination of popularized biblical and sociobiologist ideas.

An important cornerstone is the pro-marriage sociobiological argument that men, because of their "procreative instincts," are largely unable to control their sexuality around women. Simultaneously, as the pro-marriage leader David Blankenhorn said at the Second National Summit on Fatherhood in 1998, this "force" is the generative spark of the survival of the human species. Whereas women are already family oriented (because of their perceived gender-specific reproductive concerns) this argument goes, men need to become regulated and civilized into a family orientation and social order to refrain from running berserk. While "responsible" married men are the backbone of social order, "unattached males" are a menace and society's most powerful enemy (Popenoe 1998, 43). These are the men behind violent crimes, who rape and kill and have such self-destructive habits as drug and alcohol addictions, according to key pro-marriage representatives. In the fatherhood responsibility movement "manifesto," *The Fatherhood Movement* (Horn, Blankenhorn, and Pearlstein 1999), the psychiatrist David Gutmann draws on anthropology and sociobiology from the 1920s to the 1970s to make a functionalist case for marriage:

> Paternity and maternity are not expressions of power politics between the sexes, but are evolved adaptations to the special requirements of the weak

and needy human child. . . . Men are generally assigned the task of providing physical security on the perimeter, not because they are more privileged, but because they are more expendable. Thus, in the hard calculus of species survival, there is typically an oversupply of males, in that one man can inseminate many females, but women, on the average, can gestate only one child about every two years. . . . The surplus males, those over the number required to maintain viable population levels, can be assigned to the dangerous, high-casualty "perimeter" tasks on which physical security and survival are based. (Gutmann 1999, 135)

Sociobiological arguments for marriage are used to negate its gendered power dimensions. Drawing on the fear-based, loose essentialist anthropological and sociobiological arguments outlined above, pro-marriage strategies for male/fatherhood responsibility boil down to an attempt to bond men to their children with the glue of marriage. The fundamental purpose of marriage is twofold and supposedly benefits everyone: it connects fathers to their children and keeps men from causing damage outside of the androcentric trinity.

Marriage proponents present two main arguments for the centrality of marriage: (1) the "whip-men-into-shape" argument, which contends that marriage motives men to be successful breadwinners and more responsible about the well-being of themselves, their children, and others; and (2) the "child well-being" argument, which maintains that marriage is the optimal child-friendly environment. This male-centered rationale suggests that women and marriage exist mainly to accommodate and harness masculinity. Again, women constitute a structuring absence in pro-marriage rhetoric. This absence depends on notions of women and mothers as complementary but mute objects. Notions of heteronormative complementarity also permeate the pro-marriage argument that children and men need marriage; marriage completes men by pairing them with women. Women happen to be more biologically, biblically, or anthropologically suited for childcare and the "softer" familial responsibilities. In its gender-specific roles for mothers and fathers, marriage also offers what one interviewee referred to as a "complete package" to children.

The *whip-men-into-shape argument* presupposes that men lack the agency to behave "responsibly" unless external institutions and forces harness them (chapter 5 contains a detailed discussion of this). Marriage straightens men out and gives their hedonistic lives a purpose. The moral implications of this heteronormative perspective within the pro-marriage wing overlaps with and reinforces the biblical approach of the Promise Keepers. Like Promise Keepers, marriage proponents occasionally include (male) homosexuality on their list of socially destructive sexual behavior. In their view, homosexuality is illegitimate because it is detached from the moralizing heterosexual institution of marriage and from procreation. Furthermore, marriage serves to reinforce important gendered functions, according to pro-marriage notions of moral and sexual order. A speaker at the NFI's Second National Summit on Fatherhood Summit in 1998 elaborated on the need to reinforce certain male roles in families and societies. This speaker was seemingly influenced by a combination of popularized sociobiological and Freudian ideas:

> Marriage civilizes men. Tames us to the domestic yoke. Makes us responsible. . . . Men [who are] ordained by nature to be the protectors of families and the defenders of communities are stripped of those roles. The inborn aggressiveness. And I'm convinced that we're born hard-wired to be aggressive. We keep trying to fix things by trying to make us less aggressive. Wrong. We need to learn to channel the aggressive instinct. When we lose those roles, the inborn aggressiveness doesn't go away. It just gets distorted into antisocial patterns. And the result is that the men who should be the pride of their families and the strength of their communities become instead useless to their families and threats to the well-being of their communities.

According to this logic, masculinity in and of itself calls for the confines of marriage for the sake of families and communities. The "whip-men-into-shape" argument maintains that marriage has a positive impact on men and indirectly on women and children. Divorce, cohabitation, and homosexuality, however, have the opposite effect on men. Marriage proponents often draw on various pop-psychological notions (for example, John Gray's *Men Are from Mars, Women Are from Venus* [1992]) in maintaining that marriage causes and motivates fatherhood responsibility for men in general regardless of socioeconomic position. As well-known marriage proponent said in an interview:

> What do we know? When a man gets married—what happens? One, his employment rates go up; two, he drinks less; three, he does less drugs. When he gets divorced—what happens? One, his employment rates go down a bit; two, he drinks more; and three, he uses more drugs. So one could make the argument that being a married, and that's for *men* anyway, being married and committed and connected to family and children *causes* you to behave more—*motivates* you to behave more responsibly.

Again, men are thought to need marriage to be "responsible," whereas women seemingly facilitate this process and domesticate men. "Children" are a main argument for this rationale. The pro-marriage version of the *child well-being argument* focuses on the benefits of the child as opposed to the parent. This argument presupposes that parents have distinctly gendered features that affect the future of children and society more than, for instance, economic resources or the nongendered qualities of parents. Unless properly socialized within heterosexual marriage, fathers *and* their children are incomplete, which has large-scale damaging consequences. The "gender and parenting equation" has generational implications. Not only does society need to harness fathers and "tame them to the domestic yoke," but their sons need to become properly "attached" to a woman and family as well. Only fathers have the authority to curb their sons' destructive and violent behavior, and only parental responsibility tied to marital commitment can truly domesticate men into responsible fatherhood. Since there is such a big difference between men and women, there are some gendered teachings the father can do that the mother cannot (and vice versa). As examples of indispensable fatherhood characteristics, marriage proponents often mention self-control and risk taking as particularly fatherly teachings. If fathers are not living with their children and are not married to the mother of their children, their children will be less likely to be "complete."

Apparently both adults and children are positioned within the gender and parenting equation because of male or female variables. Marriage proponents believe that one has to be situated on one side or the other of their gender fence. Moreover, young males need to be affirmed in their manhood by male peers, male role models, or other authoritative and distinctively male figures. One of the father's perceived unique contributions is to role-model and illustrate for sons how to treat women and for daughters how they should be treated by men from a heterosexual male standpoint. Both fathers and sons need some "straight guy talk" with each other and with other men. If the father is absent from a child's life, marriage proponents believe that there is a "father void" and a "father hunger." Marriage proponents often argue that the father also has an irreplaceable role to model "male behavior" in interaction with the mother. Correspondingly, the mother models "female behavior." Children are thus socialized into their proper positions within heterosexual gender relations.

Despite their frequent references to "natural order" and biblical, pop-psychological, or sociobiological ideas, marriage proponents to some degree construct gender inclinations as partly subject to the impact of culture and change. Thus, the pro-marriage gender model is not 100 percent essentialist; rather, it is "loose essentialist." Marriage proponents generally believe in a basic "natural gender order" beneath cultural and historic surfaces. However, they also allow for the cultural surface to exert some influence on gender relations. For instance, this NFI representative starts at the loose end to make an essentialist point in an interview on gendered and parental differences:

> [S]ome would say, not many anymore but for a period of time I think some people would say well, gender is entirely a thing that's in flux. That it's culturally constructed and it changes over a period of time. I think there's some truth to that. And you know we're trying to stretch gender, the gender scripts in America. We think there are men that should be a lot more responsible generally at home. To help with household chores for example. And women quite naturally want to stretch the fairly confined gender boundaries that they've experienced in society. But here we're talking about men and women as parents. Mother as mother. Father as father. And here it appears to us and I think most people generally agree that fathers have a unique contribution to make that it ties back to who they are as, in *nature* if you will, if you believe there's some kind of natural law here or what have you. Something's fairly deeply ingrained.

The representative did not elaborate on this "natural law"—perhaps because he believes it speaks for itself. The general pro-marriage approach is that you can "experiment" and play around with gender relations to a certain extent, for instance, when fathers and mothers help each other out with specific tasks (laundry, driving, babysitting, and the like). But when it comes to children and marriage in general, you need to shape up and be a "serious adult," with important social and moral obligations according to a certain gendered and sexual order. Pro-marriage representatives express different degrees and versions of loose essentialism. In another interview, a well-known pro-marriage representative sounded more "scientific" than the NFI representative above in using a chromosome model of gender difference:

> I think, a father who are X-Y chromosome, brings the masculine, and they bring the feminine. Uh, they bring the justice, and they bring the mercy. The woman who is X-X, for the most part, brings the feminist, she brings the nurturing, uh, and is not as prone to bring the masculinity or to bring that other piece that men have. And so, men bring a balance for the child and the woman that does not. But it doesn't mean that she less than, because the quality of her bringing equals the quality of the man's bringing if they two are together. But if they're separate then the child are overall in the majority fare better with the father than with the mother.

According to this leading pro-marriage representative, the gender and parenting equation is built on the "balance" and complementarity of the male and the female variables. Quite literally, he argues that women lack certain masculine characteristics that only fathers can offer to children. However, marriage proponents constantly point out that equality and difference coexist in their model of marriage and family, and they reiterate that this model is selflessly concerned with children. While making this case in an interview, one (white) pro-marriage representative equated masculinity with fatherhood and used "shepherding" as a metaphor for the father's relation to his family:

> My own view on that is that masculinity generally is in a state of bad repair. Masculinity has broken down because fatherhood has broken down. I think true healthy masculinity involves a lot of tender qualities, a gentleness, a firmness, and strength combined with gentleness. A leadership and initiative that combined with a, sort of servant mentality. Not somebody's who's caught up with and obsessed with authority. Ah, the male being the physically stronger it's easy, it's all too easy for men in cultures everywhere for men to want to use their physical strength to dominate. Our view of the man is that the truly strong man is the man who does not rely on strength but relies on character and who relies on strength of his ah, qualities as a person ah, to serve others, not to dominate. I mean, that's a pretty big challenge for a culture to accomplish that. And our view is that a lot of the acting out is sort of misogynist, violent activity in our music, in our streets, in our gangs, in our rap groups, and what have you, is directly tied back to the absence of fathers who have never taught young boys how to be strong, mature men—to control themselves and to respect others. I mean, so my sense would be that, the good man is the man who is in control of himself and who does not use, does not exercise authority or strength over others but rather is one who ah, who is prepared to serve and to shepherd, in effect.

In other words, this representative feels that men and fathers should relate to women and children in their families as a shepherd relates to sheep. Although he says he believes in difference-based gender equality, there is a hierarchy at work in his metaphor, which he justifies by saying that fathers should respect and serve women and children. His statement illustrates the ways marriage proponents piece together their partly biblically founded vision that male leadership does not necessarily imply sexist inequality if a "servant mentality" is added to it. Another pro-marriage leader illustrated the pro-marriage model of difference-based equality with the following nonbiblical metaphor for the father's place in the family: "You're in the *front seat,* not in the back seat. Sometimes you're driving, sometimes your wife is driving—and you're *different.*" He seems to imply that "true masculinity" is based on difference from women, but he tries to maintain that this difference is nonhierarchical. Another leading marriage proponent put it this way in an interview: "I think true masculinity creates a sense of oneness between men and women. A sense of not sameness, but equality. There's a difference, I think, in equality and sameness, so we're not the same, I'm a male, you're a female, but we both are equal in terms of our ability to um, change environment and make a living in society."

Again, this pro-marriage belief in difference-based equality ignores gendered structural dimensions. Marriage proponents have different ways of qualifying their gendered differentiations between sometimes obviously hierarchical parental responsibilities. For instance, marriage proponents may assert that just because you're a man doesn't mean that you *deserve* to be a leader in your family, even though this is your "natural" role; you have to *acquire* this "natural," responsible servant-mindedness. From a pro-marriage male standpoint, women's subordinate positions in this picture are less interesting.

The ideal pro-marriage man has learned to control his masculinity and use it to benefit society. David Blankenhorn's *Fatherless America* (1995) and George Gilder's *Men and Marriage* (1986) are the most elaborate examples of the pro-marriage argument that men are sexually immoral/promiscuous and aggressive in their "natural" presocialized state and need to find their other "natural" roles within the confines of marriage. When a man picks up the responsibilities and roles that are "wired" into him in the capacity of a husband and father, he reaches his "height" and acquires the "crown" of his masculinity. Here (other than in their sometimes hierarchical metaphors for gender equality) lies one of the most severe paradoxes in the pro-marriage rationale: masculinity (fatherhood) is "wired" but it needs to be socialized. In other words, masculinity is "natural" but not "normal" or morally legitimate. Under the right circumstances, men are guided into marriage and domesticated into responsibility led by "The Force," that is, by their heterosexual urges and competitiveness. One marriage proponent put it this way in the NFI's newsletter, *Fatherhood Today:* "[B]ecoming a father is the crowning event of the transition from a 'natural' male state (where basic appetites and instincts dominate) to the civilized male role (where these crude impulses are productively sublimated into a quest for social honor). But fatherhood is usually only the 'clincher' in the transition from male to man; for most men it is not the main bait. The first and foremost incentive is a woman" (Zinmeister 1996, 7).

His statement exemplifies the ways many pro-marriage thinkers draw on early-nineteenth-century sexology (Weeks 1985; D'Emilio and Freedman 1997) and recent conservative (Gilder 1986; Blankenhorn 1995) ideas that posit women as morally pure and the "civilizers" of men (Kimmel 1996). The process by which women and marriage transforms men from hedonistic beasts into responsible servant leaders is not entirely clear in pro-marriage rhetoric. Moreover, marriage proponents contradict themselves by maintaining that men should simultaneously reinforce *and* change their "natural" state. Men are supposedly indispensable *and* despicable because of the same innate capacities. As will be seen in coming chapters, some of these ideas and dilemmas exist in the fragile-families wing as well. Marriage proponents refer to "nature" or moral order as their fundamental argument for the politics of gender difference. But, at the same time, the "natural" difference that masculinity constitutes is the "problem" they want to change through cultural and social means.

Androgyny and the Case for Married Masculinity

As is apparent above, the type of masculinity that marriage proponents advocate corresponds pretty well to familiar and classic notions of masculinity constructed in relation to notions of not only women but also other men, such as gay and minority men. In the words of the sociologist Michael Schwalbe, a man who lives up to notions of traditional masculinity is "rational, tough, indomitable, ambitious, competitive, in control, able to get a job done, and ardently heterosexual. He must also signify these qualities in a style befitting his ethnicity and social class" (1996, 16). As mentioned earlier, pro-marriage constructions of masculinities are grounded in conceptions of gender difference and the notion of The Force: that all men have innate urges to conquer women and are innately aggressive and competitive. According to pro-marriage thought, men can be differentiated by the ways they channel or manage The Force.

The ideal man uses The Force to benefit society as a married and responsible father and breadwinner. Marriage proponents distinguished between "constructive" and "destructive" masculinities, in contrast to the fragile-families representatives who focus on race/ethnicity and socioeconomic structural differences between men. Nevertheless, pro-marriage distinctions implicitly correspond to socioeconomic and racial stereotypes, evoking the U.S. history of equating white men with civilization and citizenship (Bederman 1995). Low-income/poor and minority men are thought to more typically misdirect The Force into violent, nonmonogamous, irresponsible "hyper"/ "protest masculinity," or "masculine excess." Such notions have contributed to the stigmatization of African American fathers throughout U.S. history and have asserted white men's centrality to the nation and civilization. Racial stereotypes often blend into socioeconomic stereotypes in pro-marriage notions of "constructive" and "destructive" masculinities. For instance, one pro-marriage representative contrasted low-income/poor men with the destructive versions of middle- and upper-class masculinities, which are distorted by feminine traits instead of "hypermasculinity." In the eyes of many marriage proponents, there is a recent "androgyny" trend among middle- and upper-class white men, especially among academics. Notions of "new fatherhood" that deemphasize gender difference are particularly troublesome to marriage proponents. Drawing on century-old concerns about "feminization," they equate such notions with "androgyny," which is perceived as a dangerous development in recent parenting discourses.

The pro-marriage androgyny concept is twofold. Marriage proponents defend against "androgyny advocacy" and construct notions of androgyny as deviance, based on gendered and sexualized notions of normality. In other words, *androgyny* is a term that marriage proponents use not only to label and discredit enemy *strategies* but also to construct "perverted" *results* of such perceived adversarial gender and sexual politics. According to leading pro-marriage representatives, there are interest groups in family policy, public debate, and education that are opposed to the very thought of gender difference and instead try to uphold an erroneous model of gender sameness. Representatives were vague about exactly who these interest groups are or represent, but some of them pointed out "feminism" as a main force behind "gender neutralization politics." For instance, Wade Horn traces the emergence of "the myth of the androgyny ideal" to the 1960s: "Out of a concern for greater social equity, androgyny advocates preached that men and women not only to be treated exactly the same, but to behave the same as well. . . . Once androgyny advocates established that most fathers were 'doing it wrong' [and should be more like mothers], it became relatively easy to argue that fathers were not really necessary to the 'modern' family" (Horn 1997, 25).

"Androgyny advocates" are supposedly against men and masculinity in and of themselves. They want to change men into something they are not: feminine. In condemning men's natures, "androgyny advocates" are perceived as wanting to make men and fathers "superfluous" to the family. In the pro-marriage view, the "androgynizers" try to undermine the legitimacy of fathers and relegate the men-marriage-children trinity to the periphery. David Popenoe, one of the leading marriage proponents who currently runs the Rutgers University–based National Marriage Project, argues that "often it is said that fathers should be more like mothers. While this is said with the best of intentions, the effects are perverse. After all, if fathering is no different from mothering, males can easily be replaced in the home by women" (1998, 40).

Despite this kind of rhetoric, it is not exactly clear what kind of damage "androgyny" does except to feminize men. In this understanding of masculinity, "too few" masculine traits seem to be as bad as "too many." From what I could gather from pro-marriage representatives, nonandrogynous masculinity is marked by the "male traits" of "aggression," "competitiveness," and heterosexual "promiscuity"; in contrast, androgynous, or feminized, masculinity is characterized by fewer of these traits. In an interview, Harry, one of the leading figures in the pro-marriage wing, depicted androgynous masculinity in terms of a "softie" type of "I-cry-at-movies masculinity." He seemed to think that it makes men look like sissies to be "Mr. Moms." He described "the androgyny ideal" as encouraging men to take on motherly roles, which he deemed "impossible" and "stupid":

> Up 'til now, a lot of parenting education programs take what mothers do naturally and say to men, "You want to be a good parent? Do like what mothers do!" And rather than say "Gee, you know, what guys do as fathers is maybe different from what mothers tend to do as mothers, but doesn't mean it's *worse*. It doesn't mean that one is doing it right, and the other is doing it wrong." You've heard of the movie *Mr. Mom* [depicting a stay-at-home father], and you've heard people refer to stay at home fathers as Mr. Moms. That's pretty insulting! I mean, why don't we call mothers that stay at home with their kids Mrs. Dads? Never! The fact of the matter is, men are men, women are women, fathers and mothers are doing things *somewhat* differently. Not that the one is doing it right and the other is doing it wrong, and what we ought to do is honor, respect and support the unique contributions of fathers and mothers. Not—And basically what this is, it's an argument against androgyny as an ideal. I think androgyny is impossible in practice and stupid in theory.

According to Harry, men think that androgyny not only is against their nature but also makes them look ridiculous when they perform what they consider mothering practices. Harry did not ponder why it might be perceived degrading for a man to be compared with a woman. Again, his pro-marriage perspective is completely detached from structural aspects. Furthermore, Harry probably equates androgyny with "too much" effeminacy and with men who do not sufficiently define themselves in binary opposite relation to women—for instance, gay men. As is apparent in Harry's statements earlier in this section, the problem he sees here is not that men *cannot* do things he conceives of as female tasks and behaviors but that they do not feel *comfortable* about it. They do not feel it is quite "them." The anti-androgyny argument against the feminization of men seems to make both culturalist and essentialist points: that men do not *want* to be more like women and that there are biological, moral, and "innate behavioral" differences between men and women that make certain changes "unnatural." It all comes back to the idea that there is no way you can erase The Force. Attempts to do so only misdirect it and turn it against society. You need to stroke and appease and carefully cultivate The Force in ways that appeal specifically to men. Furthermore, you need to do so in ways that reaffirm biological and heterosexual men's place at the center of gendered, sexual, social, and moral order.

I quote at length from an interview I had with John, another well-known marriage proponent, to illustrate the ways marriage proponents attempt to revive pro-marriage masculinity as a moral value in defending against feminist criticism. John echoes Popenoe and Horn in maintaining that social constructivist feminist scholarship is an excuse to reform men into androgyny:

> [As a] result of a lot of feminist scholarship and arguments and a lot a result of the women's movement, but also just probably a lot of other things too . . . , has really caused a questioning of the very idea of masculinity and considerable schools of thought that say basically that masculinity, as understood in traditional terms, is bad. And [that] it should be basically gotten rid of, and that it *can* be gotten rid of; it's just social construction and therefore it can be socially deconstructed and replaced by something else. Which could be more along the lines of an androgynous personality or, you know, what I think of generally as of to an idea that men should become a lot more like women. That is, they should become less aggressive, less instrumental in their treatment of others, more nurturant towards others, and so on. And so therefore tradition—masculinity, because it is viewed as emphasizing instrumentalism, aggression, competition and rule oriented behavior, it is considered *bad*—just bad.

While John defines true and innate masculinity as aggressive et cetera, he also laments that such traits are under attack and that men are *accused* of being this way, just as mythopoetics do (see introduction). Such accusations just create confusion, because, in his view, men are still left with The Force, no matter how much you criticize it. If you scold men for being their "bad" selves, the only other alternative is to be like women, who are supposed to be binary opposites. In John's view, masculinity as traditionally understood is being devalued by feminization, while femininity has extended into domains formerly defined as masculine:

> I think that, you know, to me at least, for women over the last twenty or thirty years, there's been a sense that for a lot of women it seems to me that [there has been] the *expansion* of their femininity. That is, the notion that you don't just have to be this thing, you can also be these other things. You can, in addition to being, having a satisfying, you know, relationship with your mate and with your chi—— In addition to being a mother, in addition to, you know, being sexually attractive, in addition to having a home, you can also be successful in the workplace, you can also be a full partici-

pant in public life, you can also get just as much—deserve just as much in the world of education, money—that's been the basic kind of idea for women. And so it's been an expansion of—you know, "You can be more." For *men,* I think it's been more a sense of "What you are isn't good." [Big laugh] Which is very different: not like, you know, it's like "You need to replace some parts of what you are with something really different. And therefore—and if you don't, you're a bad person. You were causing the rain forests to get smaller, you were causing nuclear weapons to proliferate, you were causing domestic violence, you are basically a *bad guy.* [Laughs] Once you're doing these things, you know you're standing in the way of social justice, you're lagging behind the changes of the modern world [in an ironic tone of voice]." You know, there's just a thousand ways of saying this. But basically, the message is: "Not good—got to change!"

In John's view, while women have *expanded* into masculine territories, men have been reprimanded for their "bad" selves. Hence, change of masculinity into traits perceived as feminine is synonymous with reduction—*less* of the traits defined as masculine:

Me: And change into something that is considered more feminine, or—?
John: Change into something that's more—more of a, toward more of an androgynous, or more of nurturant type of person: less aggression, less instrumentalism, less competitiveness, less workaholism, less competing with other men over money, sex—"Do a lot less of that which is bad— do a lot more of those other things." For all kinds of reasons [in an angry voice]: "Because if you don't, you're oppressing women, because if you don't, you're messing up your children, because if you don't you're going to have a heart attack and die because it's a terrible way to live your life. Just don't do these old bad things that your father and grandfather did— do these new things that you're supposed to do because this is the new age." And I think a lot of guys [sighs] they don't listen to that too much, *but* they know, because *enough* part of the world, that I think there's a sense of, like, what does it really mean to be a man today, you know, is there something wrong with masculinity?

John lost me here. Does he think that aggressiveness and competitiveness are flattering traits in men? Does he think it is okay for men to oppress people? When trying to explain the damage "androgyny" does, John maintains that change to gender equality is good but that beyond a certain point it becomes destructive; change is good as long as it does not disturb the general heteronormative gender order or threaten the androcentric trinity:

To me, I guess a lot of it is a question of getting a balance on things. I think that some of the changes towards more flexibility [of gender roles within marriage] has been good, and certainly towards the equal regard model. I think, to me, that's the essential issue here: towards the elimination of the notion of superiority and inferiority that is yet the core change that I think is . . . a real achievement. . . . To me it's just a question of *limiting* the point where it starts to turn into something that's bad. You know, when does a trend cease to become good and start to cause more problems than it causes solutions? And I think the notion of androgynous model of parenthood, if it really does go beyond the notion of equal regard and beyond the notion of somewhat greater flexibility in gender roles, it starts to attack the very *notion* of gender roles and it starts to attack the very notion of sex differences in parenting. I think that's when it becomes destructive for the well-being of children and destructive of the possibility of sustainable marriage. And . . . destructive of ongoing sexual attraction between men and women. So I guess the judgment is, at what point does a trend start to change from something that has positive social benefits to something that has negative social results? When we question the validity of sex roles per se and we question—view masculinity as essentially bad, we reject the idea of . . . sex difference and hold up an androgynous model, I think that's when it crosses the line and becomes destructive. I think there is *great* empirical evidence for this. . . . I think there are pretty good reasons to think that *androgyny* is not good for children, and I think there are pretty good reasons for believing that if you attack the notion of sex roles, we're going to [undermine] fatherhood. I think there are pretty good reasons for believing that sexuality—sexual happiness, the sexual relationship . . . deteriorates under . . . androgyny. I think there are empirical reasons for believing these things to be true.

Thus, androgyny (which John seems to identify both as a "model" promoted by, for example, feminists and as a feminized way of being male) is destructive to the well-being of children and society. It is destructive because it neutralizes gender difference, which destroys the basis for heterosexuality, marriage, and fatherhood. John welcomes flexibility and "equal regard" between men and women up to a certain point. But when it starts to attack the heteronormative foundations for social order, it becomes destructive. These views underscore a main point among marriage proponents: that men should get accepted in "the family" *as men* (Popenoe 1996; Blankenhorn 1995). Celebrating essentially "unique" male-parenting contributions, marriage proponents defend men against having to participate in practices considered "feminine."

Whiteness and the All-Encompassing Pro-Marriage Perspective

John speaks from and defends a perspective that traditionally has been the hallmark of white heterosexual working- and middle-class masculinities. However, one explanation marriage proponents give for the differences between the two wings of the fatherhood responsibility movement is that the fragile-families wing focuses on a *specific* and limited group of fathers, whereas the pro-marriage wing works with *all* fathers—not just one target group. Unlike fragile-families representatives, white marriage proponents are not stigmatized, stereotyped, or discriminated against in terms of gender, sexuality, race, or socioeconomic class. On the contrary, most of the leading pro-marriage representatives at the time of my fieldwork were extremely successful in their careers and politics and have held many important top-level governmental offices. For instance, Wade Horn is the former president of the NFI, the former U.S. commissioner for children, youth, and families, the former chief of the Children's Bureau, and currently the assistant secretary for children and families in the Department of Health and Human Services. Don Eberly, the CEO and chairman of the NFI, is a former key congressional and White House aide and is now the deputy director of the White House Office of Faith-Based and Community Initiatives. The marriage proponents I interviewed often had pictures on their walls and in their newsletters of themselves shaking hands with other powerful men, such as the president of the United States and famous politicians. It is not surprising that these successful men steer clear of criticizing the structures and institutions that had taken them so far. Neither is it surprising that the pro-marriage wing of the fatherhood responsibility movement calls for a confrontation with "culture"—not with the ruling class or a dominant group. They do, however, willingly confront the vaguely defined "androgyny advocates," whom marriage proponents sometimes call the "cultural elite." Marriage proponents claim that their campaigns are designed to ensure that the cultural norms uphold marriage, not to challenge any powerful political interest group. For pro-marriage groups, asymmetric social and economic arrangements, in, for example, the labor market or education, do not matter to fatherhood issues as much as cultural ideas and practices do. Needless to say, a culturalist perspective appeals more to men who are the least disadvantaged by socioeconomic opportunity structures.

Marriage proponents may or may not be white themselves, and they may or may not resonate with minority or low-income/poor men. To put it differently, an organization may have, for instance, an African American representative saying that race does not matter. The point is that pro-marriage organizations speak from an authoritative universalizing perspective in promoting norms and institutions that traditionally have reinforced the hegemony of heterosexual, white, Protestant, middle- and upper-class masculinity. Historically, the marital institution has obviously privileged men over women as household heads (Cott 2000; Moore 1988). Furthermore, marriage has been the privilege of white men, not poor African American men.

Historically and contemporarily, through slavery, segregation, discrimination, and unemployment, African American men have lacked the autonomy and resources to support a family and thus the economic foundation to make choices about marriage. In focusing on more generic, universalist notions of "culture" and gender difference, marriage proponents speak from positions and outlooks that are unmarked rhetorically by male privileges or race and socioeconomic class. Many fragile-families representatives question this rhetoric and maintain that marriage proponents represent white middle-class men's interests. However, pro-marriage representatives would not agree with any analysis that pins them down to any of these categories, and they would also be able to name exceptions that would "disprove" any generalizations about them as a group or constituency. For instance, the National Fatherhood Initiative, whose leaders were all white men at the time of my fieldwork,[3] collaborates with the pro-marriage Institute for Responsible Fatherhood and Family Revitalization, lead by Charles Ballard, who is African American. The race of representatives is sometimes less important or interesting than the premises of their approach. Charles Ballard's organization is often mentioned by marriage proponents as evidence that the pro-marriage model works with poor African American populations too.

Marriage proponents do not usually speak from an explicit *perspective.* They maintain they are just making common sense, which has little to do with the racial and socioeconomic conditions of themselves or others as far as they are concerned. White and minority marriage proponents do not think of themselves as racialized at all; rather, they see themselves as generic representatives of fatherhood responsibility. They think it is beside the point that whiteness and middle- and upper-class outlooks historically mark their notions of ideal masculinity. They therefore insist on not attributing importance to socioeconomic and racial aspects that might affect the positions of different fathers. Marriage proponents are a perfect illustration of the ways whiteness makes itself invisible by, in the American studies scholar Ruth Frankenberg's words, "asserting its normalcy, its transparency, in contrast with the making of others on which its transparency depends" (1997, 6). Whiteness, like heterosexuality (see chapter 5), is inseparable from systems of racial, sexual, and gendered dominance because each construction depends on the subordinate statuses of racial, gendered, and sexual "others" (Katz 1995). The "slipperiness of whiteness," according Frankenberg, is more about "othering" and exclusion than about the actual constructions and practices of whiteness (1997, 13). Nevertheless, to investigate whiteness and processes of "whitening," one needs to situate whiteness historically and contextually and to trace the ways specific constructions of whiteness interplay with constructions of gender, sexuality, and socioeconomic class (Frankenberg, ed., 1997). Situating marriage proponents in the wider context of racial and socioeconomic contestation between men in the fatherhood responsibility movement, as well as in their antagonistic relation to feminist and gay/lesbian politics, allows such tracing.

There is one stereotype about themselves that white marriage proponents do mention: being depicted as "bad guys" or "Neanderthals" who want to turn back the clock to the time when "womenfolk knew their place" and white heterosexual men had unlimited privileges over everybody else. Pro-marriage representatives constantly try to defend themselves against such bad-guy stereotypes by positioning themselves in adversarial relation to "radical feminist" discourses that they claim depict men as misogynist patriarchs. Marriage proponents also defend themselves against claims by representatives of African American men that they merely represent the concerns of middle- and upper-class white men. This kind of defensive rhetoric suggests that the feminist and civil rights movements have partly succeeded in making gendered and sexual privilege, as well as white middle- and upper-class masculinities, visible and problematic. Competing minority men and feminist claims increasingly challenge middle- and upper-class white men in the labor market and government policy (Robinson 2000). Moreover, the marriage proponents' protests against "radical feminist" accusations indicate that the supremacy of married heterosexual men is no longer self-evident, since they feel a need to defend these ideals.

Pro-marriage representatives who habitually spoke on behalf of "all men" did sometimes acknowledge that particularistic "subgroups" of men, such as fragile-families representatives, might have "their specific issues." Here they make a subtle distinction between themselves as generic representatives and exceptional populations with certain "problems." When speaking about problems and solutions concerning men and fathers, marriage proponents may sometimes end up excluding and discounting the outlooks of fragile-families fathers. This creates tensions between marriage proponents and fragile-families representatives within the fatherhood responsibility movement. One marriage proponent I interviewed indirectly touched on this tension:

> A lot of times when we come to cities with a large black population, they often try to whip up a discussion about race, and ask us, "How can you say this about our community?" And we say, "We're not judging, we're observing." They say that because African Americans are making a lot less money, everything would be better if they just made as much money as whites, that it's about economy. But we say that a two-parent [poor?] black

family is doing better that a one-parent white family. So it's more about something else, or maybe both.

Because most marriage proponents at the time of my fieldwork were middle- and upper-class white men, they saw no urgent need to focus on the structural positions and opportunities of different men. Some marriage proponents spoke about fatherlessness in poor African American communities in terms of an illness that now has spread to white communities or is threatening to contaminate them. Other white marriage proponents even claimed to be victims of reverse racism. For instance, Harry was annoyed by African Americans' "racist" claims that the NFI is a "white" organization that does not understand the black community:

> We talk about marriage and guys who argue with us say black people, marriage is gone in black communities so we can't expect black people to value marriage. They never say it that clearly, but let me tell you that's how clear it is. I think it's racist, I think it's patronizing, I think it's paternalistic to make those claims, and, unfortunately, it's a lot of black guys that are making those claims. I think they're doing a disservice to the black community by saying that, and I think in the long run it's quite self-destructive of their own communities. Show me the evidence that the black community can survive with 70 percent out-of-wedlock birthrate. Show me the evidence that that's possible in the absence of marriage. And you know what? I think they're disconnected from their own constituencies because, guess what, I go in and I talk to black audiences, I talk on urban black radio. And guess what, I don't get people saying, "You're a white guy, go home." What I get is, "You're exactly right. This is the problem. We've got to figure out how to make families stronger in the black community and one way to do that is to reestablish the expectation of marriage." I'm sorry, I don't know who they're talking to. They're talking to each other, I guess, but they're not talking to the same minorities I'm talking to. Guess what, minorities care about marriage. Guess what, they want to get married. Black folk want to get married. Hispanic folk want to get married. They don't go, "Marriage, what's that? I've never heard of that." They don't go, "Marriage, that's a white man's institution, I don't want marriage for my kids."

Harry seems to think that marriage should unite rather than divide different constituencies of men. He overlooks the fact that poor and minority constituencies of men (as well as white middle-class men) approach marriage from positions within particular opportunity structures that affect their ability to make choices about family formation. When prescribing marriage across lines of race/ethnicity and socioeconomic class, Harry does speak from a perspective that is more viable to some constituencies of men than to others. As many fragile-families representatives point out, the "playing field" of competing masculinities is uneven, and not all men have opportunities to become breadwinning husbands. The beauty of Harry's pro-marriage view, however, is that it makes perfect sense given its presumptions. It is like balancing an equation: one can shift its variables around, divide, multiply, and exponentialize but still come down to the same balancing principle. However, one must not forget that the pro-marriage way of making sense in its all-encompassing logic and convincing "evidence" is just one of many ways of seeing things. If one focuses too much on the pro-marriage "answer," one forgets that it is built on certain variables and assumptions that do not necessarily provide clarity or make sense to everyone, namely:

— Culture, as opposed to socioeconomic structures, is the driving force behind, and the key to, social processes.
— Gender difference and heterosexuality are innate sociobiological or biblically ordained predispositions that dictate "natural order," normality, and maturity.
— Men need an external force or authority so that they are not destructive to themselves or others.

Furthermore, these assumptions do not always fit neatly together. For example, marriage proponents may sometimes seem to contradict themselves by arguing that men should be encouraged to follow their "innate predispositions" *and* that they need to be controlled by external regulations. In making these arguments, marriage proponents simultaneously deny legitimacy to a range of alternative views and perspectives. Nevertheless, a common pro-marriage rhetorical strategy is simply to claim that they make more sense than others according to their notions of "evidence," their calculations of likelihood and generalizations. Pro-marriage representatives frequently add to their sentences "evidence supports this" or "research says that" without naming or elaborating on these sources, and they often cite bewildering statistics to support their arguments. They commonly reason through a series of rhetorical questions that lead to one answer. With such tricks, some marriage proponents tried to make me feel really "smart." After demonstrating that I managed to follow their logic, they congratulated me and made me feel that I was almost as clever as they were, as is evidenced in an interview I had with Harry:

Harry: Call me an old fogey, but I think that men ought to be married to the mothers of their children before they father children! And the reason I say that is not because I'm some old *fuddy duddy* you know stuck in some Neanderthal times, or some, you know, patriarchal, you know, misogynist who hates women, but because if you looked through the eyes of a child and you said; . . . "Here are the two fathers you can pick from— one category is a in-the-home, loves-the-mother, married father. The other category is an unwed father who is not living with the mother, but established paternity, comes by once a week and sends his *child support check* every two weeks. OK, child; pick—which father do you want?" What are most kids going to pick?

Me: Well, the first one then—

Harry: Of course! So why do we hold out as a model for the new responsible father category two instead of the first category?

With this marriage quiz, Harry helped me figure out what makes more sense from everyone's point of view: to pick the married father. When one looks at things from "a child's perspective," one supposedly moves beyond ideology, politics, or group interest. Harry made a couple of disclaimers so that feminists would not think he speaks from a masculinist perspective and to stress that he is actually just concerned about the well-being of children. But one might wonder: when do people hold up Harry's category two as a model for families? Is Harry implying that "feminists" maintain that children should *not* have fathers who are married to their mothers?

As mentioned earlier, it is typical for a pro-marriage culturalist perspective to insist on nonstructural interpretations of the social and economical processes that condition the positions of different men and women. Since their definitions of social problems and their solutions diverge from those of feminist critics (Gillis 1996; Roberts 1998; Silverstein and Auerbach 1999; Stacey 1996) as well as fragile-families representatives, marriage proponents are bound to be "misunderstood." The pro-marriage culturalist approach permeates their work with policymakers and the practitioners who work directly with fathers. For example, in describing barriers to father involvement at a practitioner workshop, Joe, one of my key pro-marriage interviewees, identified them as partly *psychological* (the other parts were legal barriers and the physical environment of the programs). As a *subheading* for psychological barriers to father involvement, Joe mentioned the especially high unemployment rates for African American teens. On the topic of legal barriers, Joe went on to say that child support awards are not enough to "cure" poverty. Again, he chose to describe a problem in medical/psychological terms rather in than economic/structural ones. Bob, another key pro-marriage interviewee, elaborated on the approach to unemployment as a psychological problem: "There is at least three barriers that men encounter . . . psychological barriers and legal barriers, and then there's also . . . environmental barriers, but those would be barriers like say within a school site or a place where there's social services. . . . And the psychological would be; 'Well gee, I don't have a job, I'm supposed to be the breadwinner, so therefore I shouldn't be involved with my kids.' And that would be a huge psychological barrier."

Marriage proponents have been criticized by fragile-families representatives for being too far removed from the everyday struggles of poor, unemployed minority men. Identifying unemployment as a psychological problem just sounds "goofy," as one fragile-families representative put it, and so does recommending marriage to men with far more urgent legal and economic problems than being unmarried. Nevertheless, marriage proponents firmly believe that there is something in the institution of marriage itself that is indispensable to men and American society. They do realize that there are marriages that do not work and that marriage does not guarantee the well-being of children, but they argue that *in general,* the structure of heterosexual marriage, regardless of its content, is the only viable counterstrategy for fatherlessness. Cohabitation is, in the words of one marriage proponent, a "very weak family form" and likely to be temporary. Nor does nonresidential fatherhood work well because it does not provide for the reliable, long-term presence of the father in the children's lives. In the pro-marriage view, the fragile-families notion of team parenting is not as sustainable as marriage. According to one leading marriage proponent, there is a big difference between their hard line on marriage and the more flexible approach of the fragile-families organizations. Whereas the fragile-families representatives maintain that men should wait until they are financially and emotionally ready to father children, marriage proponents say that men should be married before they have children.

Marriage proponents do not *intend* to discriminate against people who do not meet the ideal of marriage. In the words of one practitioner speaking at an NFI conference, they intend to "reach the unreachable and teach the unteachable." Another marriage proponent echoed a common stance in the pro-marriage wing saying, "We're just saying that marriage is important. We're not saying that it's going to solve everybody's problems." Despite their explicit policies of dealing with all fathers regardless of their marital situation, marriage proponents are often criticized by fragile-families representatives for disregarding the realities of low-income/poor, unmarried, and minority fathers. Bob described this contestation:

> Some local programs don't want to talk about marriage, because it's seen as passive judgment. We're just saying that it could be a beneficial thing. It's not the solution and it's one portion of it. With marriage, people think that you're making a value/moral judgment. People get sensitive about the topic . . . so they choose not to address it. Some organizations would put priority to working with fragile families, but we have the priority to work with all fathers. . . . What drives the differences between organizations is the different target groups among fathers. We try to address all. . . . If it

would come down to marriage, collaboration would not work. When it comes to the marriage thing, you either talk about it, or you don't—you can't compromise about it. . . . I don't think marriageability is an economic question. Even if you're very minimally employed, if you put your money together, you're already above poverty level. When you only have to work for yourself, there is less incentive to get a job. Marriage can serve as an incentive to increase employability. But of course unemployment/availability is a factor.

The reasons fragile-families representatives are "sensitive about the topic" of marriage are clarified in the next chapter.

Notes

1. Other prominent fatherhood movement figures active in the marriage movement include Wade Horn, Maggie Gallagher, Michael McManus, Theodora Ooms, and Barbara Dafoe Whitehead.

2. Many pro-marriage leaders use the notion of civilization to argue for the importance of marriage and fatherhood (see, for instance, Popenoe 1996).

3. The current president, Roland Warren, is African American.

3   Fragile-Family Fatherhood

Playing Catch-Up with The Man

See, for what we've been through and the way that we're treated, we are
expected to act as if we're white, but . . . we're treated as if we're not white,
and I'm not going to go along *with that—they're not going to make* me
schizophrenic!

—African American fragile-families interviewee

The sociologist Michael Kimmel describes U.S. masculinity as a homosocial enactment, where the quest for masculine accomplishments in the
labor market and consumption is a constant competition between men for the
sake of other men's approval (Kimmel 1994, 128–29). In line with notions of
homosocial competition, fragile-families representatives constantly point out
that men's success in the marketplace determines their marriage potential and
that, compared with white middle-class men, poor African American men are
disadvantaged in terms of their marriageability. Obtaining a job and acquiring a wife are thus interdependent goals in fragile fathers' battles to compete
with white middle-class men *as men* (Messner 1997, 69; Segal 1990). However,
fragile-families organizations also seek to construct *alternative* masculinities
based on racial/cultural/ethnic pride, independent from notions of white
middle-class culture.

Kimmel describes postindustrial U.S. ideals of *marketplace masculinity* as
characterized by aggression, competition, and anxiety in the labor and con-
sumer markets (1994, 124). Economic success since the early-nineteenth-cen-

tury Industrial Revolution has been less stable because of the unstable nature of economic forces in the marketplace (Kimmel 1996, 9). The U.S. postindustrial myth of the self-made man, writes Kimmel, is uncomfortably linked to the volatile marketplace, where the self-made man depends on continued mobility (1996, 17). Kimmel argues that ideals of self-made men in the marketplace still affect what contemporarily defines a "real" man (1996, 17). He also argues that marketplace masculinity is predicated on the exclusion of men who are not successful in the marketplace, such as low-income and poor nonwhite men (1994, 124). However, rather than critique the ideals of white middle-class masculinity and its exclusionary asymmetric implications, many fragile-families representatives envision marketplace notions of masculinity as a desired position of power and self-respect to which African American and minority men have been denied access (Segal 1990). Poor, African American, and other minority men's struggles for access and recognition *as men* are reflected at an organizational level in fatherhood politics. To gain a voice and get access to what fragile-families representatives call the "playing field" of fatherhood politics, fragile-families organizations compete with pro-marriage organizations for funds and political influence, framing their claims in terms of racial justice while simultaneously aligning themselves strategically with pro-marriage politics. At the same time, fragile-families representatives support "women's interests" in family policy that are considered anathema to pro-marriage organizations.

As we have seen in previous chapters, marriage proponents do not find race or socioeconomic class relevant to fatherhood responsibility issues. Thus, for instance, white marriage proponents do not attribute any political meaning to their whiteness. However, race and socioeconomic class are integral to fragile-families fatherhood politics. For low-income, poor, and minority men, fatherhood politics entails a struggle, in the words of one fragile-families representative, to "catch up" with white middle-class men and compete in education and the labor market. Particularly from an African American male standpoint, white middle- and upper-class men are an ever-present reference point in constructions of masculinity. While trying to compete with white middle-class men on what they perceive as a pro-marriage dominated "playing field" of fatherhood politics, fragile-families organizations risk buying into the very power structures they seek to subvert. This places practitioners—social workers, coordinators, or educators who work at the local fathers' programs—in an ambivalent position between compliance and resistance.

Practitioners who work with so-called fragile families, as well as the fathers who participate in their programs, construct African American masculinities and fatherhoods in relation to a long tradition of policy discourse. Such discourses stigmatize African American men as particularly problematic in terms of violence, criminality, and sexuality (Majors and Billson 1992; Duneier 1992; Staples 1982). Although fragile-families representatives resist racist policy stereotypes of poor and minority men, they sometimes draw on notions of violent, "sexually illegitimate," "protest masculinity" and notions of "negativity" in their promotion of "responsible fatherhood" and middle-class "respectability." On the one hand, fragile-families representatives fight the ways such stereotypes as "protest masculinity" have been used to stigmatize African American men. On the other hand, fragile-families organizations also seek to deal with the actual problems of fathers who face such issues as drug abuse, violence, and family relations. In walking a fine line between these concerns, fragile-families representatives are caught between criticizing power relations among men and competing with other men over the badges of masculinity, that is, breadwinner success and household leadership (Segal 1990).

Breadwinnerhood is at the nexus of marketplace masculinity, as well as the basis for men's standing in the marriage market. The ability to support a family and thus gain the *resources* to make choices about marriage is a core issue for the fragile-families wing. To fragile-families organizations, the racial and socioeconomic inequalities among men in the labor market, as well as the gendered relations of the marriage market, are linked in the struggles of poor and minority men to achieve recognition as men and fathers. Unlike the pro-marriage groups that use a moral/culturalist approach to family formation, fragile-families organizations apply a structuralist/economic perspective and focus on the barriers to breadwinning and marriage among poor and minority men.

Drawing on the long-standing struggles of minority men who share similar gendered, socioeconomic, and racialized histories, fragile-families organizations are sites for grassroots recognition struggles and civil rights mobilization that stretch beyond fatherhood programs. The practitioners and the fathers who participate in local programs reconfirm and support one another's aspirations for traditionally overlapping ideals of manhood and empowerment. The low-income, poor, and minority men in the fragile-families wing conceive of themselves as equal "brothers," but some "brothers" are simultaneously role models for others. Practitioners who act as "role models" could be seen as intermediary agents in their simultaneous capacities as "brothers" representing constituencies of low-income/poor and minority men *and* role models representing "The System"[1]—white mainstream society, social services, the business sector, governmental agencies, and law enforcement or all these combined. Fragile-families representatives generally perceive this "system" as a force controlled by white middle-class men, a force that feeds on the oppression of African American and other minority men. Practitioners simultaneously assume the standpoint of their constituencies *and* collaborate with government agencies they perceive as traditionally antagonistic to poor and minority men, such as Child Support Enforcement.[2] Practitioners therefore constantly need to reconfirm that they are one of the "brothers" without seeming like "sell-outs" to "the system" that employs them and with whom they must collaborate. Practitioners embody the tension between compliance and resistance to values they perceive as white and middle class.

In low-income, poor, and minority men's struggles to participate as "equal players" in the labor and marriage markets, other more powerful *men* are the primary competitors. As seen in the last chapter, this contrasts with the marriage proponents' struggles to reclaim masculinity in relation to *women*. Thus, fragile-families representatives frame gender politics primarily in terms of homosocial competition rather than in terms of a battle between men and women. However, contestations over gendered relations—in other words, the division of labor and leadership between (heterosexual) men and women—are still important in redefining minority masculinities and fatherhoods. While seeking to redefine masculinities within an egalitarian approach to gender and families, parts of the fragile-families wing draw on masculinist traditions in African American political and academic discourses that posit men's domination of women as a legitimate masculine claim (Segal 1990, 192). These contesting and contradictory elements of fragile-families masculinity politics reflect complex rhetorical strategies and alliances in the fatherhood responsibility movement.

Thomas, one of the leading figures within the fragile-families wing, framed the struggles of "fragile fathers" to compete with white men in terms of struggles for equal economic and social opportunities. "Poor people in this country want to do the same things that rich people: they want the same thing that every middle-class American does. . . . And that is: they want a job, they want to raise a family, they want to see that their kids grow up healthy and happy," he declared in an interview. He described the goals as American core values but identified a difference in the fatherhood responsibility movement over *how* to achieve "successful" fatherhood, because "all Americans didn't start in the same place." White middle-class men have been privileged over poor and African American men throughout "their entire multigenerational history." Thomas emphasized that poor African American men are particularly disadvantaged in the labor market because "employers generally hire people who look like them, who live in the same neighborhoods being like them, and the majority of employers in this country are white."

Thomas and many of his colleagues draw heavily on the work of the sociologist William Julius Wilson in describing the central issue of African American men's employment situations. In *The Truly Disadvantaged,* Wilson argues that the "sex and marital status of the head [of low-income and poor African American families] are the most important determinants of poverty status for families" (1987, 71), because families headed by a single female are more likely to be poor. He states that "the problems of male joblessness could be the single most important factor underlying the rise in unwed mothers among poor black women" (1987, 73). Wilson investigates the ways male unemployment affects "marital instability," the "decreasing supply of marriageable men," and the increasing numbers of poor African American, female-headed families (1987). He contrasts these processes with the conditions for white middle-class families, where "trends in male employments and earnings appear to have little to do with the increase in female-headed families"(1987, 83). In *When Work Disappears,* Wilson reiterates these arguments but also accounts for the interaction between "material and cultural constraints" in discussing the decreasing marriage rates among inner-city African American parents (1996, 97).

Poor and unskilled African American men face declining opportunities in the labor market because of recent changes in the nature of work. In accounting for this, Wilson contrasts a number of African American Chicago inner-city neighborhoods over time. The majority of adults in the neighborhoods under study held jobs in 1950; in the 1990s, only four in ten, one in three, and one in four worked in these same neighborhoods (1996, 19). Low-skilled male workers were jobless eight and a half weeks longer at the end of the 1980s than at the end of the 1960s. A drop in real wages and an erosion of career opportunities have accompanied the increases of joblessness among low-skilled workers (1996, 25). The sharp decline in employment among low-skilled African American men is also related to discrimination, neighborhood segregation, the decline of U.S. industry, and the expansion of the service sector, which hires more women than men (1996, 26–27). The wage and employment gap between skilled and low-skilled workers is widening partly because the new global economy requires higher degrees of education and training (1996, 28).

In addition to the barriers in the labor market Wilson discusses, fragile-families representatives identify structural barriers for "fragile fathers" in welfare policy, child support laws, public housing policies, and the social environment of low-income/poor and minority men (Mincy and Pouncy 1999). For instance, the fragile-families representative Ronald Mincy and the political scientist Hillard Pouncy mention housing subsidies as a factor that needs to be calculated in the "income/benefits trap associated with welfare." For a fatherless family, rent may be quite low, whereas the rent for a two-parent family may be more than the family can afford (1999, 100). Fragile-families representatives describe a vicious circle in which unemployed, low-income, and poor men's low self-esteem *as men* affects their labor market positions negatively, which further breaks down their self-esteem while they confront barriers to meeting society's gendered expectations and compete with (white) middle-class men. Some fragile-families representatives frame poor and minority men's struggles to obtain white middle-class male ideals as "the Ozzie and Harriet syndrome." This expression refers to a popular television show in the 1950s about a white male breadwinner and a female homemaker in a nuclear family. One representative explained the Ozzie and Harriet syndrome in an interview:

> The standard of the white male is to be the head of the household, which has to do with economic factors. The Ozzie and Harriet picture of the housewife and the male breadwinner is still prevalent in *some* sectors in society, but this is not the case in AFDC-receiving households.[3] That's not real here—not with most guys here: there are not equal opportunities for jobs and education. To these guys, to provide for a family is a struggle in itself. The Ozzie and Harriet syndrome means that men get self-respect from being a breadwinner, and this is the way his children and society looks at him. How does society look at men out there who are out on the street selling newspapers? Breadwinning opportunities are not offered to them!

In the view of this representative, breadwinner status determines men's self-respect, their recognition by the wider society, and their ability to achieve white male ideals of household headship. This is an example of the ways in which pro-marriage ideals of men as breadwinning husbands might work oppressively for low-income, poor, and minority men. The fragile-families wing highlights the dissonance between gendered social expectations for men to be natural-born breadwinners and the actual opportunity structures of low-income, poor, and minority men. Thomas, the fragile-families representative mentioned earlier, commented on this in an interview: "[T]he stereotypical notion of men [is that] men are supposed to get out there, get a job, care for their families, and if they don't get a job, it's really not the problem of the economy, right, it's the problem of lazy men. You know what I mean? Because that's how society looks at men." Representatives frequently pointed out that men are expected to succeed in the labor market regardless of their starting position—otherwise they are considered despicably lazy or insufficient *as men.* "Basically we [men] grow up, and we have to get jobs. We get jobs, and we're totally frustrated and confined in them, but it doesn't matter, but you are expected to *work;* it's one of the cultural imperatives—if you have a penis in

America you have to work! So—and if you *don't,* you had better be extremely wealthy, because otherwise you're a bum," said one fragile-families representative in an interview.

According to many fragile-families representatives, African American men have been "playing catch-up" with white men in the labor market since slavery. Some of these representatives say that white middle-class men are primarily concerned with *maintaining* their privileged labor market positions at the expense of poor African American men (and their families). One coping strategy fragile-families representatives often highlighted was for unemployed African American men and other minority men to "go underground." By going underground, these men avoid dealing with "the system" by not establishing paternity and not paying taxes.

Because of the structural barriers to supporting themselves—not to mention a family—fragile-families representatives advocate recognizing unmarried "team parenting" to increase poor and minority men's *marriageability* instead of primarily promoting *marriage.* "Team parents" are unmarried men and women who raise their children regardless of whether the biological parents live in the same household or are a couple. The rhetoric of marriageability and team parenting emphasizes the economic and structural barriers for some men to even be in a position to consider marriage and children as an economically sustainable option. Stable employment is integral to notions of marriageability in the fragile-families wing. However, marriage and marriageability rhetoric often seems indistinguishable in the fragile-families wing. Although fragile-families organizations struggle for the public recognition of unmarried team parents and call these "nontraditional," they certainly do not *promote* an *alternative* to marriage. On the contrary, most of them see marriage as a positive value and the end goal in their fostering of "responsible fathers." Fragile-families representatives almost always point out that *recognizing* non-marital family forms is not the same thing as *condoning* them (see, for example, Mincy and Pouncy 1999, 91).

For instance, one representative told a conference audience in the context of "how to work with legislators" that fragile-families organizations are not *legitimizing* unmarried couples but are providing intermediary support to these couples as a step *toward* marriage. Another representative described their approach to marriage as not explicitly *telling* people to get married but implicitly *guiding* them in that direction. At one pro-marriage conference, a fragile-families representative labeled African American and white upper-class married couples "achievers" and African American single-parent families "underachievers".

Even though fragile-families representatives stress the unattainability of marriage for the men and fathers with whom they work, their terminology sometimes posits marriage as an ultimate ideal. For example, when discussing low-income, poor, and minority men in relation to marriage, fragile-families representatives use such expressions as "not ready," "too young," "several steps before marriage," and "from point A to point B." These phrases indicate that they consider marriage to be a goal that one moves toward as one matures and becomes successful. One of the leading fragile-families representatives put it this way in an interview: "[I]f we can't get them to get married, let's at least get them to be team parents." Nevertheless, he maintained a fine distinction between approaches: whereas the marriage proponents require marriage as the *only* model for family formation, the fragile-families groups' approach is to provide the support for men to be able to make choices so that they can *end up* married.

Events involving fragile-families organizations typically feature a panel of "reformed" low-income/poor men who describe their achievement of "responsible fatherhood," which is often related to the achievement of marriage. For instance, as part of a congressional hearing on welfare reform and the Fathers Count Act of 1998, "witnesses" were invited from various fatherhood organizations. These witnesses informed the Subcommittee on Human Resources (of the House of Representatives' Committee on Ways and Means) about the barriers that face unmarried and welfare-receiving fathers in their attempts to become "good husbands" and "good fathers" (Committee on Ways and Means 1999). At this congressional hearing on fatherhood on July 30, 1998, there was a committee of white congressmen sitting on a platform facing the audience and a panel of practitioners and participants from different African American fatherhood programs. One practitioner in the panel used the term *marriage material* to describe men in an economic and legal position conducive to marriage and said that the guys who come to fragile-families-oriented programs do not constitute such "marriage material." The participants on the panel told the congressmen how "bad" they used to be, but, as a result of the program, they have now become responsible fathers. The congressmen asked such questions as, "Were you all from single-parent households?" The following exchange occurred between Congressman Jim McCrery from Louisiana and Joseph Jones, the director of a famous fragile-families program called Baltimore City Healthy Start Men's Services:

> McCrery: . . . Does your program have a marriage education component? Do you talk about marriage? Do you promote marriage in your group?
> Jones: We do not necessarily promote marriage . . . we are going to add an addendum to [our curriculum] that will outline the principles of marriage. Right now . . . they [i.e., the men with whom the program works] have

got so many other things to deal with. Most of them don't even have a
fixed address, and you want to talk about encouraging marriage. . . .
McCrery: If you get married, you will find that your fixed address will be a
lot more fixed. [The audience laughs.]
Jones: I am married, and my address is much more fixed than I ever thought
it would be. (Committee on Ways and Means 1999)

Later in the testimony, Jones says that his work is promoting marriage as
an *effect* of men's improved economic and legal conditions. Nevertheless, the
crowning event when fragile-families organizations demonstrate achievement of "responsible fatherhood" to various audiences is the father's procla-
mation that he is, or will get, married to the mother of his children. Thus, although they are somewhat critical, fragile-families representatives ultimately
promote marriage, and surely they do not question the supremacy of marriage as a heterosexual institution (see the two last chapters for discussion).
From disadvantaged starting points, fragile-families representatives struggle
for the equal participation of low-income, poor, and minority men in the interrelated labor and marriage markets, framed in terms of homosocial competition and racial justice.

Being a Player and Sitting with the Man

Fragile-families representatives' critical endorsement of marriage may partly
be a strategy to constitute themselves in collaborative dialogue with pro-
marriage stakeholders within fatherhood politics, with whom they cannot afford to have an adversarial relationship. Fragile-families representatives feel
that marriage proponents possess more influence and access in policymaking.
To gain visibility, fragile-families organizations need to compete with pro-
marriage organizations for funding and political influence. For instance, both
pro-marriage and fragile-families organizations apply for grants from such
funding agencies as the Casey Foundation and the Department of Health and
Human Services. In this context, fragile-families representatives may critically
endorse marriage. Marriage is an explicit goal in recent grant-giving initiatives,
such as the Fathers Count Act of 1999 (H.R. 3073) and the Responsible Fatherhood Act of 2000 (H.R. 4671) mentioned earlier. Some fragile-families representatives highlighted the current political "pro-marriage climate" in interviews and the economic necessity for them to buy into what they see as the
centers of power in fatherhood politics. One fragile-families representative,
Daryl, maintained that the fragile-families wing is becoming "co-opted" by
the politically more powerful pro-marriage wing, exemplified by the National
Fatherhood Initiative (NFI). Moreover, he said that many fragile-families rep-

resentatives are buying into pro-marriage rhetoric to become "marketable" in fatherhood policy:

> Some people who I would consider colleagues and allies, when they're in this [pro-marriage] setting they're going to say what they think those people want to hear, and what I think they sometimes fundamentally believe. . . . [W]e're not as connected with corporate America and government and policymakers as NFI. . . . That creates the problem that some folks from [fragile-families organizations], their idea is that we have to be able to compete, so we're going to use the same strategies and same type of language that NFI would use.

Thus, fragile-families representatives struggle to gain access to policy-making on behalf of poor and minority constituencies while strategically aligning themselves with the marriage proponents, who they think dominate fatherhood politics partly because of long-standing race and class privileges. The NFI's Second National Summit on Fatherhood in June 1998 manifested the competition between pro-marriage and fragile-families organizations for the attention of such politicians as Al Gore, who was then vice president. Daryl described the competition for political attention reflected at the summit in terms of competing "players": "We want to be players, we want to be able to sit with Vice President Gore, just like Wade Horn [president of the pro-marriage NFI] can sit with Vice President Gore. But if Vice President Gore wants to sit with Wade Horn, we just have to stay after him." Some African American fragile-families representatives explained the powerful position of Wade Horn and his National Fatherhood Initiative by referring to the fact that Horn and most of his pro-marriage colleagues are white and privileged. These fragile-families representatives identify this condition in marriage proponents' highly successful political and professional careers. Despite their critical approaches, fragile-families representatives participate in pro-marriage conferences to "get a piece of the pie," even though some consider marriage to be primarily "a white man's issue." As Daryl explained:

> See the thing is, the people I work most closely with . . . we can have dinners and have these real intellectual conversations about it, and we can [make] these dichotomies between us and them. . . . When I say that "Oh, I want to go [to a pro-marriage NFI conference] and we can check out what's going on," and first we weren't even going to spend the money to do it, because we don't even want to be *in the same room* with these people, because they're *sick*. . . . I mean, they only talk about poverty issues when it's to their advantage, and we think fundamentally that the type of family they want to create is destructive. . . . [But] we have to be able to work with these people, because they are significant players on the stage.

Fragile-families representatives see a correlation between the structural positions of low-income, poor, and minority constituencies of men and the positions of fragile-families representatives as "players" on the "stage" of fatherhood politics. On this "stage," fragile-families organizations collaborate with the most powerful "players" in family politics: pro-marriage organizations.

Strategic Alignment in a Brother's Recognition Struggle

> *This group means a whole bunch to me. I mean even if they do lose funding, we are going to still keep going. It is going to go on with or without the funding from here, Congress, wherever. Even if we have got to have our groups in our backyards, we are still going on with our group. This is my family.*

—Testimony at the congressional hearing on fatherhood, July 30, 1998

Just as the pro-marriage wing extends into the "marriage movement," the fragile-families wing builds on civil rights struggles, overlapping discursively and collaboratively with such civil rights organizations as the Urban League and the National Association for the Advancement of Colored People (NAACP). The NAACP and the Urban League are the most established civil rights organizations in the United States. The NAACP, founded in 1909, is committed to the political, educational, social, and economic equality of minorities.[4] The National Urban League, founded in 1910, is dedicated to the social and economic equality of African Americans.[5] To fragile-families representatives, fatherhood responsibility is about the equal opportunities of poor and minority men in the labor market, government, and the juridical system, as opposed to the pro-marriage emphasis on the moral/cultural obligations of men. Whereas the fragile-families wing concentrates on civil rights and racial justice, the pro-marriage wing primarily stresses men's individual moral obligations to family, society, and God. The struggle to achieve "responsible fatherhood" among low-income/poor and minority men can be seen as a struggle for the recognition and empowerment of low-income and poor unmarried men and their "non-traditional" families. Throughout U.S. history, these struggles have both converged with and diverged from white and African American feminist struggles against white male supremacy (Davis 1981).

In local fatherhood programs, practitioners mediate between "the system" and poor and minority men. On the one hand, fragile-families practitioners represent their constituencies' struggles for recognition and empowerment as disadvantaged men and minorities. On the other hand, they work for or with "the system" they criticize for discriminating against poor and minority men. When seeking to resolve problems they identify in African American communities without "blaming the victim" (Majors and Gordon 1994), fragile-families representatives are wary of reproducing racist stereotypes of violent and criminal "hypermasculinity." Distinguishing between "positive" and "negative" role models for African American and other minority masculinities, fragile-families representatives try to steer clear from reproducing the stereotypes they are trying to deconstruct. While remaining critical of racial stereotyping, fragile-families representatives sometimes express the idea that poor and men channel their frustrated aspirations for middle-class masculine success into "negative choices" (Majors 1994, 312–13; Dworkin and Wachs 2000). Most important, fragile-families organizations deal with very real issues facing their constituencies, such as drug abuse, joblessness, violence, and family relationships.

The traditional hegemony of U.S. white middle-class masculinity was partly founded in the subordination and stigmatization of minority masculinities (Frankenberg 1997; D'Emilio and Freedman 1997). By focusing on the idea that minority men need to catch up with white middle-class men, fragile-families organizations risk playing into gendered, sexual, and racial stereotypes. Fragile-families representatives' notions of male role models may exemplify this dilemma. Within the fragile-families wing, binary notions of "positivity" versus "negativity" serve to legitimize the necessity of the male role model. As a "responsible father," the role model embodies fragile-families' notions of "positivity": he works hard, is a law-abiding citizen, is involved in his community and family, and is monogamously committed to a wife or girlfriend. In contrast, fragile-families' notions of "negativity" seemingly echo marriage proponents' stereotypical notions of "protest masculinity" (Blankenhorn 1995; Popenoe 1996; Gilder 1973) and 1960s notions of outlaw "ghetto lifestyle." Conceptions of negativity refer to getting involved with drugs and criminal activity, unemployment, "womanizing," and having out-of-wedlock children one cannot support. However, fragile-families practitioners are aware that notions of "negative," "hyper," and "protest masculinity" have traditionally been used as weapons against African American men. For example, Mitchell Duneier (1992) describes past and present academic and policy discourse (Hannerz 1969; Anderson 1978; Wilson 1987) as confining African American men to two basic options: *ghetto specific* masculinity and *middle-class-aspiring* masculinity. African American men from the inner cities have become icons of economically and socially destructive masculinities, whereas middle-class African American men get to embody "respectability" according to traditional Eurocentric family values and are supposed to role-model for the former group (Duneier 1992). However, William Wilson wonders whether it is fruitful to avoid discussing "unflattering behaviors" among African American men in an attempt to sidestep sensitive topics (1996, xviii). In his introduction to *When Work Disappears,* Wilson touches on Duneier's critique of *The Truly Disadvantaged* by asserting that he did not deny that there are hardworking and family-oriented people in poor African American communities, although he did emphasize the declining numbers of "stable and employed families" (1996, xvii–xviii). Wilson also stresses the importance of recognizing issues and structural obstacles that make it difficult for "inner-city residents" to maintain their mainstream values and expectations, even if this would entail bringing up "unflattering behaviors" (1996, xviii).

The tension between challenging and reinforcing white middle-class ideals of masculinity is reflected in local fragile-families programs. In fatherhood programs, practitioners function as role models who act as catalysts of "positivity" and perform as an antidote to fatherlessness. The role model concept refers to successful men (in most cases successful breadwinners and husbands from poor backgrounds) who talk to kids in poor communities, acting as living examples of middle-class possibilities beyond the environment to which they are accustomed. A practitioner's job is to embody ideals of masculinity and fatherhood and to expose the fathers who participate in the program to mainstream values, behavior, and skills. When the participants in fatherhood programs have learned how to function successfully in mainstream society as breadwinning, "responsible" fathers, they may become role models for other men in their communities. Fragile-families representatives often frame this mainstreaming process in terms of reforming disadvantaged men from a "negative lifestyle" to a more "positive," family-oriented one.

However, considering the long history of racialized stereotypes associated with "ghetto" versus "middle-class" masculinities, the fragile-families wing is torn between buying into previously stigmatizing terminology and refuting white middle-class men as yardsticks for male success. Practitioners often point out that they are not promoting white mainstream values and that they continually expose racism and discrimination from African American or other minority male perspectives. However, when practitioners teach poor, African American/minority men ways to conform and succeed in mainstream society, they sometimes perceive a conflict between their racial identities and racialized middle-class ambitions. This became apparent during my fieldwork in a local fathers' program on the East Coast. The fathers at the local program asserted their loyalty to a generalized notion of African American "brothers" when discussing such questions as "Does one have to be like white men in order to get the same access and benefits or does promoting mainstream values entail buying into white middle-class values?" Many fragile-families representatives resist conforming to white middle-class masculinity. As one said in an interview, "There's so many people in 'African America' who have taken the comparison with whites as the standards that *so much* of what we all have become is up to what white people become. And I'm just not going along with that, I believe that *God* has made me who I am, and I'm responsible to God."

In the local fathers' program I visited regularly, participants and practitioners held up positive images of African American men in the face of white stereotypes of them as "drug pushers and evil people," who are "looking bad" and "shuffling around in a jumpsuit." One participant said in the context of discussing the conditions for African American versus white men, "[W]e seem to be caught up in other people defining who we are! Don't let anybody else determine us!" Sometimes the practitioners and participants in the programs called themselves "black kings," which set them apart from white men (and women of all colors) in a self-affirming manner. However, most representatives promoted a middle way between ethnic pride and the necessity of mastering mainstream white cultural and professional norms. An exchange between Troy, a practitioner at a fathers' workshop, and a participant illustrates the tension between compliance with and resistance to white marketplace masculinity that seems to permeate the fragile-families wing:

> Troy (practitioner): We have to learn to conform: nobody wants to change nobody. Like Dr. Jekyll and Mr. Hyde, you can be how you want to be in the hood. But we have to stay at a legitimate track. The majority of people who have a job are white. That's my understanding. We have to go to them and be like them in order to get a job.
>
> Participant: They run the country: white supremacy! . . . Why do you have to have what they have to get a job to support a family?

Apparently this group of African American men perceived a huge difference between themselves and white people. In the local fathers' program, practitioners and participants frequently contrasted white society's values and African American values, although these values were rarely specified. Conceptions of "us" and "them" and "our people" as opposed to "whites" seemed to be a platform for the participants and practitioners to situate themselves as a group of low-income and poor African American men—even when one or two non–African Americans were part of the group. Troy even compared "the white man's world" to outer space while he urged the fathers to learn to adapt to "the system":

> Troy: Ain't nobody's gonna give you nothing—there's still racism and discrimination. Keep your earrings, keep your ways . . . but keep it in the hood—to get a job you have to modify. Ain't nobody's trying to change you. What does it mean: "When in Rome, do as the Romans do?" You've

got to conform. . . . I'm not saying it's *right*. I'm a black man just like you. In order to get what you want, that's what you've got to do. We have to learn to do what The Man wants us to do. And the man can be black, white, Korean—but you have to get that job to feed your family. . . . No disrespect to you [points at me, the white observer]—the Caucasians run the juridical system.

Participant: It's a business, not a system.

Another participant: It's a conspiracy.

Troy: Our people wasn't at the table when the system was made up. They don't know how it is to grow up on the streets. For example, *I* don't know what it is like to be in outer space—I haven't learned about that.

Troy speaks from an African American male perspective when talking about "our people" versus "the system." He emphasizes that he does not necessarily agree with The Man just because he promotes strategic compliance with The Man's powerful system. However, it is clear that Troy considers the mimicking of white middle-class men necessary for low-income and poor African American men to be successful in the marketplace. One way to "do as the Romans do" within the fragile-families wing is to blend in by strategically conforming to codes of behavior and appearance. For instance, many fatherhood programs taught poor and minority men dress codes for different official settings. At the local East Coast–based fatherhood program, the African American practitioners dressed in shirts and dress pants most of the time, and sometimes they even wore suits and ties. They explicitly modeled how to "dress for success" as a male in the labor market and official settings, and they sometimes gave advice to fathers on how to look "respectable" in specific contexts. Fatherhood programs also demonstrate to low-income and poor minority men how to interact with peers, public officials, women, and children. For instance, the practitioners and participants in the programs sometimes say "Mister" and "Sir" to one another and use the person's last name. Some practitioners encourage fathers to call women "ladies" instead of "bitches" and "ho's" and to treat them accordingly. These practitioners expressed their suspicion that participants often use condescending words to describe women and were influenced by sexist rap lyrics and "street" language.

At press conferences, meetings with officials, and public events, fragile-families representatives constantly point out the lack of role models for marriage and the work ethic in poor African American communities, as well as the necessity of setting "high" standards. By associating such reform efforts with "the system," practitioners may be perceived as "poverty pimps." This expression refers to advocates and social workers who indirectly perpetuate white men's dominance over African American communities and work for the government merely to support themselves. This suspicion might be particularly prevalent among fathers who were sent to programs by the court system as part of a sentence. Practitioners, however, generally prefer to be perceived as "spindoctors for the hood" who fight for the rights and recognition of poor and minority men and their families. To appear credible to both colleagues and program participants, fragile-families representatives constantly need to "prove" that they are genuinely concerned about the individuals and constituencies they are working with and represent. Practitioners continuously point out that they fight the same battles their constituencies fight and share the experiences of low-income, poor, and minority fathers. For example, at one fragile-families conference, the president of a fragile-families organization stressed that he and the low-income/poor African American fathers who are assisted by the fragile-families organizations experience the same gendered and racial discrimination: "Being a minority male, race and discrimination is still an issue. I love being a minority male, but it sure becomes inconvenient sometimes [audience laughs]. When I drive down the highway I'm concerned with being stopped for [committing the crime of] DWB, Driving While Black."

I often heard practitioners publicly emphasize that they were from poor communities or circumstances. One clear example of practitioners' tension between representing "the system" or representing the "brothers" is reflected in the recent collaboration between fragile-families organizations and Child Support Enforcement (CSE), which historically has been a major enemy of poor fathers. CSE has traditionally served poor fathers with child support orders and sanctions that fragile-families representatives consider unreasonable and destructive to these fathers' abilities to find stable employment. Lately CSE has tightened the conditions for noncustodial fathers by, for instance, pursuing fathers with child support debts across state lines (Mincy and Pouncy 1999). Fragile-families organizations have worked to help local practitioners work out deals with CSE and judges at the local level on behalf of low-income/poor fathers. In the process of this cooperation between CSE and local fatherhood programs, both sides are trying to present a friendlier face and redefine their previously adversarial relationship. Some CSE workers are trying to understand the perspectives of the fathers the practitioners represent, whereas some practitioners are trying to understand the situation of CSE workers whose mission is to provide for children. However, this collaboration makes practitioners suspect within their own constituencies; they might be perceived as "snitches" by colleagues and program participants. At a fragile-families conference mentioned earlier, one leader said that community-based organizations are dedicated to helping their clients and that "they are concerned that if they work with [Child Support Enforcement] that they'll be seen as a snitch. They look at CSE as an enforcement entity."

The cautious approach of the fragile-families wing toward whiteness and "the system" is founded on a long history of gendered and racialized oppression and resistance that goes back to slave society. Building on racial justice traditions, fragile fathers' "brotherhood" extends beyond fatherhood programs. Poor and minority men, who often lack public or informal support elsewhere, find assistance and peer support. In meetings they sometimes talk about looking out for one another not only in the program but also on the street, in prison, in court, and so forth. For instance, at one of the local fatherhood workshops on the East Coast, the fathers discussed how to cope with being a father when locked up in jail. A participant talked about how he had met with the fathers from the program in jail:

> Participant: I had a little problem and got locked up. I saw a few brothers from the program who were locked up too. We got together as a group in jail. One of them was even wearing our T-shirt.
> Practitioner: That's deep!

At another workshop, fathers were talking about helping one another outside the program, such as on the street or in official settings. One participant said, "I think that we should stick together in and outside this group. I'm going to take care of my problems because I'm my own man. Nobody has to do nothing for me. But if we're in this situation together as a family, then we should work as a family." In dealing with the tension between compliance with and resistance to mainstream white culture, fathers in the fragile-families wing seek support from other men but simultaneously hold their ground as "black kings" and "their own man."

Teaming with Women: Refuting or Aspiring to Leadership?

> *The dominant theme in the discourse of racialized masculinity politics in the United States has tended primarily to be concerned with the need to strongly assert men of color's rightful claims to "manhood" as a means of resisting white men's racial (and often, simultaneously, social class) domination of men of color.*

—Michael Messner, *Politics of Masculinities*

> *Many of us have difficulties in sharing leadership and responsibility with our ladies. Many of us try to dominate them. There's something real wrong with that. That has a direct impact on my children. They have to see us being able to disagree and work it out. We dominate our women and our children too. Because we get pushed around outside the home, the only place we feel that*

we can dominate is in our home. I say, take care of your lady, and your lady will take care of you.
—Practitioner Bill at a fathers' workshop

Although the primary battle, as far as fragile-families organizations are concerned, is fought between men on the "playing fields" of the labor market and education, gender relations are an integral part of constructing and negotiating low-income, poor, and minority masculinities. For instance, because they historically lack financial bargaining power, low-income/poor African American men have not been able to become heads of the households as easily as white middle- and upper-class men have (Messner 1997). While dealing with deteriorating labor market conditions for poor and minority men, fragile-families representatives respond in various ways. They may seek recognition as leaders of their families regardless of their financial bargaining power, or they change traditional "Ozzie and Harriet notions" of masculinity (of men as breadwinning husbands and household heads) into more egalitarian ideals, or may do both. There is no unitary approach to the gendered division of labor and leadership within the fragile-families wing. Instead, tensions and contradictions as well as contestations and negotiations characterize fragile-families representatives' approaches to gender relations.

In his classic work *Black Masculinity: The Black Male's Role in American Society,* published in 1982, the sociologist Robert Staples argued that African American men who are denied their "rightful claims" for "manhood" displace those claims onto heterosexual relations and attempt to reconfirm "manly authority" in relation to women instead (1982, 160; see also Gibbs 1994). Staples further maintained that although white middle- and upper-class masculinity in U.S. society is characterized by privilege over women, African American men should not be concerned primarily with gender equality, because they have not been allowed access to the privileges white men have as breadwinners and heads of households (1982, 19; Staples and Johnson 1993, 138). According to Staples, African American men should instead concern themselves with their difficult conditions and their own survival, because "in the case of black men, their subordination as a racial minority has more than canceled out their advantages as males in the larger society" (1982, 7; see also Hill 1997).

Leading fragile-families representatives I interviewed sometimes claimed to be less antifeminist than the pro-marriage wing. Nevertheless, Michael, one of my key fragile-families interviewees, critiqued the entire fatherhood responsibility movement, including the fragile-families wing, by maintaining that it fundamentally seeks to reclaim male leadership in families:

Michael: [Local fragile-families organizations] may say the correct things about "treat your women with respect," and they say stuff like that, but fundamentally, when they use those rites of passage programs, most of them—not all—reinforce the idea of men that, once they get themselves together, once they get themselves in a job and they're making money, they have a responsibility to their families. And hence, that responsibility is to be the moral leader of that family . . . what they mean by "Take care of your family," they mean like, "Be a man, take the leadership role, save your family." . . . To me it's pretty simple . . . it's that when you say something like "men are hardwired different," you're implicitly saying there's something unequal. Because when you say there's difference between me and you beyond biological, I mean beyond the waist, right [laughs], then to me what's implicit in making that assumption is that then you're going to place value. Once you're saying that there's difference, you're going to place value on which is more valuable than the other. And once you do that, you go right back into the situation that we're trying to get rid of, of a society where sexism is rampant, racism is rampant.

Me: And both sides—fragile families and pro-marriage—are saying that men and women are wired differently?

Michael: Yes, I strongly believe that. I strongly believe that they believe that that's true.

Me: Are you alone among your colleagues in thinking about things this [critical] way?

Michael: Past me and [my coworker Phil] you'd be hard pressed to find someone who's in the work, who's doing this type of work who would agree with this [critique]. Other than the women's groups that we've talked to.

According to Michael, sexist and essentialist beliefs in gender difference are widespread in the fragile-families wing, despite representatives' attempts in interviews to distinguish themselves from the "traditional" views on gender relations and marriage they identify in the pro-marriage wing. However, the diverse approaches of fragile-families representatives made it difficult to discern a clear general view. For instance, fragile-families representatives claim that they "talk to" what they call "women's groups" and that fighting racism is a struggle that involves both African American men and women. Fragile-families representatives' struggles for racial equality, however, sometimes take priority over or cancel out gender equality. Representatives may argue that poor and minority men have a legitimate stake in "political, economic and social manhood" and that, if unrecognized, they turn to "illegitimate" and "negative" solutions to achieve recognition *as men*. "Anger management" and "staying at a legitimate track" (in other words, participating in the mainstream labor market instead of the illegal economy) were frequent topics in fatherhood programs. In the local fatherhood program I visited frequently, practitioners and participants often discussed the ways drugs, violence, and illegal activities keep African American men from achieving legitimacy as men in white mainstream society. As one of the practitioners, Troy, once said, "All these things are in our communities to put our people down: drugs, sex, lack of principles, and lack of self esteem." Another African American fragile-families representative said in an interview:

> Being a man *requires* self-determination, it requires *freedom*. When you are not free, the men who are free will define you and describe you. We have been defined and described as "boys," because it's easier for a man to control a boy than to control another man. They would not give us the privilege or allow us the power to call ourselves men, because they would not treat us as men, because at that point they would have to *fight*—you see? . . . How we display manhood is where we run into questions, because since political and in many ways economic and social manhood is denied, what do you do to distinguish yourself as a man while you are masculine? Well, you use your masculine powers, often body strength, sexual procreativity, sexual—well general boyish irresponsibility, you use your powers of male bonding, you use the powers of relationships with women in terms of the cross-gendered relationships, you see, that's where you describe your manhood.

This representative uses "us" to refer to African American men and "them" to refer to white middle-class men. He maintains that men whose aspirations for "manhood" are thwarted will displace these aspirations in homosocial and heterosexual arenas. Fragile-families representatives commonly identify oppression by white men as a major cause for potential "protest masculinities" of poor and minority men. The representative just quoted equates "free manhood" with power over other men and over women and the power to "define" and "describe" others. He thereby risks reinforcing the same types of power relations and pecking orders he criticizes in the first place. In other words, he implies that if African American men cannot "define" themselves as men because of their oppression by white men, at least they can "use the powers of relationships with women." At a national fragile-families conference in 1998, the keynote speaker described a pattern he argued still exists today, where African American men submit to white men and therefore need to "demonstrate" their "manhood" in "other ways":

> They [the white slave masters] had control over the black male, even if still it was patriarchal. . . . In other words, in order to adapt the black male in that kind of system, and you can realize this and appreciate this in the stereotypes, it's that the black male in order to survive, the best way to sur-

vive was for the black male to be docile. . . . So when you see, when you think of the image, the classic image from slavery and segregation, of shuffling; shuffling being bent over scratching your head and rolling your eyes, I think you'll appreciate that that's *totally: totally* a black male image. . . . Now if you're being kind of cut down by the society in terms of your images of manhood and being a man, you might gravitate into other ways of demonstrating your manhood.

As became apparent in the rest of his speech, "other ways" referred to impregnating as many women as possible without assuming responsibility for the resulting children, who mainly serve as "proof" of "manhood." The speech illustrates a partial tendency to displace competitive homosocial constructions of masculinity onto heterosexual power relations within fragile-families-oriented thought. "Demonstrating manhood" here implies displacing power relations between men into power relations between men and women. The keynote speaker articulates a long-standing academic and policy tradition that explores the many ways poor African American men with blocked "aspirations for manhood" channel their frustration in violent, sexist, criminal, and "antisocial" behavior as alternative means of empowerment (see, for example, Anderson 1990; Franklin 1994; Majors and Billson 1992; and Staples 1982). The well-known sociologist Elijah Anderson, for instance, has written at length about African American men's ways of compensating for their poor employment prospects and their subsequent inabilities to become middle-class husbands and providers (1990, 1993). In response to this situation, argues Anderson, the young, inner-city African American man "resort[s] to proving his manhood through sexual conquests" (1993, 93–94). Accordingly to Anderson (and the keynote speaker above), "The lack of gainful employment opportunities not only keeps the entire community in a pit of poverty, but it also deprives young men of the traditional American way of proving their manhood, namely, supporting a family. They must thus prove their manhood in other ways. Casual sex with as many women as possible, impregnating one or more and getting them to 'have your baby' brings a boy the ultimate in esteem from his peers and makes him a 'man'" (1993, 95–96).

Being a head of a family is another part of the "traditional American way of proving manhood" according to this logic, which is tightly connected to the provider issue. In Anderson's words, "As jobs become increasingly scarce for young black men, their roles as breadwinners and traditional husbands decline. The notion is that with money comes a certain control and say in the domestic situation. Without money or jobs many men are increasingly unable to 'play house to their own satisfaction'" (1993, 93). The keynote speaker at the fragile-families conference also touched on the related issues of African American men's and women's relative positions on the labor market and their gendered power relations within families. He said that racialized and gendered dynamics in "the corporate office" (where low-skilled women have a better chance of getting employment than do low-skilled men) have "confused us in terms of what the roles should be in a family, the issues of dominance and so on. As we know, the black woman has been dominant in many ways, but it was because the black man was not *allowed* to be so dominant [due to racist white society]."

Like marriage proponents, many fragile-families representatives occasionally use biblical essentialist ideas to support their notions of manhood. Within the fragile-families wing, biblical ideas may be used as means to empower low-income/poor minority men and to support egalitarian-sounding ideals of team parenting, but biblical ideas may also promote the familiar Promise Keepers' patriarchal-sounding view that lack of male leadership in families is "unnatural" and against God's intentions. One discussion at a local fathers' program that was supposed to motivate men to be good fathers illuminates the ways biblical notions sometimes serve to reinforce notions of male leadership. The workshop was led by two guest lecturers from another local fatherhood program, but the regular practitioners were also attending:

Guest Lecturer 2: We're supposed to be strong, you're supposed to *do*. But for real, those times are gone. Now women have become more masculine, and we need more balance. That's how I feel about being a man: I *always* represent.

Guest Lecturer 1: [reads from notes] We've got to pray, pray, pray and ask for God for wisdom, courage, strength as you lead your children. Fathers are the leaders, and when the father falls off the road—who's leading?

Participant: The mother takes over the leading.

Guest Lecturer 1: The father *is* the leader. The devil takes over if he falls off.

Guest Lecturer 2: We as men can't negotiate being the father. We can't stop watering the plant. The devil is going to start wanting the plant.

Participant: But children will go to their grandfathers or their neighbors before they go to the street.

Guest Lecturer 1: The father is the captain of the ship. The grandfather isn't. We gave that boat to our ladies, who are supposed to be our support. The devil is a very meticulous person. He takes no prisoners.

Guest Lecturer 2: He only destroys. And as fathers we can protect our children. As captain of the ship, we've got to lead the family. Captain of the ship, that's the position of integrity.

Guest Lecturer 1: If you're really a captain, and you know what's right. When we're wrong, we're going to be men enough to say we're wrong. You've got to stand up to your weakness before you move on

Guest Lecturer 2: We've got to find femininity in us, because love is a feminine thing. We're not only black men with big egos—I hate to say this just in front of anybody.[6]

In this discussion, the guest lecturers use biblical notions of gender relations much as the Promise Keepers and the marriage proponents do. However, unlike Promise Keepers and marriage proponents, they apply these biblical essentialist notions to a context that is specific to (low-income/poor) African American men. Although promoting egalitarian notions of gender relations in other contexts, neither practitioners nor the participating fathers challenged the notion of the father as the biblically ordained family leader and "captain of his ship." Moreover, there were no objections to the guest lecturers' conceptions of a hierarchical balance between men who lead and women who support them.

Another discussion in the same fathers' program mirrored the wide range of competing and contradictory approaches to gender relations in the fragile-families wing. An older father named Terrence, who often expressed his opinions and got into debates with practitioners and other participants, met strong protests when he claimed a masculinist model of male leadership. The discussion quoted below took place after Bill, the practitioner, had just argued that it is wrong for men to try to dominate "their ladies" and that men ought to "share" leadership and responsibility with "their woman":

> Terrence: I agree with what you're saying [to Bill], but *to a degree.* Because I firmly believe that the man is supposed to be the head of the house. When single women are running the homes, things are just running rampant. Men have been the heads of the house since the beginning of time. It's not about domination—it's about subjection.
> [Bill boos and laughs. Some of the participants laugh as well.]
> Terrence: When a woman is in the household, she's subjected to the man.
> Participant: If you're loving this woman, why you want to subject her?
> Terrence: It's about obedience.
> Bill: Obedience? [People laugh.]
> Bill: He's a Neanderthal [referring to Terrence]. He's a man of the fifties.
> Terrence: Let's go back to the time when children had a mother and a father: that was family structure. First alcohol came, then drugs, then the social services. That all turned the black men away from their families. That's how our society is programmed: weak family structure. So we need to be responsible.
> Participant: But does that mean the father has to be the head of the household?
> Terrence: I can't come in and be the leader. Did I not say that men and women are created equal?

Terrence seems to envision taking charge of the household—that is, subjecting women—as an African American men's resistance strategy against a "society" that sabotages "family structure." "Family structure" is therefore an issue of racial justice, and (as the Moynihan Report of 1965, described in chapter 1, argued) "weak family structure," synonymous with father absence, disadvantages African American communities. Phrasing his claims for male supremacy and African American community empowerment in blatantly masculinist terms, Terrence met strong and loud protests from the group. When framed in nonbiblical terms claiming that men should be the leaders in their families, practitioners and participants thought Terrence's hierarchical model of gender relations was hopelessly outdated. They booed and laughed at him and called him a "Neanderthal" and "a man of the fifties." Both practitioners and participants questioned his views. Nevertheless, in closing the discussion, the practitioner Troy maintained a *biblical* hierarchical model of gender relations where the father is the "protector" and "head" of the family, which he distinguished from dominance:

Terrence: The man is put to be the head. How you're going to be the head if you're not responsible for *yourself?* I'm not going to tell my wife, "You're going to wash these clothes." But she's better at washing the clothes.

Participant: The word is *dialogue*—not demand. Commanding the woman to wash—that's stereotyping the female!

Bill (practitioner): You want to treat her the way you'd like to be treated. Like a team. You're going to socialize the children.

Terrence: The Bible says that men have become weak as women. That's still true today. That's weak! We shouldn't have women out in the field fighting for us!

Participant: How can you be together in the household if one tries to rule over the household? We have to be equal.

Terrence: Family structure was instituted by the Almighty. It is now instituted by the government. This was a form of government being set down. Equal was this: the vice president can do the job of the president. But—there's only one head.

Participant: But both have to sign things.

Troy (practitioner): There's no one prescription that's going to work in all our lives. From my understanding, God created man first—I think God made the man head of the household because he was here first, but not to dominate, but to be the protector.

This discussion illustrates a point I elaborate in the upcoming chapter: in the fatherhood responsibility movement, biblical rhetoric serves as a rhetorical strategy to defy political questioning. Troy's concluding remark reconfirms Terrence's masculinist views but is couched in different terms, and no one protests or disagrees. This means that when such views are phrased in biblical terms, they become more palatable, somehow less "Neanderthal" and "fifties." The discussion clearly illustrates the ways biblical rhetoric may change sexist arguments into an unquestionable "moral dimension" and simultaneously up-hold "difference" and "equality." Again, we have a case where someone makes the contradictory claim that one can promote hierarchical notions of gender difference within a biblical rhetoric that casts men and women as equally in-dispensable in God's eyes—with a total disregard for the structural dimensions of worldly constructions of gender. The previously offensive message about male supremacy becomes indisputable and is supported when it is phrased in biblical terms that still legitimize masculinist authority.

Practitioners may use differing interpretations of the Bible to stress more or less hierarchy, and they may even advocate gender equality and male lead-ership simultaneously. They may use the Bible to say that "men and women are created equal" but also to say that men are God-ordained heads of the household (in order to protect it). Both these seemingly contradictory asser-tions fit into the same model in which God has assigned *different* but *equally valuable* tasks to women and men. According to such logic, female submis-sion is as valuable as male leadership. Troy and Bill, who are role models for the participants, object to such words as *obedience, dominance,* and *subjection,* but Troy still believes in a biblical model of the father as the (protecting) head of the household. By disregarding the power dimensions of this headship, Troy can maintain a noncontradictory belief in difference-based equality. Only one representative (Michael) in the fragile-families wing explicitly crit-icized the sexist implications of such biblical notions, which he discerned among both marriage proponents and fragile-families representatives. In cri-tiquing the programs of both these groups, Michael said in an interview:

> When you go through a program and you have rites of passage and you have other types of systems, these programs and services and preachers who are running programs, and they are quoting Bible scriptures—they are creating a potentially harmful situation where these men think that, just because they went through this program, that they can walk back into some woman's house, even though their kids may be there, . . . and take charge. And I speak to women, and I've talked to fathers who are in pro-grams and I ask them, "Where is the mother, can I go talk to her?" And these women will say to me that that's their biggest concern and their biggest fear [their men taking charge]. . . . That these men go through these programs . . . and they think they're the shit. They think they can walk back there and be that leadership and start quoting Bible scriptures.

One event at the local fathers' program illustrates how such programs may encourage men to claim biblical notions of leadership that poor and African American men, or their male ancestors, perhaps never had in their families. At the workshop led by the guest lecturers quoted earlier, there was an exchange between a seventeen-year-old newcomer to the program and one of the guest lecturers. During the workshop, the seventeen-year-old newcomer raised his hand and said, "I've got some problems with leadership. I just came out of jail." The other participants applauded to show their support for this exodus, whereupon one of the guest lecturers replied, "Today is a new day. You're the captain of the ship, the father." The guest lecturer did not tell the seventeen-year-old father *how* he was supposed to take charge in everyday family life. Because it had already been established that being the "captain" required men to take charge, however, it was clear that his empowerment required his family's submission.

Mediating Contradictory Masculinity Politics

The fragile-families wing reflects a contradictory mix of masculinist and egalitarian discourses on racialized and gendered relations. Fragile-families representatives draw on a tradition of political and academic discussion of the many ways that African American men's aspirations for "full manhood status" have been blocked and unrecognized since slavery (Madhubuti 1990; Majors and Billson 1992). The family sociologist Robert Staples is one of the scholars who have been widely criticized by feminist scholars, mainly for conservative essentialist and radical reductionist emphasis on African American men's struggles for the political and economic power that allow white middle-class men to count as "men" (see also Franklin 1994). The African American feminist scholar bell hooks is one of the most well-known critics of masculinist perspectives in African American studies. She laments that African American men have never collectively critiqued dominant norms for masculinity and instead have assumed, like Staples, that male headship is a "natural fact of life" (1992, 96–97). She argues that the "[c]ontemporary black power movement made synonymous black liberation and the effort to create a social structure wherein black men could assert themselves as patriarchs, controlling community, family, and kin. On one hand, black men expressed contempt for white men yet they also envied them their access to patriarchal power" (1992, 98).

Here, hooks contributes to the feminist critique of the civil rights movement, which its leaders often described in terms of "claims for manhood." However, hooks also acknowledges the efforts of individual African American men who oppose sexism and "subvert and challenge the *status quo*" (1992, 100). I met quite a few representatives in the fragile-families wing who claimed to promote gender-egalitarian notions of masculinity and fatherhood. None of these representatives claimed to be feminist or pro-feminist. However, there was one fragile-families representative (Michael) who made a point of applying a feminist perspective and often criticized the gender politics of his colleagues. Even though he claimed his colleagues were resistance to feminist ideas, he kept trying to promote equality-based fatherhood programs from a feminist perspective, as is reflected in these interview comments:

> I think it needs to be programs and agencies that are really helping men rethink masculinity. A lot of people say that word, but what I mean by that is: you have to have men really recognize what sexism is. You have to really help men recognize where oppression is, really work to change the power dynamics they're used to in their families. . . . And if you get men to do that, then you may have less men abandon families, because they will understand that there should be no leader in the family—there should be partnership when people decide to cohabitate or marry, or have a lifelong connection. There is no leader, no follower: people individually went together to deal with stuff. But men are so tired of all that, and they hear this from [retired Chicago Bears football linebacker] Mike Singletary, Vice President Gore, and all those other speakers, they hear that "Oh, I have to be the moral leader of my family." . . . I talk a lot to these people [policymakers and fragile-families leaders] and they think I'm crazy, but I always try to say that look, you have to teach these men a different way of thinking. . . . The ideal situation would be that all men who go through fatherhood programs, when they go through fatherhood programs they become feminists. . . . The one thing about feminism . . . it's that most feminists, by very definition, fundamentally believe that all people are equal.

This statement may articulate the ways fragile-families representatives could seek nonsexist grounds for African American masculinities, but most of them think that feminism is "crazy," according to Michael. Many fragile-families representatives seem to focus on racial justice rather than on gender equality. For instance, at the national fragile-families conference referred to earlier, the keynote speaker emphasized African American men's traditional lack of authority in their families: "The black family was patriarchal, remember it was always in a position of weakness, because they were an oppressed patriarchal structure, so that [black men] never had the power and control over their families even as a patriarch. That was not in their domain, the power over the black family was in the hands primarily of the white slave owners. . . . So it was not a position of authority as we would consider in a white family in this system, it was not."

Earlier in his speech, he maintained that structural and economic changes have "destabilized" "traditional" and "intact" families and created new demands, roles, and responsibilities within African American families that "perhaps God never intended," were "against nature," and were not "appropriate." This keynote speaker implicitly combined scholarly and biblical perspectives.

He subsequently made the point that white racism denies recognition of African American men's appropriate dominant roles in their families. As I showed earlier in this chapter, the keynote speaker thus shifts racial justice struggles into African American men's right to "be dominant" in their families. Although it is important to emphasize gender-egalitarian tendencies in fragile-families organizations, representatives of the fragile-families wing also partly reproduce notions of men as ideal main providers and heads of households, whether they attribute this role assignment to God or white middle-class norms. While comparing themselves primarily with white middle-class men, fragile-families representatives still indirectly involve (African American) women as gendered appendices within the homosocial competition among men over marketplace ideals. Although there are fragile-families representatives who support masculinist views articulated by Staples and other African American family scholars, others claim to promote more egalitarian notions of parenting. For instance, representatives from the Partners for Fragile Families, the National Center for Strategic Nonprofit Planning and Community Leadership (NPCL), and the National Practitioners Network for Fathers and Families, which are leading organizations of the fragile-families wing, promote equality-based principles for gender relations in families. Despite these principles, however, the conference featuring the keynote speaker quoted above was organized and attended by the NPCL leadership. Furthermore, the speaker's views on African American male leadership in families remained uncontested throughout the conference.

Fragile-families organizations are in a difficult situation in family politics. While pursuing strategic alliance with pro-marriage groups, they are constantly wary of compromising their constituencies. Moreover, while seeking autonomous foundations for minority masculinities, fragile-families organizations strategically but ambivalently mimic the traditional "winners" of marketplace masculinity: white middle-class men.

Notes

1. *The System* is a term fragile-families representatives and their program participants often use.

2. Child Support Enforcement is the governmental agency that collects child support from fathers. It also provides assistance in establishing paternity. The program is administered by the Office of Child Support Enforcement, under the Administration for Children and Families, which is in the Department of Health and Human Services (Mellgren 1993, 201).

3. AFDC is an abbreviation for Aid to Families with Dependent Children. This form of public aid has been replaced by TANF (Temporary Assistance for Needy Families).

Ronald Mincy and Hillard Pouncy describe the consequences of TANF: "States can use the federal grants to provide assistance to individuals who belong to families with children, and it is now easier for states to make grants to two-parent families than it was under (A.F.D.C.). Therefore, if a state wants to provide employment training services to unwed and disadvantaged fathers, it may do so as long as the father lives with his child and the child's mother. However, states cannot use federal funds to make grants to families for more than five years . . ." (1999, 96).

4. The NAACP has branches in all fifty states, about 2,200 branches in all, and its total membership exceeds 500,000. The organization works through lobbying, demonstrations, and political campaigns (*A Future of Promise* 1998).

5. The Urban League has approximately a hundred affiliates in thirty-four states and the District of Columbia. It works through advocacy, community mobilization, program services, and research (see www.nul.org).

6. The "anybody" here probably referred to me, because I was the only (white and female) outsider observer present among a group of African American men.

4   Religion and Sports as Common Grounds for Masculinization

Tools for Masculinizing Domesticity

The fatherhood responsibility movement is a reaction to the grievance that "the family" has become synonymous with mother and child and thus "feminized" (Blankenhorn 1995, 13; Gore 1996). In its claims for male participation and legitimacy in the family, the fatherhood responsibility movement anxiously seeks to masculinize domesticity by carving out specifically "male" notions of parenting. Although masculinization strategies are more explicit in marriage proponents' promotion of gender difference, the fragile-families wing also participates in practices of gendering parenthood. Two intersecting arenas are particularly widely used to masculinize fatherhood in both the pro-marriage and the fragile-families wings: religion and sport. Religious and athletic discourses and practices constitute unifying gendered and (hetero)sexualized foundations for promoting responsible fatherhood. Although fragile-families and pro-marriage organizations generally approach gendered and parental relations differently, biblical and sport images permeate both camps. These arenas for "masculine" practice provide common metaphors for male bonding and role modeling, as well as familial relations. Simultaneously, religion and sport constitute long-standing arenas for contestations between men along the lines of race and class. Pro-marriage and fragile-families representatives use religious and athletic metaphors with different meanings and with different goals in mind.

The fatherhood responsibility movement's talk of a "fatherhood crisis" (Blankenhorn 1995; Horn, Blankenhorn, and Pearlstein 1999; Popenoe 1996) echoes contemporary and past men's movements' uses of a rhetoric of crisis to negotiate shifts in understandings of masculinities (Robinson 2000). Former vice president Al Gore, a leading figure in the fatherhood responsibility movement, has declared, "Too often American society equates 'parenthood' with motherhood . . ." (1996, 13). Ideals of parenthood and notions of "the family" have become feminized and fathers superfluous according to the fatherhood responsibility movement (Popenoe 1998). In this context, sport and religion provide an abundance of masculinizing metaphors, practices, and settings. These arenas provide important tools for the fatherhood responsibility movement to negotiate and contest manhood in relation to the feminized domain of parenting. Fatherhood programs transpose the cultivation of masculinity and male parenting into sport arenas by, for instance, framing fathering practices in terms of coaching and team sport. Fathering practices become distinct from those of mothers and simultaneously heroic and appealing. Similarly, for the fatherhood responsibility movement as well as the Promise Keepers, biblical imagery serves to carve out a particularly male position in families. Fatherhood programs thus masculinize fatherhood by casting men as indispensable because they are naturally and divinely ordained "protectors" and "leaders" of women and children. As we have seen in chapter 1, marriage proponents use the Promise Keepers' notion of "servant leadership" as a model for responsible fatherhood and ideal masculinity.

Biblical Rhetoric as Common Political Strategy

> By positioning its actions as a religious war, Promise Keepers eliminates the chance for compromise or reasoned discourse. No point of entry or common agreement exists from which to counter a purported directive from Christ. . . . One either accepts men as God-given leaders, or is declared an antagonist.
>
> —Robert A. Cole, "Promising to Be a Man"

> . . . Promise Keepers encourages the exclusion and abjection of those individuals who pollute this conception of the chosen community [of divinely ordained gendered and sexual roles]. . . . Promise Keepers invites men to reject those ideas that challenge their own efforts to realize normative conceptions of masculinity by framing those challenges as blasphemous and biblically unsound.
>
> —David S. Gutterman, "Exodus and the Chosen Men of God"

The influences of the Promise Keepers and Million Man March on gender politics are not exceptional in the United States; religion permeates U.S. politics. Most scholars who discuss the inseparability of religion and politics in the

United States refer to the French historian Alexis de Tocqueville, who was struck by the religiousness of U.S. politics when he came to America in the early nineteenth century ([1835] 1990, 308). In his work *Democracy in America,* first published in 1835, Tocqueville emphasized the centrality of religion to U.S. social and political order and maintained that "from the beginning, politics and religion contracted an alliance which has never been dissolved" ([1835] 1990, 300). Tocqueville characterized U.S. society as deeply Christian ([1835] 1990, 303). Despite the separation of church and state and the limited *direct* influence of religion on laws and politics, Tocqueville maintained that Christianity regulated the state by regulating customs and domestic life. In Tocqueville's words, "Religion in America takes no direct part in the government of society, but it must be regarded as the first of their political institutions" ([1835] 1990, 305).

The fatherhood responsibility movement highlights the continuing prevalence of religion in U.S. politics (Coltrane 2001). Despite the competing and asymmetric perspectives on gendered and racial/socioeconomic relations in the fragile-families and pro-marriage wings, they both rhetorically overlap with the Promise Keepers on biblical grounds. Fatherhood responsibility movement representatives often use the very successful Promise Keepers strategy of constructing a distinction between religion and politics in order to place biblical rhetoric "beyond" politics. In other words, the Promise Keepers and parts of the fatherhood responsibility movement jointly attempt to remove themselves from criticism by speaking from a godly perspective. In some contexts, religion seems to be one of the few common grounds in the fatherhood responsibility movement, superseding such divisive issues as marriage and racial/socioeconomic stratification.

Religious rhetoric is a highly visible (and highly successful) political strategy in the Promise Keepers' masculinity politics that is reinforced by the fatherhood responsibility movement. Together with sports talk (analyzed in the next section), religious rhetoric is one of the devices the fatherhood responsibility movement uses to constitute itself as "beyond politics." Religious rhetoric seems to be a particularly popular tool for gendered and sexual politics. Many scholars analyze the Promise Keepers' religious rhetoric as an attempt to shift the grounds for masculinist politics from public to familial arenas (Donovan 1998; Faludi 1999; Messner 1997). For instance, Brian Donovan describes the Promise Keepers' concerns with men's increased power in the home as indicative of the political nature of the Promise Keepers, despite its claims to the contrary: "Looking at their advice for men in these interpersonal domains [marriage, fatherhood, and same-sex friendship] demonstrates that

Promise Keepers address a form of non-juridical power, distinguishing them from movements centered on making appeals to the state institutions. These practices are no less political or consequential than those of other new social movements because they work toward changing the dominant definition of masculinity within as well as outside the movement" (1998, 827).

Not unlike those fatherhood responsibility movement representatives who seek to differentiate concern with child well-being from gender politics, Promise Keepers distinguish between morality and politics. However, this distinction is untenable if the Promise Keepers' wider impact on gender relations is considered. Donovan argues that since economic and cultural changes have undermined older forms of masculinity, the Promise Keepers tries to move "the basis of male authority from economic to spiritual grounds" (1998, 830). In a similar rhetorical shift, the fatherhood responsibility movement attempts to move "beyond" politics. However, it is difficult to trace any unitary "masculinist interest" behind its gendered/sexual politics. Representatives speak of concerns for "spiritual renewal" and "the common good" and thus appear to be situated beyond, or even above, politics.[1] Researchers have demonstrated the rhetorical benefits of constructing a stark distinction between religion and politics to make moral arguments with political implications. The social science scholar Colleen Kelley (2000) illuminates the ways the Promise Keepers' rhetorical strategies are designed to occupy a "rhetorical high ground" by legitimizing its messages from a biblical grounding. Kelley also demonstrates the ways ideologies founded in biblical discourses are "difficult to counter since 'hidden authorities' are virtually impossible to challenge, particularly those 'parading in the guise of holy scripture'" (2000, 230). This is one of the difficulties that critics of the Promise Keepers face. For instance, according to Kelley, the Promise Keepers is "rhetorically superior" to the National Organization for Women (NOW) because of NOW's "failure to provide a comparable counter-vision and inability to ideographically trump words from The Word" (2000, 233):

> It becomes difficult if not impossible for NOW to discursively compete with Promise Keepers because it is difficult if not impossible to rhetorically surpass a vision derived almost entirely from "god terms" or ideographs, which themselves originate in The Highest Authority and the ultimate source of His Word: the Bible. . . . Promise Keepers has been successful in sustaining their vision because leaders such as McCartney say they are only relating the Word of God, directly from His Book; it is difficult to dispute that authority, as it seems to originate in the word of God itself. (2000, 233)

The Promise Keepers' aspirations for rhetorical superiority work on many levels in fatherhood politics. For instance, biblical rhetoric is a common tool to appeal to Christian constituencies. One of the most commonly cited biblical references in the fatherhood responsibility movement is the apocalyptic Old Testament message on fatherhood. Representatives are very aware of the benefits of using this message as a "rallying call" for the movement. As one marriage proponent said in an interview:

> Oh, and there's one other thing that—you need to check this out. It was pointed out to me the apocalyptic message of fatherhood . . . and if you will go to a Bible, a Protestant Bible . . . and look at how the Old Testament, that's the first part of the Jewish literature, the last words in the Bible of the Old Testament talk about fatherhood. . . . It says something like "Before the end of the world, of the great dreadful day, God will send his prophet Elijah, who will turn the hearts of the fathers to their children, and the hearts of the children to their fathers. And if this doesn't happen, the land will be struck with a curse." And that is the way that the Old Testament, the Bible, ends. And so as I have heard that and listened and heard it from others, it's interesting that this whole arena of fatherhood and this whole subject has apocalyptic and spiritual meanings to it. Whether you personally accept that or not makes no difference— many . . . believe just that, and they believe that it's important for fathers to intentionally turn their hearts towards their children as if it is God's will for them to do that. And the reason why I think that is worth while pondering and referencing and looking up is because it is the rallying call for many fathers. That they have claimed a meaningful role and experience and the meaning of society when they turn their hearts—not their heads . . . but their emotions . . . —and when this doesn't happen, the land is struck with a curse.

Not only are biblical discourses one of many rhetorical strategies in fatherhood politics, but some fatherhood responsibility movement representatives consider spirituality to be the *primary* arena and motivational call to "renew" fatherhood. It is not coincidental that many prominent leaders in the fatherhood responsibility movement (such as David Blankenhorn, Ronald Mincy, and Charles Ballard) frequently speak from biblical perspectives. David Popenoe, a pro-marriage intellectual leader, argues as the final point in his contribution to the edited volume *The Fatherhood Movement: A Call to Action* that the renewal of fatherhood requires a "religious reawakening": "It may be that a fully restored sense of moral obligation can be accomplished entirely through secular means, but I doubt it. Religion has always been the main cultural repository of morality, and it is not likely that we can have permanent moral renewal without a society-wide religious reawakening" (1999, 23).

Resonating with the grassroots evangelical Christian ethics that made the Promise Keepers so successful, many fatherhood responsibility movement leaders believe that biblical rhetoric "provides energy and urgency" for fatherhood politics, as Blankenhorn put it at the Second National Summit on Fatherhood in June 1998. This widely used discursive foundation is reflected in everyday practices at local levels as well. For instance, on several occasions in both pro-marriage and fragile-families workshops for fathers, I observed a popular exercise where the participants drew pictures of their ideal father. The majority of these drawings included a symbol (for example, a cross or the Bible) that represented "strong faith" or "spiritual principles." Wade Horn, David Blankenhorn, and Mitchell Pearlstein included "A Call to Fatherhood"—what had become the manifesto of the fatherhood responsibility movement—in their edited volume. Representatives[2] from a variety of fatherhood organizations had come together in 1996 to sign the manifesto with the aim of ending the "curse of fatherlessness" (Horn, Blankenhorn, and Pearlstein 1999, 169). The manifesto frames fatherlessness as an urgent biblical "curse" (Horn, Blankenhorn, and Pearlstein 1999, 169) to be battled for the sake of "the greater social good," as Horn explained in his contribution to the volume (1999, 7). Reflecting Popenoe's views, the manifesto states that "the renewal of fatherhood" is a necessary part of a "larger and much-needed spiritual rebirth in our society" (Horn, Blankenhorn, and Pearlstein 1999, 172). The fatherhood responsibility movement thus calls for legitimacy and authority beyond secular politics. Biblical "rallying calls" for fatherhood responsibility resonate with many constituencies. A prominent leader in the fragile-families wing spoke at a conference about the fatherhood "curse" and argued for the "healing" importance of the fatherhood movement and applied the apocalyptic biblical message on fatherhood to a specifically African American context:

> About five years ago, . . . I woke up one day, . . . and I was reading in Malacai 4:10, which most—many of you know: "Behold: I am going to send you a prophet before the great incoming day of the Lord and he will restore the hearts of the fathers to the children, and the children to the fathers, lest I come and strike the land with a curse." I live in central Harlem, and it's very clear to *me* that many of *our* communities are already experiencing that curse, and it's very clear to me that that was going to be what my life is about, but it's also been a process of healing. The early part of that scripture talks about he's going to send a prophet with *healing* in his wings, and the leaves from the trees will be for the healing of the nations. And I really believe that those of us who are involved in this work around fatherhood development are really about the work of healing our communities [agreeing sounds from the audience]. And the world of healing and peace has to do with joining and making things whole. . . . And it can't be said in simpler terms. . . . However, the work that we are really about, as we draw the hearts of the fathers to the children, and the chil-

dren to the fathers, is enabling young men to fulfill and to heal about their own father loss by helping them to experience what it is to be a father to a child. And that's why this work is fundamentally so important.

The fragile-families leader applies a biblical approach to fatherlessness and other problems in African American communities. He seemed convinced that most of the representatives who attended the fatherhood conference were familiar with a biblical perspective. Although fragile-families representatives were more likely than marriage proponents to focus on social and economic injustices than on morality, I only found *one* out of approximately twenty fragile-families representatives who openly questioned the legitimacy of biblical approaches in fatherhood politics. This representative, Michael (who was also the only representative I met who claimed to have a feminist perspective), saw biblical themes as rhetorical strategies to camouflage racial and socioeconomic power issues. In an interview, Michael criticized those in the fatherhood responsibility movement who use the Bible to avoid secular political questioning: "On paper there is supposed to be a separation of church and state, but we have a very moral and religious driven society. My challenge now is: what do you say to people who respond to your [argument] and just tell you that 'that's immoral and plain out wrong'? Where do you go from that point in trying to be an advocate on an issue? You ask them why they think it's wrong, and they show you a scripture in the Bible."

By speaking from a biblical, moral, or other religious/spiritual perspective, fatherhood responsibility movement representatives convert their politics into unquestionable "truths," which resonates with many participants in fatherhood politics. Because of its "slipperiness," biblical/spiritual rhetoric is a powerful strategy in fatherhood politics. The sociologist John Bartkowski maintains that the sometimes contradictory mix of viewpoints in the Promise Keepers maximizes its appeal to both progressive and traditional evangelical men by making this mix appear overlapping and complementary (1999, 121). The same argument goes for the fatherhood responsibility movement. Since the casual observer might not pay attention to the real divisions behind its "nonideological" concerns for child well-being and contesting approaches to gender relations, the fatherhood responsibility movement often succeeds in making itself appear as an outcome of "national consensus."

Despite the controversial nature of the gender politics of the Promise Keepers and the Million Man March, some representatives of the fatherhood responsibility movement want to situate themselves closer to those movements than to government politics. Harry, a prominent pro-marriage leader, feels close to the Promise Keepers and the Million Man March because of their emphasis on individual moral accountability, which he distinguished from government politics in an interview:

> You know, [the Promise Keepers and Million Man March] are people—[who say] "I wanna be a better dad, *I* have to change." The fathers' rights guys are: "*The system* has to change, the judges have to change, the legislature have to change" [talks in a mean sounding voice]. Promise Keepers and Million Man March say that if you think that that's the answer, you're in the wrong place—the answer is within yourself, *you* have to change. That's why I feel much closer to . . . the Promise Keepers and the Million Man March, because it's about "what can *I* do?" Now *we* do public advocacy, we do public policy analysis, but in all of our literature, and in what you see is, that is not our primary focus. Because what we want to do is to inspire men to be better fathers. So *our* goal is much more similar to the Promise Keepers and Million Man March because we're saying what we want to do is to inspire men to say, "*I* need to change, *I* need to do a better job." And that's *not* something government can do.

On the surface, Harry seems to want to operate primarily at an individual moral level removed from systemic and governmental power relations and to advocate minimum government involvement. Although fatherhood responsibility movement representatives often claim to be chiefly motivated by a higher purpose and set this moral ground apart from government politics, they *do* try to affect power relations within families and between constituencies of men through policy, social programs, and public campaigns. Structurally conditioned constituencies of men come out of competing traditions of religious politics. Nevertheless, biblical and spiritual rhetoric serves as a tool to appeal to evangelical Christian concerns about the family and simultaneously evade political questioning. This rhetorical strategy has been employed by men's movements in the United States since the end of the nineteenth century.

Marriage is inextricably linked to religious institutions in the United States (Bellah et al. 1985, 96; Cott 2000; Lasch 1977; Tocqueville [1835] 1990; Popenoe 1988, 1998). Many pro-marriage representatives I interviewed pointed out that there is no way to analyze the fatherhood responsibility movement without taking its religious/spiritual aspects into account. As I demonstrated in the previous chapters, this goes for both the pro-marriage and fragile-families wings of the fatherhood responsibility movement. In the eyes of many marriage proponents, religion and marriage are mutually reinforcing. The church sanctions and provides structure, ritual, and tradition to the institution of marriage. One of the pro-marriage representatives I talked to even said that "the Lord" is a "third partner" in marriage. He also maintained that religious people are more likely to be "successful" in their marriages (that is, have a happy, monogamous, lifelong marriage) and that married people are more likely to "come to faith." Throughout U.S. history, Christian churches have had a stake in the constellation and gendered order of the marital institution (Cott 2000). The Christian Coalition,[3] for instance, upheld the ultimate significance of the married, heterosexual, two-parent family long before the emergence of either the pro-marriage wing of the fatherhood responsibility movement or the marriage movement.

As we have seen, pro-marriage and Promise Keepers rhetoric and gender/sexual concerns about marriage overlap and continue the U.S. tradition of Christian marriage rhetoric. Many representatives in the pro-marriage wing emphasize the importance of the spiritual/moral arguments for the contestation and remaking of fatherhood. For instance, at the closing plenary of the National Fatherhood Initiative's National Summit on Fatherhood in 1998, one pro-marriage leader professed:

> Something I wrestle with and that is to recognize more clearly the moral, spiritual, religious dimension of fatherhood. . . . Is it really a coincidence that so much of the . . . work in this area is coming out of our churches and synagogues and houses of worship? . . . I don't think it's a coincidence, and . . . to me, ultimately fatherhood calls men to purposes larger than themselves. At the deepest level, it is about the giving of oneself; it is about connecting with others. Ultimately . . . it is about recognizing truths that are larger than any one man. . . . And I think that this larger spiritual and moral dimension of fatherhood and fatherlessness is something that provides much of the energy and urgency for our movement, and we need to be clear that, while we're not a ministry, . . . this is a part of our movement, and a very important part. . . . It's a . . . curse that we live under now. This curse so many men being estranged from their children and estranged from the mothers of their children. And I believe that we are called . . . in this generation to do everything we can to reverse this . . . fatherlessness.

Some representatives in the pro-marriage wing appeal to the religious/moral ethos behind discussions of fatherhood and marriage as if a spiritual revival of married fatherhood were a third stage of the fatherhood movement after its second stage, the marriage movement. One representative even envisioned a religious awakening as the next step for the pro-marriage wing. He explained the religious rhetoric that links the Promise Keepers and the marriage and fatherhood movements in an interview:

> My thing is that the marriage movement, well, I think, I think in those cases in both the marriage movement and the fatherhood movement the key . . . is going to be the role of churches and our religious institutions.

Now, that's not to suggest that they're the only key players—um, or that one could not see um, a return to strong marriages or return to strong fatherhood um, absent some type of spiritual awakening or something of that sort. But um, but it is hard for me to imagine, especially in this country, that [would] happen. And in my mind the most significant activity taking place really on the fatherhood front, at least at a grassroots level, where I think it is really making something of a difference is in, you know, this kind of Promise Keepers sort of phenomenon. Where men who are motivated by faith are taking stock of their family responsibilities and committing themselves to being good husbands and good fathers. In some ways if it's not, if these guys aren't tied to some larger purpose like that, I think the um, the gravitational pull away from family ties is so great from other forces that I'm not sure I know where, you, how you can sustain some real significant change absent a very strong um, faith factor.

At the grassroots and the policy levels of both the pro-marriage wing and the fragile-families wing men are motivated by heartfelt moral/spiritual arguments to reinvigorate their notions of responsible married fatherhood. Representatives frequently use the Promise Keepers as an example of the enormous moral/spiritual resonance of their issues. Marriage proponents in particular attempt to promote a cultural impetus that subordinates men's "innate" impulses to "something larger than the self," such as the family, community, or God. In the eyes of one leading NFI representative, the thought of God's wrath has more power over men than women have, as he made clear in an interview:

> I think that the most powerful contract to keep men's behavior in check is not the contract between the *woman* and the man, but the contract between the man and God. . . . It's a lot more powerful motivator to keep my baser instincts in check if I know God is going to hold my eternal soul accountable than if my wife is [laughs]. You know, OK that sort of has that bigger ring to it, and that's why I think faith is a more powerful motivator than just the sort of contract between men and women, although I do think that contract between men and women is important.

Again, biblical rhetoric for fatherhood issues leads back to a godly gendered order: men are assigned a position of leadership, God and Jesus are the only authorities superior to men, and women are somehow both equal and subordinate to men.

The Promise Keepers' Influence on Fatherhood Politics

> *I am convinced that the primary cause of this national crisis is the feminization of the American male. . . . I'm trying to describe a misunderstanding of*

manhood that has produced a nation of "sissified" men who abdicate their role as spiritually pure leaders, thus forcing women to fill the vacuum.

—Tony Evans, "Spiritual Purity"

The gendered and sexual politics of the fatherhood responsibility movement and the Promise Keepers cannot fully be understood without examining the historical masculinization strategies of U.S. Protestant evangelicalism (see, for example, Balmer 2000; Brickner 2000; Cole 2000; Clatterbaugh 1997; Longwood 1996; and Newton 1999). Many scholars in men's studies and religious studies argue that the Promise Keepers is the latest example of a long tradition of white Christian men's organizations characterized by "fears of feminization" in response to feminist politics (Donovan 1998; Kirkley 1996; Kimmel 1996; Messner 1997; Muesse 1996). For instance, Michael Messner frames the Promise Keepers as part of a "historical ebb and flow" in fundamentalist Christian masculinity politics.[4] He points out that the "flow" tends to occur when feminists challenge men's positions of authority in families and communities (1997, 24). The end of the eighteenth century and the beginning of the nineteenth was the golden age of (white) Protestant evangelical men's movements as well as a range of male-exclusive organizations, such as the Boy Scouts, the Young Men's Christian Association (YMCA), and fraternal orders (Kimmel 1996). Four movements during this period are often discussed as the predecessors of contemporary biblical masculinity politics: the muscular Christianity movement, the social gospel movement, the freethought movement, and the men and religion forward movement.

"Muscular Christianity" consisted mainly of a series of publications and revival meetings between 1904 and 1918 led by the preachers Dwight Moody and Billy Sunday. The term *muscular Christianity* was a trivializing label used by critics who reviewed works on "Christian manliness" (Claussen 1999, 21). American muscular Christians traced their roots to British novels that offered models of "physical manliness, chivalry and the gentleman, [and] moral manliness" (Claussen 1999, 21–22). One aim of the muscular Christians was to revirilize the image of Jesus, who they felt had become too feminized with his long hair, thin chest, and flowing gowns. Muscular Christians redesigned Jesus from, in Billy Sunday's words, an "effeminate," "sissified," "dainty," and "lily-livered" image into a tough and muscular working-class hero (quoted in Kimmel 1996, 179). Muscular Christians also sought to remasculinize the church, which they thought had become too much of a women's domain. Like the contemporary Promise Keepers and fatherhood responsibility movement, the muscular Christianity movement appealed to men through a combination of Christianity and athletic masculinity. Muscular Christians, like the Promise

Keepers, did not promote social change or try to influence social policy directly (Claussen 1999, 22).

The social gospel movement, another turn-of-century evangelical men's movement, is often compared with the Promise Keepers. The social gospel movement emerged among white middle-class Protestant men in the late 1880s and early 1890s. Social gospelers believed that Christians should address social and moral issues in men's lives, such as alcohol, prostitution, and gambling. They upheld service, sacrifice, and love as ideals for masculinity. Although these virtues were associated with domesticity (i.e., femininity), social gospelers cast Jesus and God as models of masculine virtue and thus, in the words of the historian Susan Curtis, "transformed the domestic concerns of their reforms into expressions of manly endeavor" (1990, 72). Like the muscular Christian leader Billy Sunday, the social gospeler leader Walter Rauschenbusch insisted that "there was nothing mushy, nothing sweetly effeminate about Jesus"; rather, Jesus was a "man's man" (quoted in Curtis 1990, 72).

In contrast to the muscular Christianity and social gospel movements, the freethought movement refuted Christianity as a foundation for masculinity. Between 1880 and 1920, thousands of white middle-class freethinkers argued that atheism was a more manly option than Christian belief. They argued for the separation of church and state; formed local, state, and national groups; and published books and periodicals (Kirkley 1996, 80). Freethinkers also contended that the church was feminized and that its members were therefore weak, sentimental, and irrational, unlike the scientific and rational freethinkers (Kirkley 1996, 81). Freethinking atheist men refused to be, in the words of Evelyn Kirkley, "mollycoddled by feminine superstition" (1996, 82).

Like the muscular Christianity and social gospel movements, the men and religion forward movement of 1911–12 argued that real men were Christian. Financially supported by the YMCA and Protestant brotherhood organizations, the movement involved over a million Protestant men in social service activities, including cleaning up jails and lobbying for improved garbage collection. The men and religion forward movement also organized revival meetings and social service projects in more than sixty cities (Kirkley 1996, 83). Like the muscular Christianity movement, the men and religion forward movement claimed that "women have had charge of the church work long enough" (quoted in Faludi 1999, 257).

In what ways have these turn-of-the-nineteenth-century men's movements influenced contemporary gendered and sexual claims in the Promise Keepers and fatherhood responsibility movement? On the surface, the Promise Keepers and parts of the fatherhood responsibility movement sound remarkably similar to these turn-of-century men's movements. The sociologist Brian Donovan (1998) argues that the Promise Keepers fuses masculinist and evangelical discourses and thus transforms manhood into a moral identity that is indispensable because it is different from femininity. Donovan quotes the Promise Keepers author Robert Hicks, who echoes muscular Christians and social gospelers when he declares that "we are called to worship God as phallic kind of guys, not as some sort of androgynous, neutered non-males, or the feminized males so popular in many feminist-enlightened churches" (1998, 819). Similarly, Tony Evans, a leader of the Promise Keepers, maintains that the U.S. has become a nation of "sissified" males, which the Promise Keepers has set out to correct (1994, 73). Like muscular Christians, social gospelers, and freethinkers, the Promise Keepers leaders Gary Smalley and John Trent argue that the Christian church has been feminized because of the higher percentages of female worshipers and Sunday school teachers (Donovan 1998, 819). Promise Keepers resemble the turn-of-the-century muscular Christians and social gospelers who were determined to "take the church back for men," "defeminize" it, and reclaim such "masculine" domains as family leadership (Clatterbaugh 1997, 183). Promise Keepers and contemporary marriage proponents are also similar to those in the turn-of-the-nineteenth-century Christian men's movements in their insistence on a gender-specific position for men in families to compensate for the perceived feminization of the family (Coltrane 2001).

Researchers, however, debate the complex links between the Promise Keepers and past Christian men's movements. The religion scholar Randall Balmer calls the Promise Keepers "the latest avatars of the muscular Christianity impulse in American history" (2000, 195), but the communication scholar Dane Claussen cautions against drawing too sweeping historical connections between the Promise Keepers and earlier Christian men's movements. "Only some of Promise Keepers' speakers and texts have strong flavors of Muscular Christianity; some are more similar to other revivalists, and Promise Keepers has almost nothing in common with M.R.F.M. [the men and religion forward movement] or the broader Social Gospel movement," Claussen contends (1999, 19–20). Claussen goes on to argue that, unlike the muscular Christianity movement, the men and religion forward movement was involved in social issues and was concerned about peace, education, temperance, housing, race relations, and the like (1999, 23). In stark contrast to the social gospel movement, the Promise Keepers directs attention away from economic issues and relations (Newton 1999, 37). In casting men primarily as family members, with God-given and natural roles regardless of their financial bargaining power, the Promise Keepers deemphasizes the unequal relations between men in the marketplace and between men and women in families and the labor market (1999, 39).

Nevertheless, because of the general discursive parallels between the Promise Keepers and muscular Christianity, the latter has been described as a precursor (Kimmel 1987, 123) to contemporary Christian masculinity politics (Kimmel 1996, 313). In men's studies, the Promise Keepers is commonly described as a response to a "masculinity crisis" (see, for example, Kimmel 1999; Messner 1997; and Stoltenberg 1999). The "crisis perspective" frames nineteenth- and twentieth-century men's movements as responses to first- and second-wave feminist organizing as well as social and economic changes that destabilize the positions of men as breadwinners and fathers. For instance, the political scientist David Gutterman argues that the Promise Keepers is largely a response to thirty years of feminist challenges to "divinely ordained" notions of gender and sexuality (2000, 142). Obviously, neither turn-of-nineteenth-century nor contemporary masculinity politics is homogeneous. As the sociologist Michael Kimmel illustrated in his study of various reactions (antifeminist, pro-male, and pro-feminist) to late-nineteenth-century "masculinity crisis" (1987), the complexity of men's reactions to changes affecting their positions as breadwinners and fathers needs to be taken into account. For instance, Margaret Marsh (1990) locates two opposite extremes of Christian manhood ideals at the turn of the nineteenth century, both of which were differentiated from "effeminacy." On the one hand, there was a *cult of masculinity,* which was manifested in the surge of homosocial organizations at the time. On the other hand, as I discussed in the introductory chapter, there was an ideology of *masculine domesticity,* meaning white suburban men's increasing involvement in running their households. Kimmel even mentions a "fatherhood movement" during this period that incorporated men's involvement in the home into notions of (white middle-class) manliness (1996, 159–60).

Although many feminist scholars analyze "moments" (Kimmel 1987, 123) and "tendencies" (Connell 1995, 84) of contextualized "masculinity crises" and "fears of feminization," some scholars dispute analyses of the Promise Keepers in terms of "crisis" or "fear of feminization." For instance, the English scholar Donald Deardorff argues that the Promise Keepers "does not have the nefarious, reactionary elements of past male refuges. Instead, the organization has the function of helping them combat negative images of men, discrimination against men, isolation from other men, women and themselves . . . and role confusion as husbands, fathers, friends and workers" (2000, 89). Similarly, the communication scholar John Keeler and his colleagues contest the claim that the Promise Keepers is based on fear of, or defense against, feminization. They maintain that "there is no indication that those involved in the movement are motivated by feeling threatened by other groups or by a desire for consolidating political or social power" (Keeler, Fraser, and Brown 1999, 86). Although demonstrating the importance of listening to the Promise Keepers' own representations of its gender politics, neither Deardorff nor Keeler convincingly disqualifies critical analyses that situate the Promise Keepers' intended or unintended gender politics in its adversarial relation to feminist politics. Moreover, it is important to contextualize the Promise Keepers' masculinist politics in the social, economic, and political processes that affect the structural conditions of its proponents. The English scholar Sally Robinson (2000) argues that "crisis" is the best way to understand "the contemporary condition of white masculinity." Robinson asserts that those who object to "the crisis model" mistakenly assume that crises are necessarily producing singular outcomes with a clear beginning and end. What is interesting, Robinson argues, is not whether dominant masculinity is "really" in crisis but the ways the rhetoric of crisis get used to negotiate shifts in understandings of masculinities (2000, 10–11).

Sport Metaphors as Masculinization Strategies

Throughout its different uses in U.S. masculinity politics, sport has overlapped with religious discourses. In the words of the cultural critic Marjorie Garber, "Christianity and sports have long been regarded in certain parts of the United States as not only compatible but boon companions. It's no accident that the Super Bowl is played on a Sunday" (1999, 283).[5] Muscular Christianity and the contemporary Promise Keepers are the most well-known examples of the U.S. tradition of "sports evangelism" that merges sport and religious discourses into a common masculine endeavor (Garber 1999, 284). The Promise Keepers and the Million Man March overlap discursively with the fatherhood responsibility movement and are considered part of the movement (Horn, Blankenhorn, and Pearlstein 1999).

As we have seen throughout this study, the fatherhood responsibility movement is fractured across lines of race and socioeconomic class. One way in which these divisions are cross-cut and to a certain extent bridged, other than by religion, is through sports and athletic imagery and practices. Sport is also an arena for contestation over the racial, sexual, and socioeconomic lines that divide constituencies of men (Dunbar 2000; Majors 1990; Messner 1992). Considering that sport has been a common discursive tool in U.S. men's movements since the end of the nineteenth century, it is not surprising that the metaphors, practices, and attributes of sport permeate current fatherhood politics. The writer and cultural critic Varda Burstyn describes the ways organized sport emerged as "an institution of social fatherhood to provide training in manly pursuits—war, commerce and government and a stepping stone out of the family of women and into the world of men" (1999, 45).

As I argued in the introduction, actors in the fatherhood responsibility movement draw on a century-long U.S. tradition of distinguishing the maleness of fathering from the femaleness of mothering. In this context, sport, like religion, becomes a seemingly depoliticized and familiar way to masculinize male family involvement, since sport is "just a game" and the sport and entertainment industry is supposedly removed from government politics. What is more, compared with religious messages, sport metaphors seem less controversial in the rhetorics of masculinity politics. As Burstyn puts it, the "sports-media complex" is a set of large, powerful economies and institutions that appear distance from work and politics (1999, 193). The gender politics of sport discourse and practices in the fatherhood responsibility movement may therefore go unnoticed.

Hallmarks of organized team sports, such as competition and aggression, are often viewed as male predispositions in fatherhood politics. Marriage proponents in particular argue that men tend to be more "physical" and risk taking as fathers and more innately aggressive and competitive than women. According to this line of thought, sport is a specifically appropriate "male" outlet and means for men to bond with one another and their children. Sport and athleticism constitute classic arenas for attaining and displaying masculine ideals (Kimmel 1996; Klein 1993; Messner and Sabo 1990; McKay, Messner, and Sabo, 2000). Within the fatherhood responsibility movement, athletic symbolism serves as a strategy to masculinize domestic involvement, which is perceived as "feminized," and to delineate fatherhood as an intrinsically *male* parenting practice. In other words, casting parenting in sport terms makes domesticity intelligibly male to fathers. For example, fatherhood programs urge men to assume fatherhood responsibility by comparing fatherhood to coaching. The programs challenge men to take responsibilities with such expressions as "step up to the plate" and "be a team player."

An emerging body of scholarly work on gender and sport investigates the ways organized sport and athletic masculinity are founded on sexist and heteronormative differentiations (see, for example, Burstyn 1999; Messner and Sabo 1990; McKay, Messner, and Sabo 2000). Several works on sport and masculinities highlight the ways masculine ideals validated through sport are founded on differentiating heterosexuals from homosexuals (Connell 1990; Pronger 1990, 2000). Some analyze organized sports as homosocial preserves evolving in response to historical contexts in which gendered and sexual boundaries of masculinities are threatened (Kimmel 1987; Messner 1992). Sport intersects historically with religious, political, and military masculinist discourses (Burstyn 1999; Balmer 2000). In other words, sport and masculine ideals are historically interconnected in U.S. gender politics. When describing the emergence of the self-made man in the nineteenth century, Michael Kimmel highlights a "doctrine of physicality and the body" that led to a nationwide "health and athletics craze" at the turn of the century. Sports and athletics became compulsory ways of proving manhood (Kimmel 1996, 120; Petersen 1998, 47). The sociologist Alan Petersen (1998) situates the same "vogue for physical culture" as part of the increasing popularity of Darwinism in the second half of the nineteenth century. Framed in Darwinist terms, "the valorisation of qualities such as competition, physical strength, and physical aggression—inversions of 'feminised' Victorian society—can be explained in part as a response to the growing penetration of the public sphere by women" (Petersen 1998, 47). Petersen traces notions of male aggression, competitiveness, toughness, and desire to control to Darwinist notions of men's biological predisposition to fight and protect their property, including women and children (1998, 55).

The fatherhood responsibility movement uses sports as a language for notions of male predispositions and ideals for male bonding. At public events, fatherhood organizations also use such sports figures as the boxer Evander Holyfield and the basketball player Shaquille O'Neal as role models. Representatives from fatherhood programs talked about the advantages of exclusively male settings, where men can be direct, "play hardball," and lovingly give one another a "hard time." Fatherhood responsibility movement representatives generally consider sport activities particularly appealing to men, regardless of their race or socioeconomic position. There are local organizations, such as Midnight Basketball, that specialize in sports activities as a hook to get men to participate in men's workshops and fatherhood programs. Sport metaphors permeate discourses and practices of fatherhood politics regardless of whether sport is an explicit focus. For instance, as we saw in chapter 3, many representatives in the fatherhood responsibility movement conceive of fatherhood politics in terms of a "playing field" of competing relations among men. Like the Promise Keepers and turn-of-the-nineteenth-century Christian men's movements, the fatherhood responsibility movement stresses exclusively male settings for cultivating masculine ideals.

By casting fatherhood in sport metaphors, representatives masculinize domesticity and male parenting into something men can do without being perceived as feminine. At one fragile-families conference, when discussing male mentoring, the speaker said that men, because they are men, understand such terms as *team work* and *fair play*. One of the most famous fragile-families practitioners, Joe Jones,[6] uses a football metaphor to explain his "team parenting" model to fathers: "You may be on a team with someone you don't like . . . but that doesn't make any difference, because you want to win the Super Bowl" (quoted in Dodson 1999, 21). In another example, in a fatherhood video shown at a pro-marriage workshop, a practitioner told a father that "you can wrap the diaper like a football." When I asked a practitioner from a local fatherhood program how men were matched with their male mentors, he said that they look for common interests, such as athletics, cars, and automobile repairs, and that these "guy matches" sometimes build stronger relationships than do racial commonalities. Not unlike Promise Keepers who gather in football stadiums, many in fatherhood responsibility organizations try to create, in the words of a Promise Keepers representative, a "masculine context" through sport. Such contexts make men feel that their "manhood" is "intact," as one fragile-families practitioner put it at a fatherhood conference, even though they often discuss what they perceive as "traditionally feminine" domestic matters. In all-male contexts, participants in fatherhood programs may express themselves to one another, despite perceiving men as emotionally closed, especially with other men.

One workshop at a (pro-marriage) National Fatherhood Initiative conference for family services practitioners illustrates the ways practitioners in the fatherhood responsibility movement use sports terminology to construct fatherhood and masculinity by differentiating them from motherhood and femininity. The speaker, Paul, a white man in his fifties, promoted coaching as a model for fathering. Paul urged the audience of about twenty-five people (eight of whom were women) to name good coaching characteristics. The audience divided into groups and suggested such things as being organized, knowledgeable, and patient and having a good sense of humor. One group, consisting of three women and one man, mentioned offering treats, which produced much laughter. Paul and the other men in the audience asked the man in this group how he ended up there and if he was the "team mom," that is, a "womanly" person with proclivities for nurturing and domestic tasks. From this exercise, Paul concluded that the traits the other groups suggested would make a good coach and "a pretty darn good dad too." When applying their "male" sports terminology to the family context, Paul and his audience seem to envision a parental division of labor between father and mother along the lines of "coach" and "team mom." This gendered division of labor corresponds rather neatly to the marriage proponents' overall gendered differentiation between fathers as leaders/protectors and mothers as comforters (see chapter 2). Obviously, Paul and his audience consider offering treats to be a female thing to do in a coaching/family context. Such gendering of different tasks in the world of organized sport is not uncommon. For instance, the sport sociologist Stephan Walk describes the ways women with various functions in organized male sport are designated in conventional feminine terms, such as moms, sisters, ladies, or professional "bitches" (2000). The male athletes Walk studied at a large midwestern university perceived the presence of women as an intrusion. This intrusion concerned the physical spaces of male sport as well as "certainties about gender relations and sex differences that sport serves to guarantee" (Disch and Kane quoted in Walk 2000, 44).

Using sport as a metaphor and strategy to promote responsible fatherhood does not necessarily need to be sexist or homophobic. As in the case of the Bible, there are many possible approaches and interpretations. For instance, one might stress a more "gender-neutral" coaching metaphor for parenting in which both women and men can be team coaches. Sport has multiple meanings and uses in the fatherhood responsibility movement, and it constitutes terrain for contestation over the boundaries of masculinities rather than a masculinist message per se. Although practitioners use masculinizing sports terminology to communicate with men, I also heard them criticize men's interest in sports as a distraction from more important things, such as fatherhood responsibilities. This critical approach to sport seems more common in the fragile-families wing. As one fragile-families representative said at a fathers' program, "We've got to give the kid the time we give Chicago Bulls in front of the TV." In this case, a "male" interest in sport and in fatherhood is *not* seen as mutually reaffirming. Practitioners sometimes criticized the use of sports icons and paraphernalia as manifestations of masculinity—especially in the fragile-families wing, where low-income/poor African American men seek labor market opportunities, not just athletic careers. At many levels, sports have different histories and meanings for fragile-families representatives than for pro-marriage representatives. For example, athletic careers are often stereotyped as one of the few employment options available for poor African American men (see Messner 1992; and Majors 1990). I often heard fragile-families representatives criticize low-income and poor men's excessive investments in expensive sport gear and disparage media stereotypes of African American men's physical prowess. In other words, fragile-families and pro-marriage organizations understand and articulate sport rhetoric in different ways.

Scholars who have investigated the potential of sport for racially marginalized groups of men in the United States have emphasized the oppressive rather than the empowering aspects of organized and professional sport, particularly the ways it reinforces white male economic dominance (Majors 1990; Messner 1992). The psychologist Richard Majors (1990) argues that African American men's opportunities in sport reflect their meager opportunities in U.S. society at large. Most sports mega-industries are owned, operated, and managed exclusively by whites, and the number of African American men with dead-end athletic careers is disproportionately high (Majors

1990). Particularly for African American men, athletic role models are an ambivalent symbol for empowerment through success in sport—they may also represent the scarcity of nonathletic opportunities in education and work. As one representative admonished at a national fragile-families conference, "Young men can read the sports page and tell you how many shots Jordan made, but teach them how to read the financial page: knowledge is power." In low-income and poor African American contexts, promoting male and fatherly responsibility by using sport metaphors is thus charged with mixed meanings. Compared with other educational and labor market careers, sport offers bleak power resources. One practitioner, Harold, said in an interview that he probably does not make sense to most men because "I truly don't give a damn about sports . . . my issue is with men in general; we *play! Boys* play. See that's what the difference is between a boy and a man; a man don't have a whole lot of time to play—if he's doing what he has to do." Harold continued his critique of sports metaphors:

> In America a man can—he can be considered a man having left his children, abandoned his wife, run through the little money he earns, basically do nothing, rememorized sports statistics, and be able to pontificate about the actions of Michael Jordan—and everyone's going to say, "He's *quite a man* there!" You see, whereas if he does not do the basic things in terms of his responsibilities, to his flesh and blood, his manhood is suspect! So I am opposed to manhood through sports, you see, and that puts me off in America.

Thus, sports as a masculinizing metaphor and foundation for man-to-man bonding is sometimes challenged, particularly by fragile-families representatives in the broader racial justice struggle. However, it would take some further research with a specific focus on sport to analyze the specific ways in which fatherhood responsibility movement representatives utilize, articulate, and reconstruct ideals of athletic masculinity.[7] For instance, a well-known fragile-families representative, used sport metaphors both to affirm and to critique notions of manhood at a fatherhood conference:

> If you watch any boxer, any champion, there is not a champion that seeks to gain the mantle of the championship without having an old man in his corner to see that which he could not see. . . . We must learn to teach and we must learn to understand how to distinguish between a boy and a man. You see, boys imitate, men originate. . . . You can find that among any group of boys. In fact, if we were to leave this room and go down to a basketball court, if you pass the ball to a boy, a boy will start to bounce the ball, and he will say "Oh, I'm Michael Jordan, I'm Shaquille O'Neal, I'm this one or that one," because boys imitate. But if you pass the ball to a man, he will

not call out another man's name, but rather he will go straight to the hoop to show you who he is [applause and laughter from the audience]. Because boys imitate, men originate, boys play house, men build families.

Although he criticizes imitating athlete role models, he still uses sport as a key metaphor for achieving ideal masculinity through male role models. "Real men" go straight to the hoop and show what men they are, presumably by scoring. "Real men" "build families." The fathering/coaching workshop discussed earlier exemplifies the dilemmas that masculinizing fatherhood through sport may entail for the fatherhood responsibility movement. The speaker, Paul, encouraged fathers to be like coaches by reading quotes about coaching, such as "Be yourself," "Keep it simple," "Be firm and consistent," and "Be a desirable example." He subsequently asked the audience to characterize a well-disciplined team. The groups said that the team should "be unselfish," "exercise self-control," "know limits and expectations," "learn from mistakes," "work well with others," "be goal oriented," "have a positive attitude," and "be dedicated and accountable." Paul asked, "Wouldn't you want your family to be that way? But how would you react if they called your family well disciplined?" A man in the audience said, "I don't want to have my family on a leash, and I can't discipline my wife." Paul replied that "the problem is the *word* discipline. When we talk about our family, it conjures up negative meanings like punishment and control. For coaches, discipline has different meanings." To frame Paul's problem differently, both biblical and sport metaphors for masculinity traditionally carry patriarchal connotations, which obviously is part of their appeal.

In this context, Paul runs into a recurrent problem with Promise Keepers and pro-marriage notions of gendered division of labor (see chapter 2): how does one justify "difference-based equality" between men and women while avoiding a politically controversial hierarchical framework? A number of rhetorical devices are common solutions to this problem, such as focusing on male familial *obligation* rather than male *privilege*. Biblically versed fatherhood responsibility movement representatives, as well as the Promise Keepers, often emphasize moral responsibility, sacrifice, and servanthood as God-given justifications for male leadership. Likewise, Paul focused on the responsibilities of coaching, not its authoritarian aspects. Another rhetorical strategy is to make difference-based equality "nonpolitical" by casting gender hierarchy in terms of the necessity of the game or the moral/social order. The sociologist John Bartkowski, in an article about the Promise Keepers, illuminated the dilemma of "difference-based equality," which sets "radical essentialism and domestic patriarchy . . . alongside contradictory claims about the purported 'equality' of husband and wife in God's eyes" (1999, 125). Kevin Healey also touches on this dilemma for the Promise Keepers: "[M]ovement members disclaim the inequity of this structure by, for example, defining leadership as 'submission.' Nevertheless, the operational definition of male leadership in the family is the husband's authority to make the final decision in times of crisis or disagreement. . . . [T]he potential for men to silence women's voices is ever present in the relationship" (2000, 224). This potential applies to both religious and sport discourses as masculinization strategies. A common Promise Keepers reply to such criticism is not unlike one of the fatherhood responsibility movement's favorite arguments: "masculine" parenting ultimately benefits women and children. For example, in the fathering/coaching workshop, Paul dealt with this difference-based equality dilemma by framing gender relations in a sports trope, where the coach is on the same side as the team. As in the seemingly "gender neutral" fragile-families representatives' team metaphor for fathering, fathers want their "team" to "win" whether they like the team members or not.

Promise Keepers, the Million Man March, and Racialized Masculinity Politics

Together with sport imagery and practice, "spirituality"[8] is a unifying arena and source of tools to masculinize fatherhood, but it is also a longstanding battlefield over the racial, gendered, and sexual boundaries of masculinity. African American masculinity politics is ambivalently positioned in Christian masculinity politics. African American men talk about their own structurally and racially conditioned "masculinity crisis." African American studies scholars even debate whether African American men should be viewed as an "endangered species" considering the continuing legacy of racial and gendered subordination (see Majors and Gordon 1994). The Million Man March is often described as a recent prime example of African American men's responses to socioeconomic crisis (see, for example, Messner 1997; and W. Nelson 1998). The Million Man March also exemplified long-standing connections among African American masculinity politics, African American churches, and racial justice struggles. African American civil rights struggles have traditionally been cast in terms of claims for manhood (Horton and Horton 1999; Kimmel 1996), and African American churches have always served as community centers and sites for political mobilization.[9] At times, African American churches have been the only institution that operated independent of the "white power structure" (Staples and Johnson 1993, 231). Today, local and national fragile-families organizations explicitly build on these traditions and infrastructures as a way of gaining legitimacy in African American communities. They also continue the civil rights struggles for African American and minority men's equal access and opportunities as citizens.

In contrast, the pro-marriage wing overlaps with the Promise Keepers, and its representatives situate themselves as part of a nineteenth-century Christian reform tradition of "educating" the public about moral and social obligations. The sociologists Steven L. Jones and William H. Lockhart argue that the Million Man March and the Promise Keepers have totally different foundations: the Million Man March is based on racial unity, and the Promise Keepers is based on religious unity (1999, 44). In the Million Man March, race was elevated over religion as the key to the collective identity so crucial to the movement. Since most participants were not part of the Nation of Islam whereas the leaders of the march were, organizers appealed to the one bond participants shared: race (Jones and Lockhart 1999, 48). In contrast, the Christian faith of Promise Keepers takes priority over race or socioeconomic class according to Jones and Lockhart (1999, 51).

The pro-marriage wing converges with the Promise Keepers in its emphasis on men's moral obligations as husbands and fathers (Coltrane 2001). Many pro-marriage representatives mention the enormous success of the Promise Keepers' meetings and how well they were attended (between 1994 and 1997) as evidence of the importance of the "spiritual" dimension of fatherhood. Pro-marriage representatives go to Promise Keepers gatherings, and Promise Keepers representatives sometimes speak at pro-marriage conferences. For instance, Paul Edwards from the Promise Keepers spoke at the National Fatherhood Initiative's Second National Summit on Fatherhood in 1998. Edwards's speech revolved mainly around the ways men and women are hard-wired differently, which is a major pro-marriage point. It is not surprising that Promise Keepers and marriage proponents identify similar characteristics of innate or God-given masculinity, such as aggressiveness, competitiveness, and "promiscuous" heterosexuality. Furthermore, leaders from both the fragile-families and the pro-marriage wings constantly call attention to the need for integrating "faith-based" work into the fatherhood responsibility movement and highlight the "spiritual" motivation that drives the movement.

The interracial grounds for Christian men's unity in the Promise Keepers have been unstable, but "racial reconciliation" is an increasing ambition within the Promise Keepers' leadership. In the 1997 "Stand in the Gap" demonstration, where the Promise Keepers sought to bring a million men to Washington, D.C., to "fill the void of spiritual poverty," the Promise Keepers also launched an effort to make antiracism part of its goals (Newton 1999, 41). In the program for the Stand in the Gap march, Promise Keepers were urged to "reach across racial lines" and "see each other based on the content of their character rather than the color of their skin." There has been a recent increase in African American speakers and attendants at Promise Keepers events. However, the Promise Keepers has received mixed reactions to its efforts to promote "racial reconciliation" in rallies, group meetings, and workshops. Andrew Quicke and Karen Robinson point out that Bill McCartney, the Promise Keepers' founder and CEO, is one of the religious Right's most ardent advocates of racial integration (2000, 9): "In 1993, when other high-profile Christian ministries were avoiding this topic as being too sensitive, McCartney spoke out on racial reconciliation . . ." (2000, 13). However, other researchers criticize the Promise Keepers' racial politics for being too shallow. For instance, the communication scholar Dane Claussen points out that promoting "racial reconciliation" is a far cry from making legislative proposals: "Promise Keepers may be trying to provide moral direction and fight racism, but even its opposition to racism is not the same as advocating a civil rights bill or other substantive steps" (1999, 24). Similarly, Steven Jones and William Lockhart note that "Promise Keepers's lack of interest in civil rights legislation or affirmative action programs will make its reconciliation efforts sound hollow to many blacks" (1999, 55). Michael Kimmel criticizes the Promise Keepers' reconciliation message for promoting interpersonal civility but leaving the forces behind racial inequalities untouched. In other words, he argues that the Promise Keepers' reconciliation efforts are just about individual posture instead of a collective struggle that would support institutions and programs for fighting racism (1999, 117). For instance, at gatherings, Promise Keepers are encouraged to embrace a man of a different race and say to each other, "I have failed you, things are going to be different" (quoted in Newton 1999, 40). As the women's studies scholar Judith Newton points out, here "the assumed mutuality of racism symbolically cancel[s] out the structural inequalities of race and white domination" (1999, 40).

Ironically, however, the Promise Keepers' strategy of focusing on morals instead of unequal social and economic conditions may actually end up *bridging* racial and socioeconomic divides by casting all men as equally male by virtue of their domestic leadership. In this context, achieving ideals of masculinity is perceived as "natural" and God-given despite the asymmetric economic and social conditions permitting men to achieve leadership. Kimmel maintains that the Promise Keepers "seeks to heal racial divisiveness by bringing black and white men together under the canopy of patriarchy" (1999, 116). In Kimmel's view, the Promise Keepers' alliances with "right-wing evangelists" and "liberal black clergy" are based on the reassertion of male supremacy at the "table of brotherhood." Judith Newton similarly highlights overlaps between the Promise Keepers' and the Nation of Islam's "family man rhetoric" in positing men first as leaders of family and then as leaders of community (1999, 39).

The Million Man March ostensibly brought African American men together to highlight and resolve a crisis, but, when read in terms of masculinity politics, it displays many of the same sexist and heterosexist tendencies of the Promise Keepers. Despite the Million Man March's emphasis on an inclusive message, many feminist and pro-feminist scholars criticize the march's reductionist exclusion of African American women and its silence on African American lesbians' and gay men's struggles for recognition and equal rights (see, for example, Allen 1995; V. Anderson 1998; Kimmel 1998a; and Messner 1997). According to Michael Messner, the dominant discourse of the Million Man March reflects conservative views of families and essentialist views of manhood, although there are internal disagreements between conservative and reductionist approaches to racialized masculinity politics (1997, 79–80). Victor Anderson, a philosophy of religion scholar, analyzes the Million Man March in terms of a "cult of black masculinity," preoccupied with "the classical, heroic virtues of courage, manliness, strength, self-determination, and racial loyalty" (1998, 21). The gendered and sexualized politics of the Million Man March's "cult of black masculinity" draws partly on a tradition in African American nationalist circles that bases notions of African American masculinity on differentiations from notions of homosexuality and effeminacy (hooks 1992, 112; Harper 1996, 11).

The Million Man March and the Promise Keepers overlap with the fatherhood responsibility movement when it comes to the intended and unintended gendered and sexual *effects* of masculinity politics. Overlapping religious metaphors and homosocial practices serve to masculinize men and fathers, and heterosexuality is an important point of departure in these contexts. One cannot approach the uses of sport and religious discourse in masculinity politics without taking its sexual dimensions into account. Both wings of the fatherhood responsibility movement converge with the Promise Keepers in their extreme preoccupation with the "problem" of male sexuality, sexual purity, and the harnessing of male "promiscuity" through heterosexual marriage (Clatterbaugh 1997, 187). Likewise, masculinizing sport metaphors often reinforce heteronormative ideas of masculinity. Michael Messner (1992) argues that differentiating themselves from women and gay men serves as a key bonding agent for men in organized sports. Similarly, the philosophy and sport scholar Brian Pronger approaches the domain of sport as an "arena of orthodox, heterosexual masculinity" (2000, 236), where male homosexuality traditionally has constituted an antithesis and still does, even

though in recent years several gay athletes have "come out." In the fatherhood responsibility movement and the overlapping Promise Keepers, there
is an elaborate apparatus that separates homosociality from homosexuality.
According to the philosopher Diana Fuss, the supposed distinctness of homosociality and homosexuality is itself a symptom of their conflation and am-
biguity (discussed in Garber 1999, 296). For instance, affectionate physical
contacts between men in sport contexts are paradoxically ways to "shore up
the *heterosexuality* of men's sports" (Garber 1999, 297). Correspondingly, when
Promise Keepers cry and hug other men at rallies, they do so in a masculine
setting (sports arenas) in which their heterosexual identities are reaffirmed
through consistently reiterated commitments to wives as well as the overall
antigay politics of the Promise Keepers' organization.[10]

Fathers are masculinized in the ardently heterosexual settings for male
bonding in fatherhood programs. In local programs, fathers are cast as
"coaches" or "servant leaders" who "keep their pants on" when entering the
domain of the family. By being encouraged to parent through "rough-and-
tumble play" and "servant leadership," fathers may still maintain their manliness and avoid the risk of being called "Mr. Mom."

Notes

1. Fatherhood responsibility movement representatives insist on using the more general term *spirituality* instead of *religion* and rarely position themselves as Christians.
Marriage proponents frequently stress the importance of projecting a nondenominational and "broad-based" image of the movement to avoid being perceived as conservative or part of the religious Right. Local programs may, for instance, use Native American rituals. Moreover, representatives might add disclaimers anytime they use biblical
terms, saying that they would welcome any other spiritual approach—such as Muslim,
Jewish, Catholic, or Buddhist. However, I have never heard anyone in the fatherhood
responsibility movement speak from any of these other religious perspectives.

2. Including such fragile-families leaders as Ronald Mincy and Jeffrey Johnson and
such pro-marriage leaders as David Popenoe, Wade Horn, and David Blankenhorn.

3. The Christian Coalition was founded in 1989 by Pat Robertson and Ralph Reed.
The organization lobbies on behalf of Judeo-Christian and Catholic constituencies, but
it cannot be partisan because of its tax-exempt status as a nonprofit organization. According to the Christian Coalition, its purposes are "1. Training Christians for effective
social action; 2. Combating anti-religious bigotry; 3. Alerting Christians of issues and
legislation on a timely basis; 4. Speaking out for pro-family values in the media; 5. Representing people of faith at every level of government" (quoted in Quicke and Robinson 2000, 7).

4. Andrew Quicke and Karen Robinson define *fundamentalists* as subscribing to evangelical beliefs and a literal interpretation of the Bible (2000, 8).

5. However, one might also look at this in terms of a competition between churches
and sport events for people's leisure time.

6. He is the director of the Baltimore City Healthy Start Men's Services, a fragile-families program that is used as a model in the National Practitioners Network for Fathers and Families.

7. The fragile-families notion of team parenting would be interesting to investigate further because it evokes a gender-neutral notion in which fathers and mothers are part of the same team as players, possibly on equal footing. It would also be interesting to examine how the promotion of team parenting is affected by the use of sport and sport metaphors.

8. Most organizations in the fatherhood responsibility movement are nondenominational and make a point of being inclusive of all "spiritual" perspectives. Despite organizational concerns about not being associated with any particular religious perspective, it was very common for individual leaders and practitioners to invoke Protestant biblical perspectives.

9. Scholars write about the traditional "dual responsibility" of African American churches to provide both spiritual and social services (see, for example, Billingsley 1992, 361). Many prominent leaders in the civil rights movement came from church backgrounds, such as Martin Luther King Jr. and Jesse Jackson (Clatterbaugh 1997, 160). Drawing on the work of the sociologist Andrew Billingsley, William Nelson points out that "historically, much of the organizational capacity of the Black community has resided in the influence and resources of the Black church" and that "collectively Black churches represent an unrivaled structure of power in the Black community" (1998, 251).

10. John Stoltenberg quotes a Promise Keepers policy statement in which it takes a stand against homosexuality to assure homophobic observers and participants that the Promise Keepers promotes *nonsexual* intimacy between men: "sex is a gift from God to be enjoyed in the context of heterosexual marriage. We believe that the Bible clearly teaches that homosexuality violates God's creative design for a husband and a wife and that it is a sin" (1999, 102). The speech communication scholar Robert Cole calls heterosexuality and Christianity the ultimate "non-negotiable items" of the Promise Keepers (2000, 128). The Promise Keepers' leader, Bill McCartney, is well known for his homophobic statements and calls gays and lesbians "a group of people who don't reproduce yet want to be compared to people who do" (quoted in Kimmel 1999, 119).

5   Naughty by Nature

Domesticating Masculinity

Using sport and religion as all-male sites for heterosexual masculinization partly reflects the fact that marriage proponents and fragile-families representatives, despite diverging constituencies and competing perspectives, converge in conceptions of gender-specific male sexuality. Overall, the fatherhood
responsibility movement occupies itself primarily with the "problem" of perceived innately promiscuous male (hetero)sexuality. Fragile-families representatives generally support a fairly large degree of flexibility in the gendered division of labor between parents in heterosexual families. Nevertheless, they still
seem to believe in a fundamental, more or less essentialist, gender difference
that manifests itself in sexuality and is more "basic" than socially and cultur-
ally constructed gender relations. Although marriage proponents are more rigid
on the question of gender difference, they converge with the fragile-families
wing when it comes to sexualized notions of gender difference. As we have seen,
fragile-families representatives tend to frame the "male problem" in sociohis-
torical and economic terms, whereas marriage proponents tend to emphasize
moral imperatives for controlling men's (hetero)sexual urges. Regardless of differences in emphases, however, all branches of the fatherhood responsibility
movement use notions of male heterosexuality as a foundation for male bonding. "Womanizing" defines and masculinizes men, differentiating them from
women as well as homosexuals. Male heterosexuality is considered "natural"
and good if practiced "responsibly," that is, it leads to an economically or morally viable hetero family unit. By being defined in relation to femininity, mas-

culinity engenders coherence in opposition to women and gay men. The only factor that gives heterosexual men coherence as a group in contemporary fatherhood politics is the practice of defining themselves as "normal" by steering clear of practices they consider essentially feminine or gay.

In the fatherhood responsibility movement, notions of male sexuality are partly based on what researchers have called a 1900s "hydraulic" model of gender/sexuality that depicts male sexuality as a flowing force (Weeks 1985, 8). Hydraulics refers to the flow of water (or other liquids) in rivers and channels and its confinement and conduction by dams (and other containers) as well as the use of water in driving machinery (*New Encyclopedia Britannica* 1987). The hydraulic model is based on the biblical, sexological, and sociobiological separation between nature and society that calls for "civilization's" control over "nature" through the reinforcement of heteronormative family forms. In other words, representatives of the fatherhood responsibility movement envision the control of male sexuality according to hydraulic notions of a male natural "drive." First, they construct notions of masculinity and call these "nature" or "God-given order." Then they call for cultural and social control of this nature/order, ignoring the cultural/social ideas and historical conditions that shaped these notions in the first place. The fatherhood responsibility movement's notions of "uncivilized" masculinities draw partly on pop-Freudian notions that equate maturity with reproductive heterosexuality in the "antagonism" between civilization and sexual "drives."[1] Heterosexuality is thus "natural" but still needs to be learned through "proper" socialization. Masculinity, constructed as constituted by heterosexual drives, needs to be "civilized" into heteronormativity, in other words, monogamous marriage and responsible fatherhood. These contradictory essentialist and hydraulic notions of ideal masculinity ignore the ways gendered and sexual notions have been historically and socially constituted in gendered, racial, sexual, and socioeconomic relations.

The hydraulic model and notions of "uncivilized" masculinity have informed the mythologies of "hypersexual" African American men. These mythologies have been used by white men to control and oppress African American and minority men at specific points in U.S. history, for instance, in the surge of rape accusations and lynchings that followed the abolition of slavery (Davis 1981, 172–201; hooks 1992, 87–114; D'Emilio and Freedman 1997, 85–108). The fatherhood responsibility movement reflects the ways gendered, racial, and socioeconomic power relations condition heterosexual norms of masculinity. These dynamics mirror the continuing influence of racist gender stereotypes on U.S. policy and scholarly discourses on African American men and women. Mythologies of hypermasculinity paradoxically coexisted with myths in the 1960s family structure debates that African American men were socialized into "femininity" and gender/sexual confusion because of female-headed "ghetto" households. Post–civil rights discussions of socialization and African American female-headed households framed African American un-married fatherhood and male unemployment in terms of a lack of male role models (see, for example, Rainwater and Yancey 1967).

Again, the gendered and sexual politics of the fatherhood responsibility movement cannot be understood without reference to moral and religious dis-course. The Promise Keepers' emphasis on "sexual purity" and the centrality of controlling male sexuality derives partly from biblical notions of gendered sexuality. The centrality of male sexuality in contemporary fatherhood poli-tics thus needs to be contextualized within a history of masculinity politics that goes back to the nineteenth century. As we have seen, Christian concerns with masculinization are intricately connected with "de-sissification" politics. While, for instance, the Promise Keepers attempts to de-sissify men, it also tries to masculinize men by harnessing male sexuality to monogamous marriage. The Promise Keepers and the fatherhood responsibility movement generally view men as inherently sexually "sinful" or "promiscuous" and uphold fa-therhood responsibility and monogamous heterosexuality as models of mas-culinity that are *not* defined by sexual prowess (Stoltenberg 1999, 97). How-ever, promoting male sexual restraint is fraught with anxiety in the fatherhood responsibility movement.

Discursive Grounds for Sexual Fatherhood Politics

> *Men are essentially lustful creatures whose sexual impulses and spiritual slothfulness must be governed by the clear regulations pronounced by divine command.*
>
> —Mark W. Muesse, "Religious Machismo: Masculinity and Fundamen-talism," summing up Southern Baptist thought

The fatherhood responsibility movement shares a dilemma with the Promise Keepers by discouraging men from indulging in the perceived excess of the very manliness they champion (Bartkowski 1999, 124). Promise Keepers au-thor Edwin Cole calls the dilemma of "real" but sexually undisciplined men the "playboy problem" (quoted in Bartkowski 1999, 124). Essentialist notions of male sexuality are closely connected to the emergence of homosocial are-nas and discourses for masculine ideals. For instance, late-nineteenth-century sport discourses linked physical and sexual imagery to "producer values," such as making, saving, acquiring, and investing, and they promoted the benefits of sport as a way to channel male sexual "energy" (Burstyn 1999, 78). Contemporary fatherhood politics reinvigorates these "hydraulic" metaphors. The attempts to "harness" "manliness" into fatherhood result in a dilemma that reoccurred in masculinity and fatherhood discussion throughout the twentieth century. On the one hand, fatherhood must domesticate masculinity (Blankenhorn 1995, 225); on the other hand, fatherhood needs to be masculinized through sport, religion, or other "manly" activity so that it will not appear domesticated—in other words, "feminized" or "sissified."

While serving as a basis for male bonding in religion and sport, male heterosexuality has ambiguous implications in the fatherhood responsibility movement. Throughout the fatherhood responsibility movement, hydraulic notions of masculinity are considered as natural as they are problematic, and practitioners try to help men master their "lowly" "dog impulses" or "stud instincts." I often heard practitioners address participants with such expressions as "You can't be like a dog in a meatpacking factory wanting a bite out of everything," "You've got to think with the big head, not the little one," and "Just having a penis doesn't make you a man." With these and similar expressions, practitioners and participants jokingly slap each other on the back for being naughty but "manly" womanizers, but they also criticize one another for exactly the same reason.

Despite the danger in "failing" domestication, fatherhood responsibility movement representatives often refer to their (hetero)sexual urges as men in order to create man-to-man understanding. One fragile-families leader discussed the "male problem" at a fatherhood conference attended by about a hundred practitioners:

> Studies from countries all over the world [show] that men have greater frequency for sex than do women—basic. All right? Men want sex more than women. . . . Clear—right? . . . And it is all around this question of: *how* are men going to *manage* their sexuality so that, as they grow up, they can remain faithful to their partners and to their children, and they can keep their wealth within their household and not pissing away—excuse me— [laughter and applause] on child support and maintaining two households. This is a problem that, by the way, is not peculiar to our community. That's it; it's not a problem peculiar to the black community, it is a problem that happens *all around the world*. . . . And you remember Solomon and David and Abraham, and what was the one thing, the *one thing* that took these kings and tore them down? It was their failure to manage their sexuality! [Applause] Look at Solomon, the king, the wisest man on the earth, right? So how is it that we, in the African American community, think that we're going to be able to breathe health and healing in our communities if—Look at . . . Bill Clinton. . . . [Laughter and applause.]

His reference to men "pissing away" their resources is an obvious hydraulic metaphor. However, as a fragile-families representative, he is very aware of the risks in reinforcing stereotypes that African American men are "hypermasculine." He therefore reiterates that "the problem of male sexuality" concerns men *universally*. He reinforces a hydraulic model of male sexuality by using both biblical and contemporary examples to assert that men have to "manage" their sexuality to achieve responsibility and financial stability. Throughout the rest of the speech, he used himself and his son as examples to illustrate the difficulties men have in restricting their sexuality to the one woman.

The threat of unrestrained "hypermasculine" sexuality and aggression legitimizes the fatherhood responsibility movement's claims about the importance of responsible fatherhood. These ideas date back to nineteenth-century sexological notions of sexuality (Weeks 1985, 73–79).[2] Early sexologists, in their turn, drew on deeply rooted Christian beliefs. The hydraulic metaphor conjures up the nature of male sexuality as an unruly natural force that has to be stopped and economized according to hydraulic laws. Hydraulic metaphors, such as "water dammed up" or "saving" and "spending" sexual energy, have been used in medical, legal, and political contexts since the 1800s to draw and redraw boundaries of "natural" sexuality confined to heterosexual reproduction and marriage (Petersen 1998; Weeks 1985).

There are several overlapping essentialist approaches that contrast and intertwine the hydraulic notions of male sexuality that reappear in fatherhood politics. For instance, the philosopher Kenneth Clatterbaugh (1997) describes different moral, sociobiological, and evangelical conservative perspectives, which all approach male sexuality according to hydraulic notions of "promiscuity." Clatterbaugh mentions the pro-marriage leader David Blankenhorn as a major moral conservative and discusses his book *Fatherless America* (1995), which is one of the most influential works in the fatherhood responsibility movement. *Moral conservatives* are concerned with "civilizing" male drives of aggression, "promiscuity," and so forth by means of social restrictions and the moralizing influence of women. The *sociobiological conservative* approach frames the same "male" traits in terms of reproductive strategies, where men try to have sex with as many women as possible to maximize the possibility of having offspring (Clatterbaugh 1997). Finally, *evangelical conservatives,* which the Promise Keepers exemplify according to Clatterbaugh, believe that men are naturally tempted by sexual sin and need to be made moral by women, marriage, and "Christ-likeness" (1997). Whether concerned with civilization, nature, or God, these conservative approaches locate gendered and sexual relations outside historical processes.

Marriage proponents envision the harnessing of "The Male Force" as foundational to civilization (see chapter 2) and thus indirectly recenter the (white, middle-class, heterosexual) married man as the cornerstone of social and moral order. In contrast, while making civil rights claims on behalf of poor, minority men as "respectable citizens," fragile-families representatives speak of uncontrolled male sexuality as a waste of resources. In the view of many fragile-families representatives, irresponsible "management" of male sexuality may lead poor and minority men to further financial problems through, for instance, high child support expenditures. Linking economic and sexual "energy," fragile-families representatives fuse sexual, athletic, and marketplace activities in line with mid-nineteenth-century notions of "spermatic economy" (Burstyn 1999, 78; Kimmel 1996, 45; Messner 1992, 95). The writer Varda Burstyn defines spermatic economy, coined by the sport scholar Donald Mrozek, as a Victorian notion that "conveys the idea of a closed economy of human energy requiring disciplined, renunciatory practices for success in extrasexual endeavor, as well as sexual energy figured as male" (1999, 78). The sociologist Michael Messner writes of the emergence of organized sport in the late nineteenth century and early twentieth as part of a "Victorian antisexual ethic" based on notions of spermatic economy (1992, 95). According to these notions, men have a limited amount of energy that can be invested in such activities as business, sport, copulation, and procreation (1992, 95). Similarly, both the pro-marriage and the fragile-families wings generally seem to conceive of masculinity as preconditioned by a heterosexual innate drive, which they try to get men to "invest" in "male" endeavors, such as breadwinning, responsible fatherhood, and sport (Messner 1992, 95; Dworkin and Wachs 2000, 56–57).

For instance, Joseph Jones, the director of the Baltimore City Healthy Start Men's Services, at another conference echoed the fragile-families leader's assessment of the "male problem" and evoked the hydraulic/spermatic economy imagery of "managing," "saving," and "spending" male sexual energy. After joking about wanting to have extramarital sex with the entertainer Janet Jackson, Jones discussed the importance of teaching men to control their sexuality as they would manage a stock account, with a reward at the end. Jones's exhortation to "manage" one's sexuality is an example of the way in which leaders in the fatherhood responsibility movement make a connection between marketplace economy and male sexuality and conceive of men's sexuality as natural, risky, and possibly rewarding. The trick is to make use of male sexuality the "right" way, that is, to maximize the financial and moral outcomes. And of course the optimal way to successful masculinity and fatherhood is through married heterosexual monogamy.

Gendered and Racialized Discourses on Sexuality

[M]an, when alone, and deprived of that influence which the presence of woman only can produce, would in a short time degenerate into a savage and barbarous state.

—C. W. Haskins, *The Argonauts of California*

The hydraulic metaphor for men's heterosexual "drive" corresponds to and complements early-nineteenth-century constructions of (white) female sexuality and womanhood in what researchers describe as the "Cult of True Womanhood" (Kimmel 1996, 54; Welter 1966). Basically, the nineteenth-century Cult of True Womanhood portrayed (white) women as the civilizers of men. "True Women" constrain men through domestication, Christian morals, and control of "male sexual energy" (Kimmel 1996, 54–55). During slavery, the Cult of True Womanhood was used by white men as a symbol of white female "virtue" and "honor" that needed to be "protected" from the fabricated sexual threat of African American men (Morrison 1992, 80; Aanerud 1997, 43–44; Davis 1981, 172–201). As the historian Angela Davis put it, "In a society where [white] male supremacy was all-pervasive, men who were motivated by their duty to defend their women could be excused of any excesses they might commit. That their motive was sublime was ample justification for the resulting barbarities" (1981, 187). In contrast to white womanhood, African American womanhood was portrayed as "chronically promiscuous"—an inseparable complement to the racist myth of African American men as rapists (Davis 1981, 182). Constructions of male and female sexualities are thus racialized in historically gender-specific ways.

The racial tensions resulting from the historical associations between whiteness, civilization, and citizenship in the United States are reflected in the competing ways in which the two wings of the fatherhood responsibility movement construct notions of hypermasculinity (Bederman 1995). Perspectives on hypermasculinity are racially and socioeconomically conditioned in the fatherhood responsibility movement. In the pro-marriage view, hypermasculinity is one type of deviance from the ideal—harnessed masculinity.[3] Hypermasculinity, which is also called "protest masculinity" by such marriage proponents as David Blankenhorn (1995) and David Popenoe (1996), denotes excessive attempts to "prove" manhood by means of violence, sexual prowess, and the like. In their influential books on fatherhood, Blankenhorn and Popenoe mention African American fatherhood only in the context of social disorder and fatherlessness (Blankenhorn 1995, 43; Popenoe 1996, 26). According to the pop-Freudian views espoused by leading fatherhood responsibility movement figures like Blankenhorn and Popenoe, hypermasculine men are produced by a lack of male "role models" and fears of identifying too much with their mothers. Pro-marriage representatives tend to reserve such notions of hypermasculinity for low-income and poor (minority) men. For instance, David L. Gutmann writes that "Mama's boys" in "the fatherless inner city" (code word for poor African American neighborhoods or "ghetto") are the men who are most likely to "prove" their manhood by "savaging" women (1999, 142). Popenoe writes that "hyper" and "protest" masculinity "of course" is most associated with "inner cities" (again, read: neighborhoods of color) but that it now threatens to "spread" (1996, 157). These continuing implicit forms of stigmatizing African American fathers contribute to the tensions between the pro-marriage wing and the fragile-families wing. One of the most fundamental purposes of fragile-families organizations is to extend civil rights claims to poor minority fathers and to defeat the many stereotypes of African American masculinity that have haunted African American men since slavery.

U.S. family politics is, and has been, obsessed with images of "African American men misbehaving"—especially sexually misbehaving (Messner 1997, 66–67). Sexuality has constituted an uneven battleground between white and African American men throughout U.S. history. For instance, the abolition of slavery posed political and economic threats to white men and marked a period in which sexuality was white men's "weapon of terror," as manifest in lethal rape accusations against African American men, to keep former slaves from pursuing equality with whites (Segal 1990; D'Emilio and Freedman 1997, 106). Another wave of attention to "problematic" African American masculinity followed the 1965 "Moynihan Report," entitled *The Negro Family: The Case for National Action,* by Daniel Patrick Moynihan, who was assistant secretary of labor. According to this report, African American "hypermasculinity" was both an outcome and a cause of the "tangle of pathology" in the African American "matriarchal structure" (quoted in Rainwater and Yancey 1967, 75). Citing the sociologist Franklin Frazier, Moynihan traced African American "matrifocal" (mother-centered) family patterns back to slave society, where African American women were "accustomed to playing the dominant role in family and marriage relations" (quoted in Rainwater and Yancey 1967, 63). Moynihan argued that "matriarchal" family structure was a central problem in the "tangle of pathology," because it led to "reversed roles of husband and wife" in an otherwise patriarchal society (quoted in Rainwater and Yancey 1967, 76). Since male leadership was undermined, the socialization of boys was impeded.

In the post–civil rights era, academic and policy discussions about the "matrifocal" African American "family structure" partly portrayed African

American men raised in female-headed households as too "feminine" (see, for example, Rainwater and Yancey 1967; and Staples 1998). Ulf Hannerz discusses the logic of such socialization research:

> Our point of departure is the commonly accepted opinion that a boy growing up in a household where the father is more or less absent comes to suffer from confusion over his sexual identity. First of all, the person with whom the boy ought to identify is missing, so the boy has no appropriate model for his sex role. The information about the nature of masculinity which a father would transmit unintentionally to his sons merely by going about his life at home is lacking. Furthermore, the adult who is available, the mother, is inappropriate as a role model for him; if he starts to identify with her, he will sooner or later find out that he has made a mistake. . . . This misidentification with mother would lead the young males to become more feminine. Some commentators on black family structure do indeed cite examples of men out of matrifocal families of orientation inclined toward feminine behavior. . . . Cases such as these would serve as examples of rather overt tendencies toward femininity among some men coming out of matrifocal families. Very casual observations in the ghetto also lead one to believe that male homosexuality is not particularly infrequent in the community. . . . Are we to believe this? (1969, 118–19)

Hannerz highlights the ways notions of "sex identity confusion" (Rainwater and Yancey 1967, 364) spilled over to notions of sexual orientation in the discussion on the "matrifocality" of African American family formations. As in the rhetoric of turn-of-nineteenth-century Christian men's movements and the contemporary Promise Keepers (see chapter 4), the lack of a proper male role model was believed to cause "femininity" in men, which was sometimes equated with male homosexuality (Staples and Johnson 1993, 88).

Past policy and academic contestations, which portrayed African American men as simultaneously "hypermasculine" and "effeminate," constitute a political and cultural repertoire to which fragile-families representatives have to relate in one way or another when they talk about African American men. On the one hand, there is the middle-class ideal of the "respectable" married father and successful breadwinner, generally represented by white middle-class men in the public imagination (see, for example, Duneier 1992). On the other hand, there are stereotypes of African American men that have in themselves barred African American men from obtaining the ideals of respectability: racist stereotypes of African American men as a bunch of idle slackers and hypersexual superstuds. The sociologist Robert Staples calls this situation the "double bind" that traps the African American male, who "always had to confront the contradiction between the normative expectations attached to being male in this society and the proscriptions on his behavior and achievement of goals. He is subjected to societal opprobrium for failing to live up to the standards of manhood on the one hand and for being super macho on the other" (1998, 467).

The psychology scholar Lynne Segal identifies one of the sources of the contradictions inherent in current constructions of African American masculinities: "Anxiety about the 'emasculation' of the Black man coexists with anxiety over the super-sexual, super-macho nature of the Black man. Is he not man enough, or is he too-masculine-by-half?" (1990, 184–85). In contrast to white middle-class marriage proponents, fragile-families advocates constantly need to defeat such contradictory sexual, racial, and gendered stereotypes. In constantly seeking to disprove stereotypes of responsible but poor fathers, fragile-families representatives critique and expose the continuing legacy of racist imagery in social policy and the privileges white men enjoy in the labor market. But, as we saw in chapter 3, they also want to even out the "playing field" and compete for the same goals of masculine success.[4]

Although fragile-families and pro-marriage representatives "converge" over hydraulic notions of masculinity and sexuality, they do so with different meanings and from asymmetric viewpoints.

The Imagined Unity of Heterosexual Men

Despite the structurally diverging perspectives in the fatherhood responsibility movement, the two wings come together on grounds of heterosexuality when they differentiate the notion of masculinity from notions of femininity and gay masculinity. Fatherhood responsibility movement representatives, as well as the Promise Keepers and the Million Man March, often claim that there is certain gendered knowledge that men need to share with one another. By virtue of being male, men are capable of understanding one another. One of the preconditions for this male standpoint approach is men's perceived gendered sexual difference from women and their related heterosexual desires. Hydraulic sexuality is a central aspect that sets masculinity apart from femininity in the fatherhood responsibility movement. According to these conceptions, all "real" men share the same struggle to channel and control their heterosexual womanizing energy. In contrast, women's sexual desires are considered relatively lax and geared toward heterosexual love and familial commitment. Both practitioners and participants in fatherhood programs are supposedly familiar with men's struggles to constrain themselves around women because they all have personal experience with the "male problem." Not only does the fatherhood responsibility movement strive to affect men's relationships with women, but also local fatherhood programs attempt to cultivate all-male settings for man-to-man and father-to-son bonding based on notions of gendered and heterosexual sameness. As one fragile-families representatives put it in an interview, men "transmit what's male" when parenting, and they "communicate in a male way." Representatives from both wings of the fatherhood responsibility movement expressed such ideas as "As iron sharpens iron, so one man sharpens another." Or, as one fragile-families representative put it at a national fatherhood conference, men have "manly" things to learn from one another, "like birds teach birds how to fly and fish teach fish how to swim." This bird/fish metaphor even suggests that men and women are different species.

Homosociality is one site in the fatherhood responsibility movement for the contestation and negotiation of masculinities and heterosexualities in response to changing conditions affecting differently positioned men. In man-to-man settings, men express themselves in ways they sometimes perceive as unconventional. Because they sometimes talk about topics they consider "feminine"—such as feelings, childcare, and relationships—practitioners are often cautious about interfering with participants' "manhood." Practitioners and participants seem to feel that their heterosexuality may become dangerously suspect by being emotionally close to other men and doing "unmanly" things, such as talking about clothes, children, or relationships. It was therefore common for practitioners to reconfirm that the seemingly fragile heteromasculinities of the men in the group were intact. For example, when discussing an upcoming fashion show for the local East Coast–based fathers' workshop where I did the bulk of my local in-depth participant observation, Troy, the practitioner, assured the participants that nobody would think they were "sissies" by participating. He apparently felt that only women and gay men are interested in fashion, and he wanted to protect the men in the group by distancing them all from gay men ("sissies"). In doing so, he reinforced the homophobia that underpinned their imagined unity as heterosexual men. This unity is imagined because not once did the men seriously discuss sexual orientation or their feelings about it.[5] Members of another fatherhood group with which I frequently interacted continually made homophobic jokes and "accused" one another of being gay. In an interview, the practitioner who coordinated this group compared homosexuality to immorality, addiction, and violent behavior. Distinguishing themselves from gay men was central to the ways these men constituted themselves as masculine.

At one major fragile-families fatherhood conference, the moderator introduced one of the keynote speakers as an icon of manhood, a man women want as their husband and boys want as their father and role model. The keynote speaker began his speech by assuring the five hundred or so men in the room that their heterosexual identities could remain intact even if they express brotherly, as opposed to sexual, feelings for other men:

> I want to say something first to the men in the room, because it's not frequent enough that as men that we have a chance to acknowledge each other. I *love* men. I *love* brothers, and if you're in this room, and you're black, white, red, brown or yellow, you're still my brother: I *love* brothers. Because I come from a family where men were respected and men were honored and *loved* each other. . . . And so I say to you out loud and [in] a plain voice that *I love men.* Because not often enough is that said to men *by* men. In fact, we shy away from that because some people will think "Well, then maybe this guy is homosexual." No, you can love a chicken, it doesn't make you a chicken! [*Big* laughter and applause from the audience. The speaker laughs too.] *No,* I just—and I love men, and I love being around men and I *love* my brothers. I *love* them.

What made his chicken metaphor so funny to the audience was the implication that "homosexuals" are like chickens and thus not even human—unlike the "real" men in the audience. Furthermore, *chicken* is a term for someone who is not manly enough—like women ("chicks"). This incident illustrates that if men express homophobic fears of homosocial bonding, it does not make them less of a man in the fatherhood responsibility movement—on the contrary. Reconfirmation of imagined heterosexual unity is one of the ways to masculinize homosociality in the fatherhood responsibility movement, often in conjunction with biblical and athletic metaphors and practices. For the speaker and his audience to feel comfortable about the topic of love between men, he feels that he has to distinguish himself from gay men by making nonheterosexual men seem like a nonhuman species. The chicken metaphor even appeared on a billboard sponsored by a fatherhood organization, which reportedly said that men who "fly the coop" are chicken.[6] Such shaming messages tell "irresponsible fathers" that they are being unmasculine or feminine.

The ongoing concern with heterosexualized "brotherly" unity in the East Coast fragile-families fatherhood program may further illustrate the ways masculinity is constructed as the opposite of homosexuality in racialized contexts. During a discussion about male sexual self-control and "womanizing," Troy asserted that "we all love women" and that he was not "knocking anybody" because he was "a man too." In closing this discussion, he celebrated brotherly love and the importance of male bonding. At a later workshop on the "unity" of African American men, Troy and a group of about ten fathers who participated in the program discussed male homosexuality as a possible threat to racialized "brotherhood":

Terrence (participant): Did you know that Martin Luther King was homosexual?

Participant 1: The picture wasn't painted only by whites—by blacks too. If Martin Luther King was homosexual, we need *everyone* to be homosexual! He did a lot of good things.

Troy: Did Martin Luther King like women? That he was married doesn't mean he liked women.

Participant 2: This is about unity. Now when we're talking about painting negative pictures, I think [to Terrence] that there was a very negative picture that you painted there. We all need to be a bit more selective about what we're talking about—is it going to be a positive picture or one of negativity?

Terrence: Martin Luther King was something that was negative for the people. People are *stupefied*. Why did they shoot Martin Luther King in the head?

Participant 1 (to Terrence): What does sexuality have to do with what he has done? Unity is to bring peace in a collective manner. If we let accusation divide us we're going to focus on negative. Even if he [Martin Luther King] had some negative things in his life, the positive was put forth. . . .

[The group discusses whether Martin Luther King was homosexual, and it is pointed out that people often say negative things about African American men who are doing good things, such as the basketball star Michael Jordan.]

Troy: That's how the enemy wants us to feel: that we have nobody to look up to, that we don't have self-worth!

Participant 2: They say, "United we stand, divided we fall." Negative breeds negative. . . .

Troy: [in closing] The dialogue today has been good, and it does bring unity.

It is clear here that when Troy tries to establish whether someone likes women, he is referring to sexual orientation. An important basis for the homosocial bonding and racial unity of the group seems to be the collective assertion that "we all love women." Whereas group members disagree about whether homosexuality tarnishes a man's accomplishments, they seem to agree that homosexuality falls under the category of "negativity" and is an accusation that threatens unity. The concern in this discussion is the unity of heterosexual African American men and fathers, not pondering why homosexuality is synonymous with negativity. However, the discussion also provides a moment of contestation when one participant suggests that everyone should be homosexual, though perhaps it is not contestation that takes place here but just a rhetorical way of saying that Martin Luther King is so positive a symbol that not even homosexuality can tarnish his accomplishments. Since nobody reacted to this particular statement, it is hard to make anything out of it.

In sum, the men's defensive assertions of their imagined unity as African American heterosexual men reveal their constant need to prove their masculinity (Kimmel 1996). These practices of defining groups through exclusion and othering is not uncommon in social movements (Merton 1972). Reflecting the politics of men' movements at the turn of the nineteenth century, as well as contemporary biblical masculinity politics, the fatherhood responsibility movement manifests the long-standing homosocial foundations for heterosexual masculinity politics.

Homosociality, Evangelicalism, and Fears of Sissification

At the end of the nineteenth century, homosexual men emerged as a social category and a screen upon which heterosexual men projected their fears of feminization (Kimmel 1996). Preoccupations with the boundaries of masculinity at the turn of the century were thus related to the emerging notion of homosexuality (Katz 1995). During this era, the conflation of femininity and male homosexuality became established in the public imagination (Burstyn 1999, 100). Heterosexuality emerged as the hallmark of masculinity, and heterosexual men defined themselves in opposition to everything they considered effeminate and "sissy-like," which included gay men (Burstyn 1999, 100; Kimmel 1996, 100). Subsequently, such early sexologists as Richard von Krafft-Ebing and Karl Heinrich Ulrichs defined manliness as distinctly nonhomosexual and distinguished homosexual men from heterosexual men on the basis of effeminacy (Petersen 1998, 60).

Homosociality has been a crucial Christian theme since biblical times and was a particularly important one in nineteenth-century Christian men's movements. In conjunction with late-nineteenth-century male concerns about sissification, male bonding became problematic (Yacovone 1990). The religion scholar Mark Muesse argues that twentieth-century Christian fundamentalist "fears of feminization" were related to wider U.S. beliefs that religiousness and controlled sexuality are "effeminate" characteristics. According to Muesse, Christian men use "hypermasculine" rhetoric to compensate for such characteristics (1996, 90). Contemporary fatherhood politics partly draws on late-nineteenth-century Christian anxieties to distinguish male homosociality from femininity and "sissiness." Male-exclusive bonding in the fatherhood programs is an important tool to reinforce and redraw the boundaries of heterosexual masculinity. It is mirrored in the Promise Keepers and the Million Man March. The biblical metaphor for male bonding as "iron sharpening iron" is popular with the Promise Keepers, as well as the fatherhood responsibility movement. In an interview, one white Promise Keepers representative used the iron metaphor as follows:

> We need a relationship with a few other men, committed relationships with a few other men. Understanding that we need our brothers to help us keep our promises. There's something about having a close relationship, an intimate relationship, with a man. Intimacy: in-to-me-see, means I'm transparent with some brothers that aren't afraid of getting in my face and say "Hey . . . , you're messin' up." . . . Holding me accountable. A proverb in the Bible talks about "iron sharpening iron as one brother does to another." That's about iron sharpening iron; we're here to help sharpen each other. . . . A key part of that is we realize, we want to make sure that men understand the need for having other men in their lives that aren't afraid to ask them a tough question.

This Promise Keepers representative emphasizes a nonphysical and non-sexual notion of intimacy among men who display manly toughness as a means to male affection. His metaphor for male intimacy assumes that men are enough alike (since they are made up of the same matter: iron) to understand one another and strong enough (like iron) to challenge one another. The metaphor reflects one of the ways male bonding in the Promise Keepers and the fatherhood responsibility movement rests on a standpoint essentialist belief that only men can teach and validate manhood, because women cannot fully understand what it is like to be a man (Cole 2000, 123). This assertion justifies the insistence that Promise Keepers meetings and many "manhood training" and "rites of passage" programs in the fatherhood responsibility movement remain exclusively male (Cole 2000, 127). The biblical iron allegory for male camaraderie also asserts that men are made of a solid and impenetrable essence (iron) that they need to perfect in homosocial (as opposed to heterosocial or homosexual) interaction. Referring to his son and his son's friend, one fragile-families leader used the biblical iron metaphor at a regional fatherhood conference: "There's a proverb that says as iron sharpens iron, so one man sharpens another, and it's been my pleasure to watch these two young men as they were in junior high school . . . to grow up and mature in this way, and I didn't grow up with my father. That's very important. I share the same experiences of many of the people that you serve, and many of the people in this room."

The fragile-families leader first refers to his son and his son's friend and then goes on to extend the iron rationale to a father-to-son relationship. He uses this biblical metaphor for male bonding to make the point that men lack something essential in life unless they can "sharpen" themselves against other men. For the rest of his speech, he talked about the difficulties he and his son share in trying to restrict their sexuality to monogamous marriage. He and his son support each other in their efforts to "manage" their sexuality. Thus, in both male role modeling and all-male peer support, homosociality fosters heteronormative masculinity. The ways male bonding strengthens heterosexual manhood and brotherhood can be seen in the Promise Keepers. Bryan Brickner, who has written on the Promise Keepers, notes that "as the successful coach of a team sport, [Promise Keepers leader] McCartney knows the value of enduring life's battles with the support of teammates; thus the significance of Pro. 27:17, a commonly cited scripture in the Promise Keepers organization: 'As iron sharpens iron, so one man sharpens another'" (2000, 207).

When it comes to the Promise Keepers, only men can be part of this team; their meetings and messages are for men only. Promise Keepers men sharpen one another by keeping themselves on a track where anything other than heterosexual monogamy counts as sexual sin. The Promise Keepers' definition of "sexual purity" entails abstinence outside of marriage. The Promise Keepers defines sexual sin as all sex that takes place outside of heterosexual marriage—including homosexuality (Stoltenberg 1999, 98). In other words, all forms of sexuality that are not monogamous, heterosexual, and marital are considered "wrong" and against God's will.

If Christian males constitute a tough iron team, what team are they competing against? The answers have shifted throughout the history of Christian men's movements. In the case of the fatherhood responsibility movement, the "enemy" has been proclaimed to be "family relativism" by the pro-marriage leader Wade Horn (1999). Upon closer look, the pro-marriage argument against family relativism constitutes a direct and indirect politics of heteronormativity.[7]

The Hetero Closet and Pro-Marriage Sexuality Politics

One of the most ironic and cynical dimensions of the fatherhood responsibility movement is that the pro-marriage representatives cast their heteronormative perspectives as subversive. In the article that Wade Horn says galvanized the fatherhood responsibility movement (1999), Barbara Dafoe Whitehead claims that "every time the issue of family structure has been raised, the response has been first controversy, then retreat, and finally silence" (1993, 48). Whitehead also makes the point (also quoted by Horn) that "not all family structures produce equal outcomes for children" (1993, 48). In his influential book *Life without Father,* David Popenoe argues that "welfare, government programs and tax policies should be formulated to *privilege* married, childrearing couples rather than be neutral toward them (for fear of stigmatizing 'alternative lifestyles'), much less economically penalize them. We should acknowledge alternative lifestyles, but that does not mean we have to affirm them as equivalent to marriage" (1996, 222).

Marriage proponents believe that since the 1960s "sexual revolution," there has been a general cultural decline in the institution and value of marriage, and they often maintain that they are silenced about this in the media and in politics (Whitehead 1993). As discussed earlier, marriage is a sensitive topic in the fatherhood responsibility movement, and marriage proponents often say that they feel it is not safe to even mention "the M-word." Consequently, the pro-marriage wing has "subversively" started to "break" what it asserted was "silence" on this topic in U.S. family politics. Recent congressional efforts to bolster heterosexual marriage as a national value, however, starkly contradict pro-marriage assertions that marriage is "disestablished" as a hegemonic and governmentally privileged institution (Cott 2000). For instance, in response to the threat of a few states' validation of same-sex partnership, Congress quickly passed the Defense of Marriage Act in 1996, where "marriage" and "spouse" explicitly referred to one man and one woman (Cott 2000, 218). The welfare reform of 1996, which initiated major cutbacks of public assistance, reiterated that marriage is "the foundation of a successful society" and an "essential institution" for the "interests of children" (quoted in Stacey 1998, 62). The Fathers Count Act of 1999 (H.R. 3073) and the Responsible Fatherhood Act of 2000 (H.R. 4671) are extremely pro-marriage. Marriage is mentioned as a primary goal in the first sentences of the mission statements of both these acts. The Responsible Fatherhood Act also says, "States should be encouraged, not restricted, from implementing programs that provide support for responsible fatherhood, promote marriage and increase the incidence of marriage" (U.S. House 2002, 3). The Responsible Fatherhood Act proposes funds for a national clearinghouse "with and emphasis on promoting married fatherhood as the ideal, such as the National Fatherhood Initiative" (U.S. House 2002, 8). Moreover, the act seeks to include religious organizations as eligible for responsible fatherhood block grants to "promote the formation and maintenance of married two-parent families, and strengthen fragile families" (U.S. House 2002, 10). Considering the congressional support for these bills, one might question the accuracy of pro-marriage claims that there is an antimarriage political climate.

I often heard marriage proponents talk about a "marriage movement" as the logical continuation of the fatherhood responsibility movement. As a speaker said at a marriage conference I attended, "We had to first be able to say that daddies do matter before we could connect the next dot back up and say 'Well, maybe marriage is important.'" The marriage proponents in the fatherhood responsibility movement and the recently self-proclaimed "marriage movement" to a large extent promote the same fundamental ideas. For instance, such organizations as the National Marriage Project, the Institute for American Values, and Marriage Savers work on behalf of both movements. Representatives of both the marriage movement and the pro-marriage wing of the fatherhood responsibility movement envision the fatherhood responsibility movement as the "icebreaker" and "forerunner" of the marriage movement. Furthermore, the marriage movement uses the fatherhood responsibility movement as its model for how to succeed in building a bipartisan consensus movement. In addition, the pro-marriage wing of the fatherhood responsibility movement connects the marriage movement with both political and grassroots networks.

The pro-marriage wing of the fatherhood responsibility movement and the emerging marriage movement stem from similar ideas, such as loose essentialist sociobiologist/biblical approaches to gender, parenting, and sexuality. They also use similar rhetorical/political strategies, such as the "child well-being" and "whip-men-into-shape" arguments and notions of heterosexual complementarity, the idea that men and women complement each other by contributing binary opposite male and female "parts" to the heterosexual "whole." The marriage proponents who started the fatherhood responsibility movement are now helping to start the marriage movement. However, some of them are careful not to get too closely associated with the conservative connotations of the marriage movement so that they can maintain the carefully crafted bipartisan image of the fatherhood responsibility movement. Both movements try to bring about a "cultural awareness" of fatherhood and marriage (Coltrane 2001). However, within their common conceptions of an androcentric trinity, centered on men-marriage-children, there are some differences. Whereas the pro-marriage wing of the fatherhood responsibility movement focuses on fathers, the marriage movement focuses on marriage. Furthermore, the marriage movement works on divorce legislation and couple therapy to a larger extent than the fatherhood responsibility movement does. Harry, a leading person in the National Fatherhood Initiative, said in an interview that a serious fatherhood movement needs a marriage movement:

> I think it [the marriage movement] is the natural progression. Look, once you say fathers matter, and not just because they're a second pair of hands, but because they contribute something that is unique and irreplaceable in the lives of children. Once you sort of win that argument, then the next argument is, well how do we get more men to be good fathers? . . . Marriage is *by far* the effective and most reliable pathway to a lifetime father

for a child. Not perfect—not 100 percent, no guarantee, but it's better than the other two answers [child support and cohabitation]. . . . And if you're *really serious* about having every child getting a father, there's *no contest* between those three options. And once you then settle on the fact that there's no contest, and that marriage is the most effective pathway, then you have to confront the fact that marriage is such a weak institution in America. And you have to do something to strengthen it, but if you're going to strengthen marriage—guess what you need? A marriage movement.

Although marriage proponents in the fatherhood responsibility movement claimed to be forced into silence, I also met marriage proponents who definitely spoke out on the issue. When it comes to issues of sexual orientation, however, there is a complex politics of silence within the fatherhood responsibility movement. On the one hand, marriage proponents claim to feel too silenced by the "feminists" and the liberal "cultural elite" to even bring up marriage. On the other hand, most representatives choose to be silent on nonheterosexual orientations because they think topics of sexual orientation are either too politically sensitive or irrelevant to "their" issues. For instance, in the marriage report *Toward More Perfect Unions: Putting Marriage on the Public Agenda,* Theodora Ooms, the director of the Family Impact Seminar and a key figure in both the marriage and fatherhood responsibility movements, states in a footnote, "We do not discuss the controversy about same-sex marriage or domestic partnerships in this report since these are highly divisive issues and the Family Impact Seminar is seeking to find arenas of common ground on marriage" (1998, 44). When I asked Harry whether the National Fatherhood Initiative deals with issues of gay and lesbian parents or children, he answered:

No. And the reason is—We just don't. And the reason is well because look, the problem with America is not that a half-percent of American children are being raised in gay families, the problem with America is that 36 percent of children are not living with their fathers. The analogy I like to use is, you're a physician, you come across an accident scene, a guy has been thrown out of his car. On his right hand he has a broken pinkie. On his left hand—his left arm has been torn out of its socket, it's sixteen yards down the road, he's bleeding profusely by the socket of his arm, of his left arm, which has literally been ripped out of his shoulder. You're the physician; do you put a splint on the pinkie, or do you put a tourniquet on the left shoulder? I'm putting a tourniquet on the left shoulder. I'm not going to deal with the pinkie. Plenty of time to deal with the pinkie years from now; if we take the 36 percent fatherlessness rate and we drop it down to 5 percent, but *that's* where I'm putting my energies. I'm not putting it at the gay fathers. And I just don't get into those issues. I think to get diverted

into those issues is to, it's either going to be done—there's only two reasons to get diverted into those issues; one is to bait conservatives into saying—to get them into sort of the homosexual debate, which then diverts
attention away from the central issue. *Or* it's to, from the sort of left wing,
it's to promote a different agenda, a *gay rights* agenda as opposed to a *fatherhood* agenda. And, you know, those are different agendas, it doesn't
mean that those are not debates that shouldn't happen—of course they
should. People should have those debates, I'm not just going to be part of
it. . . . I think world hunger is a terrible thing too, but we don't do world
hunger. . . . You know, it's a terrible thing. Thank God there are people
out there dealing with world hunger, God love them—wonderful. But I
don't do it, and that's what I—that's my response to the gay father issue.

Harry considers gay rights to be *opposed to* a fatherhood agenda and com-
pares homosexuality with medical problems or world hunger. In the same
way marriage proponents assume an all-encompassing (white) middle- or
upper-class perspective that is blind to its own racial and socioeconomic positioning, representatives like Harry and Ooms were blind to their heteronormative approach and were reluctant to even discuss the sexuality politics
they advocate. Nonetheless, just as white people "have a race/ethnicity,"
straight people "have a sexual orientation." When some representatives
"broke" the silence they had constructed, they commonly expressed heterosexist views in line with biblical or sociobiologist ideas.

Marriage proponents use a reversed "political correctness" strategy to construct their imagined imposed silence. "Political correctness" emerged as a
liberal, feminist, and multiculturalist challenge to the idea of a universal and
neutral language, and in leftist discussions, debates connected to political correctness revolved around whose set of values are symbolically affirmed by
public discourse (Cameron 1995, 120–21). The linguist Deborah Cameron argues that political correctness has now been appropriated by right-wing com-
mentators and political conservatives who use *political correctness* as an ironic
"snarl term" for their own ends (1995, 120). Appropriating the discourse in
this way, marriage proponents claim that marriage has been made so politically incorrect and stigmatized by liberals and feminists that it must be coded,
as mentioned earlier, as "the M-word" (see, for example, Blankenhorn 1999,
xiv; and Ooms 1998). The writer Barbara Dafoe Whitehead describes a political situation in which the married, nuclear-family norm has become a silenced issue and "the dominant view is that the changes in family structure
are, on balance, positive" (1993, 50). As with their use of "androgyny advocacy," marriage proponents like Whitehead and Popenoe (1988, 1996) use, in
Cameron's words, "the rhetorical strategy of crediting your opponents with
self evidently absurd positions which in point of fact none of them have ever

subscribed to" (1995, 141). For instance, Popenoe argues that the decline of marriage and fatherhood indicates that "at the extreme, we are becoming a nation of asocial hedonists and narcissists" (1996, 46).

Those in the marriage movement openly resist what they seem to perceive as the "closeting" of their married heterosexual lifestyle by appropriating sexual minority rhetoric that celebrates the "natural" and biblically condoned bond between men and women. One of the participants at a marriage conference I attended urged married heterosexuals to "come out": "I think we're all in agreement that we have an infant movement and I don't know of any infant that doesn't let us know they're there loud and clear. I am really concerned with the self-discounting, self-effacing, even the phrase 'the M-word'—I'd like to erase that! Let's call it what it is: it's marriage. Let's say it loudly, let's say it proudly, let's stand up for it and help it to become a movement and not just something to be embarrassed about! [Big applause]."

Marriage proponents have appropriated and reversed gay and lesbian rights/minority rhetoric in order to speak of themselves as a sexually subversive and marginalized minority. For instance, in his book *Disturbing the Nest: Family Change and Decline in Modern Societies* (1988), Popenoe fears that what he calls the global postnuclear-family trend will "destroy" the nuclear family and the heterosexual married family in which pair bonding, sexual activity, and child bearing are tightly associated. According to Popenoe, "the bourgeois nuclear family, based on a marital pair bond between two adults, was an institution that simultaneously governed the intimate, long-term heterosexual relationship between adults, the practice of human sexuality, and the procreation of children" (1988, 300). Popenoe goes on to critique what he calls "alternative families" as a major threat to social order. While Popenoe does not directly mention gays and lesbians as representatives of these "alternative families," David Blankenhorn clearly states that gay and lesbian parenthood constitutes "the most radical assault possible on the idea of fatherhood as a coherent social role for men" (1995, 304–5).

Marriage proponents rarely spell out their sexual politics, but their silence on the utter centrality of heterosexuality to their politics speaks as loudly as any of the antigay statements I heard in face-to-face interviews with many representatives. The idea that gay and lesbian relationships and families would be as valid as heterosexual marriage would go against everything that the pro-marriage "gender and parenting equation" asserts in its mutually reinforcing notions of gender and sexuality. In the words of one leading marriage proponent I interviewed, "It's too radical a distortion of the institution of marriage to start incorporating same-sex couples. . . . I suspect that there is a, if you want to say, a natural order [laughs], and that is not it." John, another leading pro-marriage representative, demonstrated the exclusionary aspects of pro-marriage gender/sexual politics when he explained in chapter 2 "the androgyny theory" by equating nontraditional gender relations with androgyny and asexuality. In John's view, sexuality ceases to exist if its proper male and female components are not in place. He simply chooses to ignore the reality and legitimacy of all sexualities except straight ones. However, the brilliant logic of the gender and parenting equation becomes slightly dim when you speak to someone with an explicitly heterosexist perspective. Contradictions in the pro-marriage gender and parenting equation surfaced in the following conversation I had with Tom, a central figure in both marriage and fatherhood politics. Tom's statements illustrate the ways "scientific evidence" and moral/godly "truth" simultaneously serve to make the case for heteronormativity. As a bonus, Tom volunteered to share his feelings about anal sex and nature to underscore his point:

> Tom: We are competitive from the very outset of our lives. Men are. Women, they jump rope. They play house; they play things that include people. Not things that exclude people or where you have clear winners and losers. And, these differences are really profound and each gender needs to understand the differences between the genders if they're going to be able to make the relationship work. A man has to realize that my wife needs to talk in order to explain, to share her day with me and I need to listen to this. Even if I don't feel like it. That's a way that he can love her, by listening.
>
> Me: But then, homosexuals would get along better—relationships work better if they understand each other or—
>
> Tom: Homosexual relationships *do not* work.
>
> Me: Oh.
>
> Tom: You cannot find me one study that shows that, that long-term relationships between homosexuals work. One study I know of men who were together five years or more, 165 couples, in every case, one or both parties were cheating. Adultery is not that common in America. Only 2 percent of people or 3 percent of people cheat in a year who are married. Over half of all marriages have never had any adultery. I'm saying that, men, homosexual couples, simply, this is not how God made us.
>
> Me: Hmmm—
>
> Tom: It is uh, unworkable and most homosexuals are *profoundly* promiscuous! They have *hundreds, even thousands* of sexual encounters which have no meaning to them *whatsoever* and the average homosexual who does not have AIDS, dies at age 42. 42! . . . Why do they live only until 42? Because there are all these other sexually transmitted diseases that they pick up and they lead very violent lives. A higher percentage of suicides and murders. Lesbians live only to be 44 according to obituaries of 10 or 12 gay newspapers. A study of the obituaries of gay couples, show that these

people do not live long lives. They are unhappy and it's not natural. *It's not natural. Anal sex . . . anal sex is not natural.* I mean, that's the way, that's the way that AIDS is passed most commonly.

Me: Hmmm—

Tom: So, this program that we're talking about is *not* for homosexuals. We're talking about *heterosexual* couples [reemphasizing]. In cultures where homosexuality is discouraged there is a very small percentage of homosexuals. Where it is encouraged, you have more. . . . Which I think is unhealthy. It's not good for the people, it's not good for the culture.

Tom's remarkable use of statistics (although I didn't ask for his sources) exemplifies a tendency, especially among the more religiously grounded marriage proponents, to combine biblical and "scientific" arguments (Coltrane 2001). Tom seems to discount contemporary social scientific standards for "evidence," even as he appeals to those standards in his use of "statistics." Furthermore, Tom illustrates the boundaries and logic of his biblical, gendered, and sexual essentialism. When he first talks about the problems of bridging the gender gap, he says that there is an inherent problem in heterosexual relationships because the huge difference between men and women results in difficulties understanding each other. But then this "problem" is somehow preferable to same-sex couples, which seem to be unthinkable to Tom and thus brings him beyond the realm of worldly arguments. When introduced to the possibility of homosexual relations, Tom simply argues that God intended men to be straight. Since Tom's understanding of gay men's' relationships is informed by visions of hedonistic sex, murder, and death, he considers homosexuality to be "against nature." It did not occur to him that oppression and hate crime by people with views similar to his might help explain the violence, suicide, and death among young lesbians and gay men. Instead, he goes off on the "unhealthy," "promiscuous," and destructive characteristics he perceives ruin the lives of homosexuals and the "culture" around them. However, Tom did not elaborate on why homosexuality is "not good for the culture." He also seems to consider AIDS to be the proof, and perhaps God's punishment, of the "unnaturalness" of anal sex. One may wonder what explanations Tom would offer concerning heterosexuals who have AIDS, or are "unhappy," or "lead violent lives."

Pro-marriage constructions of gay masculinities are in line with their notions of destructive masculinities. Because they are not properly "attached" and civilized by women, gay men supposedly display the antisocial behavior of "unattached males" described in previous chapters (such as violence, drug or alcohol addiction, or promiscuity). Gay men, as well as unmarried heterosexual men, are therefore considered destructive for "the people" and "the culture" and should be discouraged, as one discourages violence and disease. This view is illustrated in an essay in *The Fatherhood Movement,* the edited volume that serves as a fatherhood responsibility movement manifesto.[8] One of the contributors to this volume, the psychiatrist David Gutmann, equates gay men's sexuality with addiction and an immature flight from their mother and their destiny as fathers:

> Multitudes of young men have recently discovered another, more drastic means for achieving social distance from their mothers, while at the same time avoiding fatherhood: the homosexual community. Again, like liquor bottles or drug vials, homosexual sex tends to be impersonal and its participants tend to be replaceable to each other. In the gay community, as with other centers of addiction, one can find pleasure without risking intimacy and the possibility of irreplaceable loss. At the same time, distance has been gained from the mothers. (Gutmann 1999, 142)

Gutmann conceives of gay male sexuality as a result of weak men's fear of women's civilizing powers. He echoes ancient nineteenth-century sexological conceptions of homosexuality as deviance and pathology (D'Emilio and Freedman 1997). Despite such outright attempts to stigmatize and undermine gay and lesbian families, marriage proponents feel free to appropriate the rhetoric of sexual minorities. Within the pro-marriage wing, representatives seem to perceive themselves as ridiculed and misrecognized, as if they were a subversive minority oppressed by a "leftist cultural elite." They manufacture the idea that married heterosexuals have become a "silenced" group for whom they courageously dare to speak out. For instance, in their report *Marriage in America,* Blankenhorn, Popenoe, and others claim that "our current national debate has been curiously silent on the subject of marriage. Who, today, is still promoting marriage? Who is even talking about it? In place of a national debate about what has happened there has been silence-—stone-cold silence" (Council on Families in America 1995, 5). A common "resistance strategy" is to speak on behalf of an imagined heterosexual *majority.* Marital heterosexual pride sounds like heteronormalism when marriage proponents openly seek to undermine other family forms and sexual practices, including the divorces and cohabitation of monogamous heterosexual couples.

For all marriage proponents' talk about being silenced, nobody tells heterosexual couples—in contrast to gay and lesbian couples—that they cannot get married. The need for a heterosexual struggle for sexual recognition and rights therefore seems far-fetched. I heard representatives compare other family forms to trash that should not be encouraged anymore than littering is encouraged. In their report, *Marriage in America,* Blankenhorn, Popenoe, and others admonish various leaders, media people, and officials: "Don't glamorize unwed motherhood, marital infidelity, alternative lifestyles, and sexual promiscuity. Imagine depicting divorce and unwed childbearing as frequently and as approvingly as you currently depict smoking and littering" (Council on Families in America 1995, 16). As one speaker at a marriage conference phrased this trash analogy, "[M]arriage is in the public interest—just as keeping the streets clean." Nonmarried family forms represent everything that is impure and chaotic—immorality, epidemics, addiction, dirt, and brutality— whereas the institution of marriage brings order out of chaos (Douglas 1966). Despite their negative imagery for nonheteronormativity and nonmarriage, marriage proponents often say that their political agendas have been misunderstood. In their minds, they are just providing a choice and the possibility of benefits—not trying to force people into marriages they do not want (Coltrane 2001, 396). For instance, Tom told me that "cohabitation is an embracing of evil," but he was not suggesting that we should send all heterosexual cohabiting couples to burn in hell. Rather, his agenda was to "help" them to "realize" and achieve the benefits of marriage in a "well-meaning" Christian spirit. Likewise, some representatives from the pro-marriage wing endorsed ex-gay ministries.[9]

The pro-marriage wing of the fatherhood responsibility movement is united with the marriage movement in its opposition to the "increasing tolerance" for nonmarriage, divorce, and out-of-wedlock childbearing. Seemingly, the children of gay and lesbian parents or the gay and lesbian children of heterosexuals do not deserve the blessings, legal protection, or benefits of marriage. Marriage proponents rarely mention lesbian and gay family forms other than under the rubric of "alternative lifestyles" that should be discouraged. This way, they are structuring a silence of their own, one that denies any legitimacy for these families whatsoever. In response to the perceived disintegration of the "marriage culture," marriage proponents seek to reintroduce moral and legal incentives that discourage nonheteronormative family forms. Despite the current dominance of pro-marriage values in U.S. government politics, marriage proponents strategically construct an "under-dog" rhetoric. They do so to appeal for the already ongoing reconfirmation of the "moral superiority" of the marital heterosexual norm, as evident in the Defense of Marriage Act, Fathers Count Act, and Responsible Fatherhood Act, as well as President George W. Bush's marriage initiative of 2002.

While the pro-marriage wing is more proactive in its politics of heterosexuality, it is joined by the fragile-families wing on the subject of masculinizing fatherhood by differentiating men from women and gay men. Drawing on a overlapping hydraulic, biblical, and other essentialist discourses that emerged at the end of the nineteenth century, the fatherhood responsibility movement is founded on the imagined unity of heterosexual men.

Notes

1. The model has been influential in Freudian and pop-Freudian understandings of sexuality as "drives" that strain to burst out and must be contained by moral injunctions if civilization is to continue (Weeks 1985, 127–81).

2. Made popular by such sexologists as Richard von Krafft-Ebing in the nineteenth century and Alfred Charles Kinsey in the twentieth.

3. The other deviances are androgyny and homosexuality.

4. Fragile-families interviewees often used the expression *playing field* to describe the competing relations between constituencies of men.

5. At least it was not discussed during my fieldwork, which followed a core group with occasional newcomers and dropouts throughout one workshop season.

6. I have not personally seen this billboard, but an interviewee told me about it.

7. The section on the politics of heteronormativity focuses on the pro-marriage wing, which is more proactive in its sexual politics than the fragile-families wing, although representatives from both wings share many sexualized notions of gender.

8. David Blankenhorn writes in the introduction, "The contributors of this book are among the people most responsible in the 1990s for publicly naming this problem and initiating a movement to confront it. Think of these essays, then, as working papers for the new movement, vision statements and marching orders from the conceptual frameworkers and front line leaders" (1999, xi)

9. Ex-gay ministries are religious organizations that seek to "redeem" lesbians and gays by "converting" them to a heterosexual lifestyle.

Conclusion

The Challenges and Dilemmas of Fatherhood in U.S. Masculinity Politics

The closer we come to uncovering some form of exemplary masculinity, a masculinity which is solid and sure of itself, the clearer it becomes that masculinity is structured through contradiction: the more it asserts itself, the more it calls itself into question. But this is precisely what we should expect if . . . masculinity is not some type of single essence, innate or acquired.

—Lynne Segal, *Slow Motion: Changing Masculinities, Changing Men*

Based on the heteronormative and essentialist belief that men are "naughty by nature," contemporary fatherhood politics tries to harness the perceived "promiscuity," competitiveness, and aggression of men. The fatherhood responsibility movement places the control of innately "promiscuous" male heterosexuality at the center of social and moral order and thus differentiates masculinity from women and gay men. But the same "indispensable" traits that make men male in this view also constitute a central problem in the fatherhood responsibility movement. Here, the fatherhood responsibility movement runs into a century-old dilemma in U.S. discussions of "new" fatherhood: how do you domesticate masculinity in fatherhood and at the same time masculinize domesticity? The fatherhood responsibility movement's contradictory attempts to virilize *and* control the maleness of fatherhood are emerging in response to feminist politics and are crystallizing racial and socioeconomic asymmetries between men. Asymmetrically positioned men construct masculinities with different points of reference. Whereas primarily white middle-class marriage proponents tend to construct masculinity in binary opposition to notions of women, fragile-families representatives of poor and minority men primarily conceive of themselves as men in structural relation to other men (i.e., white middle-class men).

The two wings of the fatherhood responsibility movement are in strategic alliance, but they come out of different, sometimes competing, historical struggles, which sometimes leads them into divergent politics. Whereas the fragile-families wing extends into civil rights struggles, marriage proponents extend into the marriage movement in opposition to something they call "androgyny advocacy" and "radical" feminism. The fatherhood responsibility movement has achieved its enormous political success by converging on mainstream political "family values," such as child well-being and the importance of fathers and family to social order. Despite these general points of convergence, the two wings diverge over the competing claims and positions of different constituencies of men. Most notably, the pro-marriage and fragile-families wings differ on marriage and work and the relative importance of morals and structure. These divisions reflect long-standing battles of white and minority groups over the rights and obligations of asymmetrically positioned men. While marriage proponents see marriage as key to all social problems, fragile-families organizations worry more about the impact of unemployment, racism, and discrimination on fatherhood responsibility.

Promoting male family involvement is fraught with anxiety in fatherhood politics. Since domesticity became associated with femininity in the nineteenth century, family involvement has been considered contrary to maleness. Because heterosexuality became crucial to definitions of masculinity, male gendered and sexual differentiation from women and gay men is deemed crucial to (heterosexual) men's "natures" and parental features. In its efforts to masculinize fatherhood, the fatherhood responsibility movement uses religious and athletic metaphors for masculinity as unifying grounds for male bonding across racial and socioeconomic divisions. Sport and religion thus constitute central and overlapping arenas for competing over the boundaries of masculinities, with ambiguous implications for African American men. Casting parenting in biblical metaphors and promoting ideals of athletic masculinity are ways to make domesticity intelligibly and appealingly "male" to fathers. For instance, local organizations attempt to "channel male energies"—in other words, perceived innate male aggression, competitiveness, and promiscuity— through sport discourse and homosocial practice. For another example, by drawing on the shifting elements of late-nineteenth- and early-twentieth-century Christian men's movements and the Promise Keepers' rhetoric, the fatherhood responsibility movement masculinizes fatherhood in contested "spiritual" arenas. Biblical notions of "servant leadership" cast men as divinely ordained protectors of families and guarantors of social order, presenting specifically "male" versions of parenthood.

The inseparability of sexual politics and masculinity politics in the contemporary vogue for U.S. fatherhood responsibility is a theme throughout this study. The "de-sissification" efforts of turn-of-nineteenth-century Christian men's movements presaged the ways contemporary notions of masculinity have been defined by heterosexuality. Heteromasculinity is continuously asserted in the fatherhood responsibility movement. For instance, fatherhood programs teach that the key to fatherhood responsibility and social/moral order is to constrain men's sexuality through marriage or to encourage heterosexual "team parenting." Within fatherhood politics, constructions of masculinities and femininities are founded in complementary and more or less essentialist notions of gender-specific heterosexuality. Marriage proponents in particular seek to reestablish lifelong, monogamous, and heterosexual marriage as the norm in all public and private sectors and believe that the "Male Force" otherwise will turn antisocial. Drawing on century-long discussions of the "new" father, marriage proponents translate heteronormative notions of masculinities into "masculine" father characteristics considered indispensable to family and society. On the basis of a loose essentialist and male-centered combination of sociobiological, biblical, and pop-Freudian arguments, marriage proponents make the case that marriage is the only viable way to bind men to their offspring and to reinforce social and moral order. Marriage proponents choose to ignore the ways their notions of masculinity are historically situated and derived from gendered, sexual, racial, and socioeconomic relations. Ignoring the whiteness and heteronormativity of their own outlooks, marriage proponents claim to speak from a universalized male perspective and out of "objective" common sense. Ironically, marriage proponents simultaneously appropriate minority rhetoric to make the case for heterosexual masculinity politics in "subversive" terms by "daring" to spell out "the M-word" in government politics. The constructed silencing of the M-word is a rhetorical maneuver that perversely constitutes the heterosexual norm as oppressed by a "politically correct" feminist/liberal "elite."

In contrast, the gendered politics of the fragile-families wing is focused more on the structural relations between men. Fragile-families representatives approach marketplace ideals of breadwinning fatherhood from the standpoint of poor and minority men. They do so by constantly illuminating the dissonance between the expectations placed on poor and minority men and their actual labor market conditions. Fragile-families organizations are fighting a range of contradictory racist, sexual stereotypes of African American men as "uncivilized," rapacious predator superstuds *and* effeminate "mama's boys." Simultaneously, fragile-families representatives are trying to increase the "marriageability" of poor and minority men and to deal with very real issues, such as joblessness, drug abuse, violence, and family relations. In the eyes of many fragile-families representatives, men's marriage potential and fatherhood responsibility depend on their success as breadwinners and their "management" of their sexuality. When role-modeling financially and sexually "responsible" fatherhood, fragile-families practitioners are always cautious about reinforcing the problems they seek to solve. Fragile-families representatives are constantly forced to relate to loose essentialist notions of masculinity as constituted by promiscuity, which could play into racist stereotypes that have stigmatized African American men at different points throughout U.S. history. Fragile-families representatives also get entangled in the perceived contradictions between compliance with and resistance to white middle-class ideals of masculinity when seeking to embody "manly" marketplace ideals.

Domestication and Compulsory Womanizing

While the "Male Force" is a central problem to the fatherhood responsibility movement, it also forms an important basis for male bonding and role modeling. Practitioners embody this contradiction by simultaneously aspiring to domesticated sexuality but also behaving according to beliefs in compulsive male promiscuity. A professional requirement for practitioners in the fatherhood responsibility movement is to be role models who demonstrate "responsible fatherhood"—preferably domesticated through marriage and monogamy.[1] Role models' "management" of their own sexuality may affect their credibility in the fatherhood responsibility movement. For instance, two representatives expressed worries that their "failure" to stay married would affect their currency as representatives of the fatherhood responsibility movement. One representative even claimed that he got fired from a fatherhood program because he got divorced.

In everyday interaction, representatives often made a point of being the "gentlemen" they role-modeled for their program participants. For instance, they insisted on such things as opening doors since they were "The Man" and had to "treat The Ladies right." One situation that often came up in my interaction with representatives reflects the gendered, racial, and sexual meanings at play: the issue of who was going to pick up the check. For these men, one of the characteristics of "treating the Ladies right" entailed paying for drinks. However, I sometimes insisted on paying at cafes and restaurants as a gesture of compensation for having taken representatives' time. My insistence on picking up checks was also an effort to define the situation as a "professional" one rather than a sexualized man-woman situation. Only one of my key interviewees did not have a problem with my picking up checks at cafes and restaurants. That I am white and that many of the representatives were African American complicated the "who-pays-the-check" situation even more. African American representatives often explicitly (and rightly) contextualized my whiteness and academic endeavors within a history of socioeconomic racial oppression. For instance, Tony, one African American representative, used to "joke" about my racial outsider status and call me a "spy" who was sent out by the white community to investigate the African American community. Once when I reached for the check, Tony said, "Just when I start thinking you're *not* an agent, I realize again that you're a spy." My paying the check not only disturbed the man-woman scheme of things but also took on racial meanings in this context.

My interaction with Robert, a middle-aged African American who was a key fragile-families interviewee, crystallized the contradictions in joining beliefs in hydraulic "manliness" with ideals of domestication and highlighted the racial implications of gendered practices. When I went to see Robert, I would attempt a somewhat "gender neutral" appearance, little or no makeup, pants or long skirts, and so forth. I had gathered from his remarks to me and to others that he considered it appropriate for women to dress that way around the men in his fatherhood program so that they would not be tempted to be "bad." Furthermore, men in father groups seemed to think that women with a certain sexy look are out to trick them. For instance, once a fatherhood group was discussing the fictive case of "Susie," who represented scantily dressed and sexually inviting women. One father said, "They're thinking their body is like a paycheck," whereupon the practitioner replied, "So why do you think you need to buy something?" The point of the discussion seemed to be that women who are deemed "slutty" may sabotage men's endeavors to exercise sexual "self-control" and "responsibility."

Robert did not want to be seen with me, a white young woman, in his community, where he was a role model with racial and gendered loyalties to the "brothers." Instead, he preferred to meet at cafes and bars, or he sometimes came to my apartment for interviews.[2] Once when Robert visited me at my place, he criticized a coworker for not adhering to practitioner codes of sexual conduct. Practitioners are required to "walk their talk" both on and off duty and never to "womanize"—even when program participants are not around. In one of our interviews, Robert echoed other fragile-families leaders in stressing how important it is for role models to "manage" their sexuality: "Women manage their sexuality more so than men. The problem is men's lack of control. . . . You can see it in the lives of the guys that I'm working with. They have the attitude that nothing's going to happen to them. As a man, you have to manage it better. As practitioners we need to model and encourage a much more responsible approach to sexuality. As practitioners, what we do speaks louder than what we say."

According to Robert, one coworker openly ogled women all the time, which Robert disapproved of because he maintained that it looked very bad in front of the participants. "You have to be very aware of the appearances," he said. As an example, Robert mentioned that it did not look good for us to be seen together because his coworkers and the program participants would automatically assume we had a sexual relationship. He maintained that this was related to my whiteness. According to Robert, people would think there could be only two reasons he would hang out with a white woman in his community: either that I was a social worker or that he had a sexual relationship with me.

Despite Robert's condemnation of role models that "womanize" and his expressed concern about being accused of having an extramarital affair with a white woman,[3] he attempted to seduce me a few moments later. He began by suggesting that we have some kind of international love affair that he could write about in his autobiography. Then he played a tape with "smooth jazz" and moved closer and closer to me until he was leaning against me. He proceeded to kiss me on the shoulder, wanted to hug me, and suggested that we dance. This situation ended rather awkwardly when I declined his invitation. Robert's sexual moves struck me as very random. Although I never asked him about his perceptions of this situation, I think he might have felt a contradiction between mutually exclusive expectations. He displayed the womanizing "manly nature" he believes in and simultaneously aspired to domesticated role modeling. Perhaps Robert tried to live up to both his ideals of male responsibility and expected male heterosexual behavior.

Robert sometimes expressed his fascination with meeting someone from overseas, which was a rare experience for him and many of the men in his community. There might have been a dimension of sexual and cultural miscommunication in which my behavior and appearance somehow signaled to Robert that we were in a sexual situation rather than in a nonsexual interview situation. Robert and I often met in informal settings on informal terms. In addition to discussing fatherhood, we talked about all kinds of other things friends discuss, such as music, travel, and relationships. Although we never directly talked about what happened, Robert told me several times afterward in abstract terms that he had had second thoughts about "our last encounter" (when he had tried to seduce me) and had learned a lot from our time together. My impression is that he was referring to his attempts to come to grips with the ambiguities inherent in hydraulic notions of male sexuality and the racial and socioeconomic dynamics of our interaction.

In contrast, Hugh, a white, middle-aged, upper-middle-class pro-marriage representative, treated me primarily as a subordinated sexual conquest. While maintaining principles of male sexual "responsibility," he also lamented the sexual powers he believed that women possess over men. To Hugh, there did not seem to be a contradiction between "womanizing" and maintaining principles of sexual responsibility. When I thanked him for our latest interview, Hugh responded, "I only agreed to it because I am sexually interested in you." I asked if he did not take our discussions seriously, and he said that sure, he took them seriously, but that did not have to mean he was not sexually interested in me. During the interview, he bought me lunch and "romantically" tried to feed me the food with his hands while I was trying to ask questions. Every time I met Hugh, he openly proposed that we have sex, and, regardless of how many times I fended off his sexual advances, he still continued to try. After my final interview with him and after the tape recorder had been turned off, he suggested that we could have "wild sex" before I left for Sweden. My marital status and sexual orientation seemed irrelevant. I do not even think that my appearance and behavior mattered or that he was particularly attracted to me. He probably behaved the same way with any young woman with whom he had contact—I had seen him interacting similarly with other young women at his workplace. Hugh *claimed* my participation in his heterosexual, intergenerational, and womanizing quest. He explicitly pursued me in a gendered power play in which he had the advantage as a wealthy white man in a position of professional authority. This is to be contrasted with Robert, who primarily dealt with the hazards and structural disadvantages of his position as an African American man from a poor background interacting with a white middle-class woman in a traditionally racist society. Hugh's womanizing endeavors were of course quite separate from his marital ideals. To use a sports trope that Hugh would certainly understand, our interviews were like a game with two competing teams where only one could win—not unlike his descriptions of the battle between men and "radical feminist" women. If I played the game, I would lose my personal integrity and professional credibility by prostituting myself for information. If I stayed out of the game, I would lose access to "his" part of the field. Either way I would lose. Eventually, I had to cancel my plans for future interviews with Hugh because his attempts to have sex with me became overbearing. I therefore did lose access to "his" part of the field.

The case of Tony, a college-educated, African American fragile-families representative in his forties, may serve as yet another example of the contradictions in the fatherhood responsibility movement. On the one hand, the movement has a message of domesticated "responsible male heterosexuality," and, on the other hand, it assumes men are "masculine" studs. As with Robert, I often met Tony in informal settings, and we sometimes met at bars, with or without his friends or mine. There was serious sexual miscommunication with Tony. The last time I saw him, he told me that if he had known in the beginning that he could not have sex with me, he would not have let me interview him. Tony had repeatedly suggested that we have sex, even while he made passes at my female friends and their sisters, whom he sometimes met when we went out for drinks after our interviews. He abundantly proved that he "liked women." At one point, Tony complained that women and other men *expect* him to hit on all women, thereby asserting his manhood. He described his womanizing as just a routine and was very open to me about his affairs and other women he was interested in.

Tony said that his colleagues criticized him for his "irresponsible" sexual attitudes, but he did not seem to care about this or about risking his professional credibility. Perhaps this was because Tony's job did not require too much contact with fathers and thus his sexual lifestyle did not seem to affect his career. On the contrary, Tony and his colleagues seemed to have a well-developed "man-to-man" understanding. When I met Tony's colleagues, they told him that they understood why he took time to socialize with me, meaning they could understand that he, a notorious "womanizer," wanted to spend his time with a young woman. For Tony, there were no contradictions, because he did not share Robert's ambition to be nonwomanizing in *all* situations. The responses of his more "domesticated" colleagues, however, point at a contradiction between the rhetoric and the practice of domesticating hydraulic masculinity. They both acknowledged and reprimanded Tony for the same reason. The line between being too "masculine" and too "unmasculine" seems confusingly blurred in the practices of fatherhood responsibility movement representatives.

These field experiences may seem coincidental and open to many interpretations. For instance, the majority of representatives did *not* seek to "womanize" me. However, I do think the representatives described above point in two important directions in the analysis of contemporary fatherhood politics. First, they illustrate the depth of the paradox of masculinizing domesticity while domesticating masculinity. Second, they indicate ways in which gendered and sexual politics are personalized in fatherhood politics.

Pro-Feminist Men and the Fatherhood Responsibility Movement

To contextualize the heterosexual masculinity politics embodied by the representatives above, one needs to look beyond the fatherhood responsibility movement. For instance, gay male and female fatherhood provide challenging contrasts to the gendered, racial, and sexual claims of the fatherhood responsibility movement. Pro-feminist men—men who support the struggle for gender equality (Kimmel 1992, 3)—take an interesting approach to some of the gendered and sexual politics of personal behavior in the fatherhood responsibility movement. These differences may also help explain why pro-feminist organizations are not part of the fatherhood responsibility movement, despite the movement's claims to be for gender equality and to speak for the benefit of women and children. To be able to contrast the fatherhood responsibility movement within a wider field of masculinity politics, I conducted a few interviews with representatives from the National Organization of Men against Sexism (NOMAS), a pro-feminist men's organization.

NOMAS was founded in 1975 mainly by a group of academics attending "The First National Conference on Men and Masculinity" in Knoxville, Tennessee (NOMAS 1998). The "movement" became a national membership organization in 1982, and the name NOMAS was adopted in 1990. NOMAS's statement of principles include antiracism, pro-feminism, and gay affirmation (NOMAS 1998). Pro-feminist men try to make their political stances personal. In other words, they struggle to "follow through" and integrate their pro-feminist approaches in their personal lives and relations (Kimmel 1992, 4). When I went to one of NOMAS's national conferences during my fieldwork in 1998, I briefly observed the ways pro-feminist men endeavor to integrate notions of gender equality and "gay-affirmation" into daily interaction. In a homosocial behavior radically different from what I witnessed in the fatherhood responsibility movement, NOMAS men spontaneously hugged, kissed, cried, and danced with one another. In utter contrast to the antifeminist and antigay Promise Keepers, NOMAS men combined their physicalness with a continuous discussion of their own and other peoples' sexism and homophobia. I observed many instances of everyday interaction in which participants made a point of being pro-gay or openly bisexual or gay. Unlike fatherhood responsibility movement representatives, who assumed everyone was heterosexual in meetings and conversations, pro-feminist men did not make such assumptions.

In the program for the conference there was a section called "Appropriate Personal Behavior at an M&M Conference: The Personal Is the Political," which listed behavior considered "inappropriate" at the conference. Participants were urged to refrain from "unwelcome sexual come-ons, touching, or intrusive personal comments." They were reminded to "refrain from any one-way or uninvited personal overtures, sexual or otherwise, that might be experienced as unwelcome, frightening or inappropriate." The program also asked participants to welcome and honor "all races, classes, ages, body types, genders and sexual preferences." At the conference I heard none of the participants or speakers express worries that the women who were there would "tempt" men by dressing inappropriately or interfere with intermale homosocial expression. NOMAS members were extremely careful about not sexually harassing people at the conference; every time they for some reason had to touch someone, they asked for permission, which was also called for in the program. Having been a participant observer in the fatherhood responsibility movement for an extended period of time, I found the personal politics of NOMAS members a telling contrast. These men continuously and explicitly struggled to embody their politics of gendered, racial, and sexual equality. They constantly illuminated and questioned the everyday expressions of racial, sexual, and gendered injustices.

As mentioned in the opening chapter, critics have often questioned the "manliness" of pro-feminist men. For instance, men who supported woman suffrage were called "momma boys" or "miss-Nancy's" and accused for being feminine or gay (Kimmel 1992, 6–7). Feminizing everyday struggles to defeat sexist and homophobic notions of gender and sexuality seems to be a major turnoff to the fatherhood responsibility movement. Instead, building on century-long traditions in U.S. fatherhood politics of carving out "male" parenting features, the fatherhood responsibility movement seeks to constitute men as the opposite of "effeminacy" and "sissiness." It is no coincidence that one of the most prominent leaders in the fatherhood responsibility movement thinks it is "insulting" to fathers to be called "Mr. Mom," whereas pro-feminist men suggest that fathers should become more like mothers. While never (with one exception) purporting to be feminist, those in the fatherhood responsibility movement with whom I spoke often claimed they were not antifeminist. However, they often failed to acknowledge the historical connections between racial, sexual, and gendered inequalities and to incorporate notions of gender equality into notions of gender relations and into everyday interaction. Some felt more compelled to demonstrate heterosexual "manliness" than to integrate notions of gendered and sexual equality in their relations with one another, women, or gay men.

The Future of Masculinized Fatherhood

> *I think that you have to take a step back and ask yourself: if women were as*
> *powerful as men, socially, and given what they deserve and equal status in the*
> *world—would boys feel that they were lacking something if they thought that*
> *their mothers were every bit as good as their fathers, if they thought that wom-*
> *en were every bit as good as men? Would they need to have a strong male role*
> *model to show them how to be different from women? And part of it is, and I*
> *think in the subtext of this positive male role model is the devaluation of the*
> *woman as a role model, as somebody who can raise a boy.*

—NOMAS representative, interview

Like many other anthropologists and sociologists, I have moved between the
two poles of critically analyzing and seriously attempting to understand representatives' points of view in this study. Throughout the study, particularly
in chapters 2 and 3, I attempted to piece together the concerns, ideas, and perspectives of representatives. One message I tried to convey throughout this
book is that I do not doubt that representatives are sincere in their beliefs and
intentions to work for the well-being of children. The fatherhood responsibility movement and its representatives have strengthened and assisted thousands of men, fathers, and families and have fought for issues of crucial importance to their constituencies. But the U.S. "family wars," of which the
fatherhood responsibility movement is part, are not primarily about child
well-being in the broader sense of childcare, education, and health. The simple fact that there are competing notions of what constitutes child well-being
in fatherhood politics underscores that this rhetorical device may mask a wide
range of agendas. Ignoring the rights and recognition of lesbian, gay, and other
nonheteronormative families in and of itself contradicts the claim to be about
child well-being. Moreover, urging men to be nice to children in their spare
time does not substantially transform the conditions for children. To a certain
extent, however, the fragile-families wing does seek to impact the social programs and the structural and economic conditions of fathers, which has an indirect effect on children.

What is ultimately at stake in the contestations over "the family" and masculinizing domesticity are gendered, racial, and sexual struggles over recognition and redistribution rather than moral and philanthropic values (Fraser
1997; Hobson 2002; Stacey 1996; Hunter 1991). This is why it is so important
to look at the structurally conditioned perspectives of men in the movement
and to highlight the politics of whiteness in the fatherhood responsibility
movement. Despite denials, the fatherhood responsibility movement is a

men's movement, though it is far from unitary and represents a wide variety of claims, grievances, and strategies.

An analysis of contemporary U.S. fatherhood politics needs to take into account the consequences for heterosexual women; single, nonmonogamous, and transgendered people; as well as lesbian, gay, and other nonheteronormative families, especially since fatherhood organizations claim that they have not been antagonist to feminist politics while avoiding issues of sexual orientation and the rights and recognition of nonheterosexuals. This entails making a distinction between representatives' *strategic claims* and the *intended and unintended consequences* of their politics. Despite its internal conflicts and differences, the pro-marriage wing in the fatherhood responsibility movement is one of the most powerful political forces behind the continuing legal and structural difficulties faced by nonheteronormative families in the United States, such as single mothers, lesbian and gay families, and transgendered peoples' families. Just being strategically "sensitive" to "women's issues" is a far cry from promoting reforms that would have a positive impact on the conditions of motherhood. As fragile-families representatives point out, the most urgent needs of households headed by single mothers are often economic. A low-income or poor mother might most need not a husband, boyfriend, or servant leader but a wider system of opportunities and social benefits.

The fatherhood responsibility movement's promotion of noncompulsory fatherly responsibilities leaves the social and economic structures of the gendered division of paid and unpaid labor largely untouched (Hobson 2002). I have not heard representatives promote any measures that would legally obligate men to share housework with women. In the case of lesbian, gay, and other nonheteronormative families, one of the greatest obstacles in achieving recognition and equal rights is the kind of rhetoric that has made the fatherhood responsibility movement so successful. Echoing a long Christian tradition that celebrates the white, married, and heterosexual "American family," the fatherhood responsibility movement claims the superiority of the heterosexual (married) family. It does so in the name of "child well-being" based on heteronormative notions of gender, parenthood, and sexuality. The fatherhood responsibility movement insists on the supremacy of the (married) two-parent heterosexual family despite abundant evidence that heterosexuals, married or not, do not parent more successfully than, for instance, gay or lesbian parents or single mothers (see, for example, Benkov 1994; Dunne 2000; Dowd 2000, 8–9; Laird 1999; Silverstein and Auerbach 1999; Stacey 2001; and Tasker and Golombok 1997). Labeling such ideas "nonpolitical" is an extremely clever strategy.

Because the fatherhood responsibility movement insists on regendering parenthood and recentering biological men to conform to a social, moral, and familiar order, it gets caught up in the paradoxes of masculinizing domesticity. Moreover, loose essentialist notions of gendered and sexualized difference within the fatherhood responsibility movement sometimes reinforce hierarchical constructions of masculinity and femininity. For instance, marriage proponents compare men and women to leader/follower, shepherd/sheep, coach/team mom and captain/crew member. Not coincidentally, in all these cases, men are assigned the position of authority. Fathers are typically portrayed as aggressive, promiscuous, and competitive disciplinarians, leaders, and protectors, whereas women are usually depicted as soft and comforting nurturers apt to accommodate men and children. The sociologist Scott Coltrane warns that the fatherhood responsibility movement's promotion of such "gender-segregated" notions of fatherhood "carries a profound risk" (2001, 403). In Coltrane's words, "accepting gender-segregated parenting as natural and inevitable . . . serves to maintain hierarchical structures both inside families and in the larger society (2001, 403).

However, it is also important to highlight egalitarian tendencies in the fatherhood responsibility movement. For instance, some fragile-families representatives argue that fathers can do anything that women can do except give birth to children. While primarily struggling for the rights and recognition of low-income and poor men, fragile-families organizations do collaborate with women's organizations concerned with domestic violence and child support. Furthermore, fragile-families organizations do to some extent work in heterosocial settings, and more research needs to be done on team parenting programs. It remains to be seen in what ways heterosexual women may benefit from the fatherhood responsibility movement in everyday life. Heterosexual mothers may possibly get more help from the social or biological fathers of their children as a result of the efforts of the fatherhood responsibility movement. However, the extent of this help may depend on which burdens and obligations husbands or boyfriends find "manly" enough to assume in the light of the loose essentialist, occasionally masculinist framing of parenting by the fatherhood responsibility movement.

Like advocates, reformers, and "experts" promoting "new" fatherhood at the end of the nineteenth century, the fatherhood responsibility movement begins with the assertion that fathers, *because they are men,* are needed for the well-being of children, family, and society. Without this assertion, there would be no need for a movement mobilized around the importance of male family involvement. Since the movement argues that biological men are irreplaceable as parents, there is a more or less essentialist aspect at the root of the fatherhood responsibility movement. In Scott Coltrane's view, the fatherhood responsibility movement can be seen as a backlash against men who mother (2001, 402). In an article that stirred enormous opposition from such pro-marriage leaders as Wade Horn, Michael McManus, and David Blankenhorn, the psychologists Louise B. Silverstein and Carl F. Auerbach argued that the movement's promotion of essentialist notions of fatherhood is part of a back-lash against gay and lesbian rights as well as feminist movements (1999, 404). They argue that the movement employs a "neoconservative" framework that discriminates against cohabiting couples, single mothers, and lesbian and gay parents (1999, 399; see also Stacey 2001). Since the movement represents a wider range of competing perspectives, I would not go as far as Judith Stacey in her assertion that it is nothing more than proxy rhetoric for antifeminist and antigay sentiments (1998, 73). However, many of the gendered and sexu-alized ideas and practices of the fatherhood responsibility movement do re-inforce unequal conditions regardless of representatives' intentions or claims to the contrary. Since gendered and sexual notions are inseparable from poli-tics in the fatherhood responsibility movement, loose essentialist notions of masculinity need to be considered in conjunction with the heteronormative foundations of contemporary U.S. fatherhood politics.

Gender/sexual essentialist notions of male promiscuity certainly have not helped African American men. Such notions have been used to reassert white, heterosexual, and middle-class men's centrality to "civilization" and the na-tion (Bederman 1995). Neither are homophobic distinctions between het-erosexual and gay men helpful in promoting fatherhood responsibility. By creating an urgency for men to prove that they are not gay, homophobic fa-therhood politics reinforces obsessions to prove heterosexual prowess. In-ability to recognize other masculinities may inhibit alternative constructions of parenthood. What about men who "mother," women who "father," and people who parent in ways that cannot be described in binary-gendered terms? Gay men, pro-feminist men, lesbians, single parents, and transgen-dered persons may have knowledge about grappling with issues of gender, sexuality, homosociality, and marriage. Alternative constructions and prac-tices of parenting may undermine binary-gender/sexual distinctions, as well as the tensions and contradictions between womanizing and heterosexual re-straint. In other words, excluding alternative masculinities and fatherhoods from the politics of fatherhood responsibility is counterproductive to con-temporary families.

Even though the fatherhood responsibility movement sometimes uses nonhierarchical notions of parenting and tries to reshape male parenting to include nurturing and mentoring, some of the gendered notions in the movement may be potentially oppressive to both men and women. For instance, characterizing men as innately "aggressive," "competitive," and "promiscuous" stereotypes men as prone to violence and authoritarianism. Fatherhood organizations may benefit from discussing, from a nonessentialist perspective, why fathers need to be what they perceive as distinctively male in the first place. Perhaps deemphasizing notions of gendered/sexual difference in heterosocial and nonheteronormative settings would help liberate fatherhood programs from the dilemmas of masculinizing domesticity while domesticating masculinity.

The fatherhood responsibility movement has accomplished much at many levels. It has transformed policy systems, increased funding for programs and research, made it easier for low-income fathers to pay child support, and worked to redefine public definitions of fatherhood to include nurturing (Mincy and Pouncy 2002, 578–79). Another recent gain, mainly for the pro-marriage wing of the fatherhood responsibility movement, is President George W. Bush's campaign to promote marriage and responsible fatherhood as central national concerns. It will be interesting to see what will result from the fatherhood responsibility movement's work. As I mentioned before, Wade Horn, the former president of the National Fatherhood Initiative and a leading marriage proponent, has become the assistant secretary for children and families. Will Wade Horn use his position primarily to promote marriage, and will the pro-marriage wing of the fatherhood responsibility movement transform into a full-fledged marriage movement? In that case, where will that leave the fragile-families organizations and their struggles for men to obtain equal social and economic opportunities so that they can parent responsibly?

This book provides analyses and material necessary to discuss the implications of future developments. Of crucial significance are the ways diverging constituencies in fatherhood politics share the fundamental conviction that masculinities and femininities are founded in binary and complementary heterosexual differences. Building on and contesting centuries-old notions of fatherhood, the fatherhood responsibility movement partly translates gendered, sexualized, and racialized ideas into constructions of parenthood. Although not spelled out, the politics of heteronormativity is central to the politics of fatherhood responsibility, guiding notions of what men and fathers are and should be. Reinvigorating century-old dilemmas of masculinizing domesticity, the fatherhood responsibility movement strives to make sense of the changes and conditions that affect the positions of men in family and work. However, this effort needs to be contextualized in intersecting structural relations and struggles. Naive attempts at "difference-based equality" are a far cry from promoting initiatives and programs that shift some of the burdens and obligations of parenthood to fathers. Moreover, heteronormative notions of gender, sexuality, and social/moral order reinforce the legal, economic, and social disadvantages of families that do not correspond to this template. As long as U.S. fatherhood politics is based on the binary differentiation of masculinity and femininity and the exclusion of alternative masculinities, it will remain caught up in the dilemmas of masculinization.

Notes

1. Although the fragile-families organizations do not explicitly promote this preference, most fragile-families practitioners I talked or listened to made a point of indicating they were married and monogamous.

2. It is not uncommon for anthropologists to do their fieldwork in whatever environments and at whatever times their interviewees find convenient. This may entail meeting interviewees at bars or at home and at night if this is where and when they are available. It is actually preferable to meet representatives, especially the types of professionals under study, in informal settings to get a more multifaceted impression of their ideas and practices. However, because of the time constraints of interviewees, most of my interviews and participant observation did take place in public settings near their workplaces, such as offices, coffee shops, conference centers, and restaurants. The environments in which the interviews took place did not seem to make a difference when it came to the sexual overtures of some interviewees.

3. He had earlier mentioned that it is not acceptable in his community and in his generation for African American men to have white girlfriends.

APPENDIX: FIELDWORK PROCESSES

From 1992 to 1993, I attended an American university, Lawrence University, as an undergraduate. During that year, I became fascinated with the ways notions of "the family" crystallize moral and structural issues around race, gender, and sexuality in U.S. politics. When I returned to the United States in 1996 to prepare for my graduate fieldwork, I wanted to investigate U.S. debates on "the family" and "family values" in relation to cultural notions of gender, sexuality, race, and socioeconomic class. I focused on the intersecting dimensions of family politics partly because of feminist and queer interests,[1] but I was not sure exactly how these theoretical interests would apply to my specific field of study. In the beginning of my graduate project, I became involved in the international and cross-disciplinary book project and workshop series "Fatherhood and the State" at Stockholm University, headed by the sociologist Barbara Hobson (see Gavanas 2002). Collaborating with the distinguished scholars involved in this project helped me focus on men and fathers in relation to family policy and the labor market.[2] Hobson's book project also enabled me to include cross-disciplinary discussions from the inception of my anthropological study.

Policy anthropology takes power relations, discourses, and practices as its objects of study in investigating political institutions (Shore and Wright 1997). In this study I combine policy anthropology with men's studies and queer studies to analyze not only traditional anthropological ethnography based on interviews and participant observation but also articles, newsletters, policy material, and reports. I contextualize policy material and political/academic discourse through formal and informal interviews, ethnographic accounts of my interaction with representatives, and accounts of representatives' interaction with one another. This anthropological study contributes to cross-disciplinary discussions by bringing together several empirical dimensions instead of being based only on literary and other secondary sources or solely on ethnographic fieldwork.

Throughout my fieldwork, I revised my approaches and adjusted my research questions on the basis of my continuous interaction and dialogue with representatives of the fatherhood responsibility movement. For instance, after spending time in the field, I realized the centrality of religion, sport, and notions of male sexuality to the fatherhood responsibility movement. I had not set out to focus on these issues, but I revised my research questions to include them. The sexual aspects of my interaction with representatives affected my fieldwork and added another dimension to my analysis of representatives' gendered, racial, and sexual politics.

Before and during fieldwork, I was determined not to take an adversarial approach to the fatherhood responsibility movement despite my biases about gendered and sexual equality. Although I approached my study from critical theoretical perspectives, I did not see the point of doing fieldwork merely to confirm preconceived ideas. My aim was to listen closely to the diverse voices of the actors in the fatherhood responsibility movement. While I carried out interviews and participant observation, I tried to maintain a sympathetic and open approach to the movement and its representatives. For instance, rather than conceive of masculinity politics as a unified interest in maintaining "traditional" male privileges, I sought to nuance the competing and ambivalent claims and stakes of men in different positions and to highlight egalitarian tendencies as much as sexist and heterosexist ones.

Not unexpectedly, it was a struggle to obtain access to the internal activities and meetings of the fatherhood responsibility movement. A large part of my fieldwork consisted of trying to get past the secretaries and assistants of representatives to get just a moment of their time. When I did get to talk to representatives, they often tried to make routine statements I had heard previously in conferences and texts. The organizations under study, especially the national ones, were very skilled in managing media and researcher representations of the movement. Representatives of the fatherhood responsibility movement had good reasons not to be accessible for studies. However, many representatives did express an interest in the international book project of which my study was a part (Hobson 2002) and were willing to participate in an international and comparative project. Representatives of fatherhood organizations were generally interested in research about fatherhood, and some even used earlier versions of my texts in their own presentations. For instance, Ronald Mincy from the Ford Foundation's Strengthening Fragile Families Initiative quoted one of my earlier texts at a congressional hearing on fatherhood (Committee on Ways and Means 1999, 46).

Pro-Marriage Experiences

As a female observer, I seemed to be perceived by the pro-marriage wing as a potential feminist intruder. The simple fact that I was an academic made me a potential member of what pro-marriage leaders dismissively labeled the "liberal cultural elite." However, most marriage proponents politely answered my questions, and I even socialized with some of them in informal settings. Importantly, as I just mentioned, my intention was not to prove preconceived notions about marriage proponents as sexist, heterosexist, conservative, fundamentalist Christian, or whatever. Although it is impossible to be completely void of biases, my purpose was to start out with an open mind and piece together representatives' outlooks, concerns, and perspectives. Not until after completing my fieldwork and processing my material did I formulate my critical analysis of pro-marriage notions of gendered and sexual order and the workings of loose essentialist and heteronormative ideas.

Apart from going to conferences, workshops, and interviews, I spent a lot of time with two pro-marriage representatives, Joe and Bob. They invited me to join them in both formal and informal settings and offered to drive me to remote events. By socializing with these representatives, I could participate behind the scenes at fatherhood events and discuss representatives' immediate reflections and analyses of what was going on. I also had dinners with both Joe and Bob at my place and at their places. Bob introduced me to other people as his friend and occasionally said that he enjoyed hanging out with me. I enjoyed hanging out with Bob and Joe too. I talked to both of them about pretty much anything, such as our backgrounds, friends, and families.

I met most of the other pro-marriage representatives only a few times and on much more superficial terms. These encounters sometimes made me feel dishonest, for instance, when representatives expressed antigay and antifeminist sentiments. I rarely had a chance to be up front with my own perspectives in such cases. Some representatives even gave me marriage advice and invited me out with them and their wives, accompanied by my "future husband." Had they asked me directly about my sexual orientation, relationships, or approach to marriage, I would have been open about these matters, but this never occurred. As I demonstrate in the concluding chapter, it was common for representatives to enmesh me as part of routine gendered and sexualized interaction. In these contexts, women were automatically assigned to a "Lady" status and a counterpart in the politics of role modeling/womanizing. On the one hand, interviewees often behaved like the "responsible gentlemen" they sought to represent in relation to women by, for instance, opening doors and paying for checks. On the other hand, a few interviewees took their conceptions of "manly" behavior to an explicitly heterosexual level by pursuing me sexually.

Fragile-Families Experiences

While being white made it easier to "blend in" when doing fieldwork in pro-marriage settings (where the majority was white), fragile-families representatives often assumed that my whiteness and educational status implied wealth and privilege. They also tended to associate social science with a history of white racist politics. As discussed in chapter 3, fragile-families representatives and the fathers who participated in their programs are partly united by the very oppression whiteness represents. Consequently, I was often required to account for my own positions, ideas, and approaches. My interaction with one of my key interviewees, Bill, exemplifies the questioning that came with my structural position in the fragile-families wing. Bill was not a typical interviewee insofar as he studied me and kept questioning all sorts of things about my behavior, language, looks, questions, and agendas. He checked my notes and questioned the ways I quoted him and what I selected to write down. He asked what my material would be used for, interrogated me about my political views, and constantly reminded me that race mattered in my interaction with representatives. Sometimes he suddenly stopped talking and demanded my interpretations of what he just had said. He rarely let me tape him and insisted on choosing the conditions, time, and place for our meetings. Bill explicitly wanted to challenge me and put me through tests before he told me "the real stories," and he often pushed topics beyond the frames I laid out, which I think inspired a mutually interesting and productive dialogue. Actually, many fragile-families representatives, as well as the fathers who participated in their programs, were very friendly and helpful to me—despite all the complex structural issues involved in our interaction.

When racial oppression was discussed in the all-male, fragile-families workshops, I implicitly or explicitly got to represent whiteness. When gender relations were discussed in these workshops, I often got to represent women. In cases where representatives and participants were African American men with fewer educational degrees, my whiteness and perceived socioeconomic status sometimes seemed more significant than my being a woman in an all-male environment. For instance, during an interview prior to a local fatherhood meeting, one African American fragile-families representative told me that the people who work with a program should "look like the people they are working with" (in other words, be African American when working in the African American communities) and "not come from a suburb somewhere." Implicit here is the U.S. connotation of the suburbs as a place where middle- and upper-class white people live. At the meeting he introduced me to the group of low-income and poor African American men as "someone who comes from a suburb, but one that lies far away." In general, however, my being Swedish seemed to encourage fragile-families representatives to talk to me. Overall, the representatives I met from the fatherhood responsibility movement seemed interested in a foreign perspective and had many questions about fatherhood issues in Sweden or about Sweden in general (such as "Is it true what I've heard about the women in Sweden?").

Despite the many factors that excluded me from full participation in activities in the fragile-families wing, I do not think a researcher has to be an African American man to carry out research on fragile families. Actually, some of the representatives I talked to mentioned being perceived as outsiders in communities or groups with which they work even though they were African American men whose backgrounds were similar to theirs. For instance, Harold and Phil, two young African American fragile-families representatives, told me not to be discouraged about being perceived as an outsider. They told me that, because they were university educated, they had similar experiences in groups where the majority of men were unskilled and unemployed. Despite being African American men from similar communities and backgrounds, they were still perceived as outsiders because of their educational status.

In sum, as a young (twenty-five to twenty-six years old at the time) white Swedish woman in all-male heterosexual settings, I was sometimes positioned as an outsider but also was able to experience the fatherhood responsibility movement differently than had I been male and/or African American. Coming from a Swedish background enabled me to notice phenomena Americans might take for granted, for instance, the prevalence of religion and sports. Moreover, as I demonstrate in the concluding chapter, gendered, racial, and sexual dimensions cannot be left out. These dimensions permeate constructions of masculinity and fatherhood in the fatherhood responsibility movement. Furthermore, gendered, racial, socioeconomic, and sexual aspects impact the practices and discussions between men and between men and women. Being treated according to representatives' ideas about male-female relations led to insights about the dilemmas of their gendered and sexual practices. Gendered, racial, and sexual dynamics affected my position and access in the field as well as my fieldwork material in not always predictable ways. While in the field, with the help of the people I met, I gradually discovered the ways my whiteness affected my position in the field. Similarly, I adapted my feminist, queer, and critical race studies analyses to my observations in the field.

Selection, Interviews, and Fieldwork Details

I started preparing for this study in 1996 by investigating organizations involved in family politics at a general level. I selected the organizations from a large number of nonprofit organizations in Chicago and Washington, D.C. These initial organizations—such as the Illinois Family Policy Counsel, the Catholic Charities, Youth Struggling for Survival, the Family Impact Seminar, and the Christian Coalition—dealt primarily with family issues and issues of low-income youth, sexuality, and "delinquency" (in other words, gang and teenage-mother organizations). The interviews were open-ended and focused on the structure, aims, opposition, and networks of the organization as well as the representatives' perceptions of, and reasons for involvement with, the social problems with which they worked. It became apparent that issues of youth, fatherhood, teenage motherhood, and family values were interrelated in the minds of many of the people interviewed. Subsequently, I investigated differences and similarities in explanations and solutions to social problems as well as conceptions of social processes.

My preliminary fieldwork took place during the summer of 1997 and focused specifically on fatherhood organizations, mainly in Washington, D.C., New York, and Baltimore. These organizations were selected because of their centrality in the national fatherhood responsibility movement. They all operate at the national level and represent and coordinate hundreds of local organizations. The representatives interviewed were either the leaders/directors or other significant staff. I interviewed twenty representatives (ten pro-marriage representatives and ten fragile-families representatives) from seventeen organizations at least once. I also conducted informal interviews with fifteen more people who had significant connections to the fatherhood responsibility movement. I selected the organizations from different directories and through consultations with several representatives experienced in their fields.

Interviewees were professionals involved in research, policy advocacy, or local fatherhood programs. All except two interviewees were married with children. All but two of the fragile-families interviewees were African American, whereas all except one of the pro-marriage interviewees were white. Most interviewees could be characterized as middle-class professionals, although some fragile-families interviewees were from poor or working-class backgrounds, and some pro-marriage interviewees were from upper- or upper-middle-class backgrounds.

All twenty interviewees brought up the following topics: (1) social processes concerning fatherhood and masculinity and their relation to family, the state, and the labor market as well as social ills, (2) strategies for grappling with the problems identified, (3) parental features and the implication of father absence, and (4) allies and opponents. At the beginning of the interviews, I asked standardized open-ended questions, but the representatives steered the topics into what they considered key notions and focuses. This partially open-ended method had the advantage of letting the actors under study define the categories under contestation. However, the method also means that the collected data differ somewhat in coverage. After talking to all twenty representatives and transcribing the audiotapes, I thought that I had a good grasp of the field and its lines of agreement and contestation. I prepared a text in which I summarized my own understandings of the fatherhood responsibility movement (revised version published as Gavanas 2002), and I let a few key interviewees from each wing read and discuss this text.

The main fieldwork took place over eight months, from the beginning of February to the end of September of 1998. I did regular participant observation at conferences and workshops and interviewed new and old representatives. On the basis of the preliminary fieldwork, I added interview questions about the evolution of the movement, the significance of the marriage issue, and the impact of religion.

Some of the events I attended were:

Bipartisan Congressional Task Force Press Conference, Washington, D.C., June 12, 1997
Promise Keepers Rally, Washington, D.C., June 13, 1997
Seminar of the Senate National Campaign for Preventing Teenage Pregnancy (focusing on young men), Washington, D.C., June 18, 1997
Department of Health and Human Services Fathers Work Group Meeting, Washington, D.C., July 17, 1997
Congressional Hearing on Fatherhood—Early Childhood, Youth, and Families Subcommittee, Washington, D.C., July 24, 1997
Virginia Fatherhood Campaign, Richmond, Va., March 24, 1998
One More River to Cross: African American Families in the Twenty-first Century, University of Maryland, April 16, 1998
Association of Family and Conciliation Courts Thirty-fifth Annual Conference, Washington, D.C., May 27–30, 1998
California Department of Social Services Fourth Annual Fathers, Families, and Communities Conference, Los Angeles, Calif., June 10–14, 1998
National Fatherhood Initiative's Second National Summit on Fatherhood, Washington, D.C., June 15, 1998
National Council of La Raza 1998 Annual Conference, Philadelphia, Pa., July 19–22, 1998
Congressional Hearing on Fatherhood Initiative, Washington, D.C., July 30, 1998
National Organization for Men against Sexism: Pro-Feminist Men 2000, SUNY, Stony Brook, Long Island, August 6–9, 1998

Connecting Fathers: Strengthening Families through Public/Private Partnerships, Oakland, Calif., August 27 and 28, 1998

Notes

1. Feminist anthropology, in Henrietta Moore's words, is "the study of gender as a principle of human social life" (1988, 188). It is concerned with not only cultural constructions of gender but also the fundamental differences between men and between women and the ways gender, socioeconomic class, and history are experienced, constructed, and mediated in relation to one another (1988, 196). Queer theory, which emerged in the 1990s out of feminist as well as gay and lesbian studies, focuses on heteronormativity as an ideological and social problem (Kulick 1996, 9).

2. Some of the other researchers were Ann Orloff, Jeff Hearn, David Morgan, Trudie Knijn, and Ilona Ostner.

WORKS CITED

Aanerud, Rebecka. 1997. "Fictions of Whiteness: Speaking the Names of Whiteness in U.S. Literature." In *Displacing Whiteness: Essays in Social and Cultural Criticism,* edited by Ruth Frankenberg, 35–59. Durham, N.C.: Duke University Press.

Allen, Ernest, Jr. 1995. "The Farrakhan Speech—Toward a More Perfect Union: Commingling of Constitutional Ideals and Christian Precepts." *Black Scholar* 25 (4): 27–34.

Anderson, Elijah. 1978. *A Place on the Corner.* Chicago: University of Chicago Press.

———. 1990. *Streetwise: Race, Class, and Change in an Urban Community.* Chicago: University of Chicago Press.

———. 1993. "Sex Codes and Family Life among Poor Inner-City Youths." In *Young Unwed Fathers: Changing Roles and Emerging Policies,* edited by Robert I. Lerman and Theodora J. Ooms, 74–98. Philadelphia: Temple University Press.

Anderson, Victor. 1998. "Abominations of a Million Men: Reflections on a Silent Minority." In *Black Religion after the Million Man March: Voices on the Future,* edited by Garth Kasimu Baker-Fletcher. Maryknoll, N.Y.: Orbis Books.

Balmer, Randy. 2000. "Keep the Faith and Go the Distance: Promise Keepers, Feminism, and the World of Sports." In *The Promise Keepers: Essays on Masculinity and Christianity,* edited by Dane S. Claussen, 194–203. Jefferson, N.C.: McFarland.

Bartkowski, John P. 1999. "Godly Masculinities Require Gender and Power." In *Standing on the Promises: The Promise Keepers and the Revival of Manhood,* edited by Dane S. Claussen, 121–30. Cleveland, Ohio: Pilgrim.

Bederman, Gail. 1995. *Manliness and Civilization: A Cultural History of Gender and Race in the United States, 1880–1917.* Chicago: University of Chicago Press.

Bellah, Robert N., Richard Madsen, William M. Sullivan, Ann Swidler, and Steven M. Tipton. 1985. *Habits of the Heart: Individualism and Commitment in American Life.* Berkeley: University of California Press.

Benkov, Laura. 1994. *Reinventing the Family: The Emerging Story of Lesbian and Gay Parents.* New York: Crown.

Berger, Brigitte, and Peter L. Berger. 1983. *The War over the Family: Capturing the Middle Ground.* London: Hutchinson.

Bertoia, Carl, and Jane Drakich. 1993. "The Father's Rights Movement: Contradictions in Rhetoric and Practice." *Journal of Family Issues* 14 (4): 592–615.

Billingsley, Andrew. 1992. *Climbing Jacob's Ladder: The Enduring Legacy of African-American Families.* New York: Touchstone.

Blankenhorn, David. 1995. *Fatherless America: Confronting Our Most Urgent Social Problem.* New York: Basic Books.

———. 1999. "Introduction—Toward Fatherhood." In *The Fatherhood Movement: A Call to Action,* edited by Wade F. Horn, David Blankenhorn, and Mitchell B. Pearlstein, xi–xv. New York: Lexington Books.

Brickner, Bryan W. 2000. "Building a Social Evangelical Organization: The Lincoln Bedroom or Oval Office Model?" In *The Promise Keepers: Essays on Masculinity and Christianity,* edited by Dane S. Claussen, 204–14. Jefferson, N.C.: McFarland.

Burstyn, Varda. 1999. *The Rites of Men: Manhood, Politics, and the Culture of Sport.* Toronto: University of Toronto Press.

Butler, Judith. 1997. "Merely Cultural." *Social Text* 15 (3 and 4): 265–88.

Cameron, Deborah. 1995. *Verbal Hygiene.* New York: Routledge.

Chateauvert, Melinda. 1998. *Marching Together: Women of the Brotherhood of Sleeping Car Porters.* Urbana: University of Illinois Press.

Clatterbaugh, Kenneth. 1995. "Mythopoetic Foundations and New Age Patriarchy." In *The Politics of Manhood: Profeminist Men Respond to the Mythopoetic Men's Movement (And the Mythopoetic Leaders Answer),* edited by Michael S. Kimmel, 44–63. Philadelphia: Temple University Press.

———. 1997. *Contemporary Perspectives on Masculinity: Men, Women, and Politics in Modern Society.* 2d ed. Boulder, Colo.: Westview.

———. 2000. "Review Essay: Literature of the U.S. Men's Movement." *Signs: Journal of Women in Culture and Society* 25 (3): 881–94.

Claussen, Dane S. 1999. "What the Media Missed about the Promise Keepers." In *Standing on the Promises: The Promise Keepers and the Revival of Manhood,* edited by Dane S. Claussen, 17–33. Cleveland, Ohio: Pilgrim.

Cole, Robert A. 2000. "Promising to Be a Man: Promise Keepers and the Organizational Constitution of Masculinity." In *The Promise Keepers: Essays on Masculinity and Christianity,* edited by Dane S. Claussen, 113–32. Jefferson, N.C.: McFarland.

Collier, Richard. 1995. *Masculinity, Law, and the Family.* New York: Routledge.

———. 1996. "Coming Together? Post-heterosexuality, Masculine Crisis, and the New Men's Movement." *Feminist Legal Studies* 4 (1): 3–48.

Coltrane, Scott. 2001. "Marketing the Marriage 'Solution': Misplaced Simplicity in the Politics of Fatherhood." *Sociological Perspectives* 44 (4): 387–418.

Committee on Ways and Means, U.S. House of Representatives. 1999. *Fatherhood and Welfare Reform: Hearings before the Subcommittee on Human Resources of the Committee on Ways and Means, House of Representatives* 105th Cong., 2d sess., July 30, 1998. Serial 105-78. Washington, D.C.: U.S. Government Printing Office.

Connell, R. W. 1990. "An Iron Man: The Body and Some Contradictions of Hegemonic Masculinity." In *Sport, Men, and the Gender Order: Critical Feminist Perspectives,* edited by Michael A. Messner and Donald F. Sabo. Champaign, Ill.: Human Kinetics Books.

———. 1995. *Masculinities.* Cambridge: Polity.

Conolly, Ceci. 1999. "Gore's Anti-poverty Plan Alarms NOW." *Washington Post,* Oct. 23, A8.

Cott, Nancy F. 2000. *Public Vows: A History of Marriage and the Nation.* Cambridge, Mass.: Harvard University Press.

Council on Families in America. 1995. *Marriage in America: A Report on the Nation.* New York: Institute for American Values.

Curtis, Susan. 1990. "The Son of Man and God the Father: The Social Gospel and Victorian Masculinity." In *Meanings for Manhood: Constructions of Masculinity in Victorian America,* edited by Mark C. Carnes and Clyde Griffen, 67–78. Chicago: University of Chicago Press.

Daniels, Cynthia R., ed. 1998. *Lost Fathers: The Politics of Fatherlessness in America.* New York: St. Martin's.

Davis, Angela Y. 1981. *Women, Race and Class.* New York: Vintage Books.

Deardorff, Don. 2000. "Sacred Male Space: The Promise Keepers as a Community Resistance." In *The Promise Keepers: Essays on Masculinity and Christianity,* edited by Dane S. Claussen, 76–90. Jefferson, N.C.: McFarland.

D'Emilio, John, and Estelle B. Freedman. 1997. *Intimate Matters: A History of Sexuality in America.* Chicago: University of Chicago Press.

Digby, Tom. 1998. Introduction to *Men Doing Feminism,* edited by Tom Digby, 1–14. New York: Routledge.

Dodson, Angela. 1999. "Bringing Fathers Back into the Fold." In *Ford Foundation Report,* 20–21. New York: Ford Foundation.

Donovan, Brian. 1998. "Political Consequences of Private Authority: Promise Keepers and the Transformation of Hegemonic Masculinity." *Theory and Society* 27 (6): 817–43.

Douglas, Mary. 1966. *Purity and Danger: An Analysis of Concepts of Pollution and Taboo.* Binghamton, N.Y.: Vail-Ballou.

Dowd, Nancy. 2000. *Redefining Fatherhood.* New York: New York University Press.

Dunbar, Michelle D. 2000. "Dennis Rodman—Do You Feel Feminine Yet? Black Masculinity, Gender Transgression, and Reproductive Rebellion on MTV." In *Masculinities, Gender Relations, and Sport,* edited by Jim McKay, Michael A. Messner, and Don Sabo, 263–86. Thousand Oaks, Calif.: Sage Publications.

Duneier, Mitchell. 1992. *Slim's Table: Race, Respectability, and Masculinity.* Chicago: University of Chicago Press.

Dunne, Gilliam A. 2000. "Opting into Motherhood." *Gender and Society* 14 (1): 11–25.

Dworkin, Shari Lee, and Faye Linda Wachs. 2000. "The Morality/Manhood Paradox: Masculinity, Sport, and the Media." In *Masculinities, Gender Relations, and Sport,* edited by Jim McKay, Michael A. Messner, and Don Sabo, 47–66. Thousand Oaks, Calif.: Sage Publications.

Eberly, Don. 1999. "No Democracy without Dads." In *The Fatherhood Movement: A Call to Action,* edited by Wade F. Horn, David Blankenhorn, and Mitchell B. Pearlstein, 25–34. New York: Lexington Books.

Ehrenreich, Barbara. 1989. *Fear of Falling: The Inner Life of the Middle Class.* New York: Harper Perennial.

Evans, Tony. 1994. "Spiritual Purity." In *Seven Promises of a Promise Keeper,* edited by Al Janssen and Larry K. Weeden, 73–82. Colorado Springs: Focus on the Family Publishing.

Faludi, Susan. 1999. *Stiffed: The Betrayal of the American Man.* New York: William Morrow.

Frank, Stephen M. 1998. *Life with Father: Parenthood and Masculinity in the Nineteenth-Century American North.* Baltimore: Johns Hopkins University Press.

Frankenberg, Ruth. 1997. "Local Whitenesses, Localizing Whiteness." In *Displacing*

Whiteness: Essays in Social and Cultural Criticism, 1–34. Durham, N.C.: Duke University Press.

———, ed. 1997. *Displacing Whiteness: Essays in Social and Cultural Criticism.* Durham, N.C.: Duke University Press.

Franklin, Clyde W., II. 1994. "'Ain't I a Man?' The Efficacy of Black Masculinities for Men's Studies in the 1990's." In *The American Black Male: His Present Status and His Future,* edited by Richard G. Majors and Jacob U. Gordon, 271–83. Chicago: Nelson-Hall.

Fraser, Nancy. 1997. *Justice Interruptus: Critical Reflections on the "Postsocialist" Condition.* New York: Routledge.

A Future of Promise: The New NAACP. 1998. Baltimore: NAACP.

Gallagher, Maggie. 1996. "Is Marriage Necessary for Good Fatherhood? A Fatherhood Today Symposium Discussion." *Fatherhood Today* 2 (1): 6–7.

———. 1999. "The Importance of Being Married." In *The Fatherhood Movement: A Call to Action,* edited by Wade F. Horn, David Blankenhorn, and Mitchell B. Pearlstein, 57–64. New York: Lexington Books.

Garber, Marjorie. 1999. "Two-Point conversion." In *One Nation under God? Religion and American Culture,* edited by Marjorie Garber and Rebecca L. Walkowitz, 280–311. New York: Routledge.

Gavanas, Anna. 2002. "The Fatherhood Responsibility Movement: The Centrality of Marriage, Work, and Male Sexuality in Reconstructions of Masculinity and Fatherhood." In *Making Men into Fathers: Men, Masculinities, and the Social Politics of Fatherhood,* edited by Barbara Hobson, 213–42. New York: Cambridge University Press.

Gibbs, Jewelle Taylor. 1994. "Anger in Young Black Males: Victims or Victimizers?" In *The American Black Male: His Present Status and His Future,* edited by Richard G. Majors and Jacob U. Gordon, 127–43. Chicago: Nelson-Hall.

Gilder, George. 1973. *Sexual Suicide.* New York: Bantam.

———. 1986. *Men and Marriage.* Gretna, La.: Pelican.

Gillis, John R. 1996. *A World of Their Own Making: Myth, Ritual, and the Quest for Family Values.* New York: Basic Books.

———. 2000. "Marginalization of Fatherhood in Western Countries." *Childhood* 7 (2): 225–38.

Ginsburg, Faye. 1989. *Contested Lives: The Abortion Debate in an American Community.* Berkeley: University of California Press.

Gore, Al. 1996. "Father to Father." *Fatherhood and Family Support* 15 (1): 13.

Gray, John. 1992. *Men Are from Mars, Women Are from Venus.* New York: Harper Collins.

Griswold, Robert L. 1993. *Fatherhood in America.* New York: Basic Books.

Gutmann, David L. 1999. "The Species Narrative." In *The Fatherhood Movement: A Call to Action,* edited by Wade F. Horn, David Blankenhorn, and Mitchell B. Pearlstein, 132–46. New York: Lexington Books.

Gutterman, David S. 2000. "Exodus and the Chosen Men of God: Promise Keepers and the Theology of Masculinity." In *The Promise Keepers: Essays on Masculinity and Christianity,* edited by Dane S. Claussen, 133–52. Jefferson, N.C.: McFarland.

Hannerz, Ulf. 1969. *Soulside: Inquiries into Ghetto Culture and Community.* New York: Columbia University Press.

Harper, Phillip Brian. 1996. *Are We Not Men? Masculine Anxiety and the Problem of African American Identity.* New York: Oxford University Press.

Haskins, C. W. 1890. *The Argonauts of California*. New York: Fords, Howard, and Hulbert.

Hawkins, Alan. 2000. "U.S. Senate to Consider Responsible Fatherhood Bill." *Fatherhood Today* 5 (1): 8.

Healey, Kevin. 2000. "The Irresolvable Tension: 'Agape' and Masculinity in the Promise Keepers Movement." In *The Promise Keepers: Essays on Masculinity and Christianity*, edited by Dane S. Claussen, 215–25. Jefferson, N.C.: McFarland.

Hill, Robert B. 1993. *Research on the African-American Family: A Holistic Perspective*. Westport, Conn.: Auburn House.

———. 1997. *The Strengths of African American Families: Twenty-Five Years Later*. Washington, D.C.: R & B.

Hobson, Barbara, ed. 2002. *Making Men into Fathers: Men, Masculinities, and the Social Politics of Fatherhood*. New York: Cambridge University Press.

hooks, bell. 1992. *Black Looks: Race and Representation*. Boston: South End.

Horn, Wade F. 1997. "You've Come a Long Way Daddy: After Being Pilloried and Left for Dead, the Fatherhood Ideal Is Making a Comeback." *Policy Review* (July/August): 24–30.

———. 1999. "Did You Say 'Movement'?" In *The Fatherhood Movement: A Call to Action*, edited by Wade F. Horn, David Blankenhorn, and Mitchell B. Pearlstein, 1–16. New York: Lexington Books.

Horn, Wade F., David Blankenhorn, and Mitchell B. Pearlstein, eds. 1999. *The Fatherhood Movement: A Call to Action*. New York: Lexington Books.

Horton, James Oliver, and Lois E. Horton. 1999. "Violence, Protest, and Identity: Black Manhood in Antebellum America." In *A Question of Manhood: A Reader in U.S. Black Men's History and Masculinity*, vol. 1, edited by Darlene Clark Hine and Earnestine Jenkins, 382–98. Bloomington: Indiana University Press.

Hunter, James Davidson. 1991. *Culture Wars: The Struggle to Define America*. New York: Basic Books.

Jones, Steven L., and William H. Lockhart. 1999. "Race and Religion at the Million Man March and the Promise Keepers' Stand in the Gap." In *Standing on the Promises: The Promise Keepers and the Revival of Manhood*, edited by Dane S. Claussen, 44–55. Cleveland, Ohio: Pilgrim.

Katz, Jonathan Ned. 1995. *The Invention of Heterosexuality*. New York: Penguin Books.

Keeler, John D., Ben Fraser, and William J. Brown. 1999. "How Promise Keepers See Themselves as Men Behaving Goodly." In *Standing on the Promises: The Promise Keepers and the Revival of Manhood*, edited by Dane S. Claussen, 75–88. Cleveland, Ohio: Pilgrim.

Kelley, Colleen E. 2000. "Silencing the Voice of God: Rhetorical Responses to the Promise Keepers." In *The Promise Keepers: Essays on Masculinity and Christianity*, edited by Dane S. Claussen, 226–237. Jefferson, N.C.: McFarland.

Kimmel, Michael S. 1987. "The Contemporary 'Crisis' of Masculinity in Historical Perspective." In *The Making of Masculinities: The New Men's Studies*, edited by Harry Brod, 121–53. Boston: Unwin Hyman.

———. 1992. Introduction to *Against the Tide: Pro-feminist Men in the United States, 1776–1990: A Documentary History*, edited by Michael S. Kimmel and Thomas E. Mosmiller, 1–51. Boston: Beacon.

———. 1994. "Masculinity as Homophobia: Fear, Shame, and Silence in the Constructions of Gender Identity." In *Theorizing Masculinities,* edited by Harry Brod and Michael Kaufman, 119–41. Thousand Oaks, Calif.: Sage Publications.

———. 1996. *Manhood in America: A Cultural History.* New York: Free Press.

———. 1998a. "The Struggle for Men's Souls." In *Men's Lives,* 4th ed., edited by Michael
Kimmel and Michael Messner, 592–94. Boston: Allyn and Bacon.

———. 1998b. "Who's Afraid of Men Doing Feminism?" In *Men Doing Feminism,* edited
by Tom Digby, 57–68. New York: Routledge.

———. 1999. "Patriarchy's Second Coming as Masculine Renewal." In *Standing on the
Promises: The Promise Keepers and the Revival of Manhood,* edited by Dane S. Claussen,
111–20. Cleveland, Ohio: Pilgrim.

———, ed. 1995. *The Politics of Manhood: Profeminist Men Respond to the Mythopoetic Men's
Movement (And the Mythopoetic Leaders Answer).* Philadelphia: Temple University
Press.

Kimmel, Michael S., and Michael Kaufman. 1995. "Weekend Warriors: The New Men's
Movement." In *The Politics of Manhood: Profeminist Men Respond to the Mythopoetic
Men's Movement (And the Mythopoetic Leaders Answer),* edited by Michael S. Kimmel,
15–43. Philadelphia: Temple University Press.

Kirkley, Evelyn A. 1996. "Is It Manly to Be Christian? The Debate in Victorian and Mod-
ern America." In *Redeeming Men: Religion and Masculinities,* edited by Stephen B. Boyd,
W. Merle Longwood, and Mark W. Muesse, 80–88. Louisville, Ky.: Westminster John
Knox.

Klein, Alan M. 1993. *Little Big Men: Bodybuilding Subculture and Gender Construction.* Al-
bany: State University of New York Press.

Kulick, Don. 1996. "Queer Theory: vad är det och vad är det bra för?" *Lambda Nordica*
2 (3–4): 5–22.

Laird, Joan, ed. 1999. *Lesbians and Lesbian Families: Reflections on Theory and Practice.*
New York: Columbia University Press.

LaRossa, Ralph. 1997. *The Modernization of Fatherhood: A Social and Political History.* Chicago: University of Chicago Press.

Lasch, Christopher. 1977. *Haven in a Heartless World: The Family Besieged.* New York:
Basic Books.

Leonard, Mary. 2001. "Bush Pledges Funds for Fatherhood." *Boston Globe,* June 8, A2.

Lingard, Bob, and Peter Douglas. 1999. *Men Engaging Feminisms: Pro-feminism, Back-
lashes and Schooling.* Philadelphia, Pa.: Open University Press.

Longwood, W. Merle. 1996. "Changing Views of Fathering and Fatherhood: A Christian
Ethical Perspective." In *Redeeming Men: Religion and Masculinities,* edited by Stephen
B. Boyd, W. Merle Longwood, and Mark W. Muesse, 238–51. Louisville, Ky.: West-
minster John Knox.

———. 1999. "'Standing on the Promises' and the Broader Conversation." In *Standing
on the Promises: The Promise Keepers and the Revival of Manhood,* edited by Dane S.
Claussen, 1–13. Cleveland, Ohio: Pilgrim.

Madhubuti, Haki R. 1990. *Black Men: Obsolete, Single, Dangerous.* Chicago: Third World.

Majors, Richard G. 1990. "Cool Pose: Black Masculinity and Sports." In *Sport, Men, and
the Gender Order: Critical Feminist Perspectives,* edited by Michael A. Messner and Donald F. Sabo, 109–14. Champaign, Ill.: Human Kinetics Books.

———. 1994. "Conclusion and Recommendations: A Reason for Hope?—An Overview of the New Black Male Movement in the United States." In *The American Black Male: His Present Status and His Future,* edited by Richard G. Majors and Jacob U. Gordon, 299–315. Chicago: Nelson-Hall.

Majors, Richard G., and Janet Mancini Billson. 1992. *Cool Pose: The Dilemmas of Black Manhood in America.* New York: Touchstone.

Majors, Richard G., and Jacob U. Gordon, eds. 1994. *The American Black Male: His Present Status and His Future.* Chicago: Nelson-Hall.

Marsh, Margaret. 1990. "Suburban Men and Masculine Domesticity, 1870–1915." In *Meanings for Manhood: Constructions of Masculinity in Victorian America,* edited by Mark C. Carnes and Clyde Griffen, 111–27. Chicago: University of Chicago Press.

Marsiglio, William, ed. 1995. *Fatherhood: Contemporary Theory, Research, and Social Policy.* London: Sage.

McKay, Jim, Michael A. Messner, and Don Sabo. 2000. "Studying Sport, Men, and Masculinities from Feminist Standpoints." In *Masculinities, Gender Relations, and Sport,* edited by Jim McKay, Michael A. Messner, and Don Sabo, 1–11. Thousand Oaks, Calif.: Sage Publications.

Mellgren, Linda M. 1993. "Creating Federal Leadership in Research and Policy Development." In *Young Unwed Fathers: Changing Roles and Emerging Policies,* edited by Robert I. Lerman and Theodora J. Ooms, 193–212. Philadelphia: Temple University Press.

Merton, Robert K. 1972. "Insiders and Outsiders: A Chapter in the Sociology of Knowledge." *American Journal of Sociology* 78: 9–47.

Messner, Michael. 1992. *Power at Play: Sports and the Problem of Masculinity.* Boston: Beacon.

———. 1997. *Politics of Masculinities: Men in Movements.* Thousand Oaks, Calif.: Sage Publications.

Messner, Michael A., and Donald F. Sabo. 1990. "Introduction: Toward a Critical Feminist Reappraisal of Sport, Men, and the Gender Order." In *Sport, Men, and the Gender Order: Critical Feminist Perspectives,* edited by Michael A. Messner and Donald F. Sabo, 1–15. Champaign, Ill.: Human Kinetics Books.

Mincy, Ronald B. 1999. "The Forum: Should Legislation Promoting Responsible Fatherhood also Promote Marriage? Three Perspectives." *Fatherhood Today* 4 (3): 7.

Mincy, Ronald B., and Hillard Pouncy. 1999. "There Must Be Fifty Ways to Start a Family." In *The Fatherhood Movement: A Call to Action,* edited by Wade F. Horn, David Blankenhorn, and Mitchell B. Pearlstein, 83–104. New York: Lexington Books.

———. 2002. "The Responsible Fatherhood Field: Evolution and Goals." In *The Handbook of Fatherhood Involvement: Multidisciplinary Perspectives,* edited by Catherine S. Tamis-LeMonda and Natasha Cabera, 555–97. MahWah, N.J.: Lawrence Erlbaum Associates.

Moore, Henrietta. 1988. *Feminism and Anthropology.* Cambridge: Polity.

Morrison, Toni. 1992. *Playing in the Dark: Whiteness and the Literary Imagination.* New York: Vintage.

Muesse, Mark W. 1996. "Religious Machismo: Masculinity and Fundamentalism." In *Redeeming Men: Religion and Masculinities,* edited by Stephen B. Boyd, W. Merle Longwood, and Mark W. Muesse, 89–102. Louisville, Ky.: Westminster John Knox.

"National Fatherhood Initiative Leads 'A Call to Fatherhood.'" 1997. *Fatherhood Today* 2 (4): 1–2.

"The Nation of Islam, 1930–1996." 1996. *Black Scholar* 26 (3–4): 1.

Nelson, Dana D. 1998. *National Manhood: Capitalist Citizenship and the Imagined Fraternity of White Men.* Durham, N.C.: Duke University Press.

Nelson, William E. 1998. "Black Church Politics and the Million Man March." In *Black Religious Leadership from the Slave Community to the Million Man March: Flames of Fire,* edited by Felton O. Best, 243–57. Lewiston, N.Y.: Edwin Mellen.

New Encyclopedia Britannica. 1987. Vol. 6. Chicago: University of Chicago Press.

Newton, Judith L. 1999. "A Reaction to Declining Market and Religious Influence." In *Standing on the Promises: The Promise Keepers and the Revival of Manhood,* edited by Dane S. Claussen, 34–43. Cleveland, Ohio: Pilgrim.

NOMAS. 1998. "Pro-feminist Men 2000: Committed to Justice, Working for Change." Program for the Annual Conference of the National Organization for Men against Sexism, August 6–9, State University of New York at Stony Brook.

Ooms, Theodora. 1998. *Toward More Perfect Unions: Putting Marriage on the Public Agenda.* Washington, D.C.: Family Impact Seminar.

Petersen, Alan. 1998. *Unmasking the Masculine: "Men" and "Identity" in a Sceptical Age.* Thousand Oaks, Calif.: Sage Publications.

Popenoe, David. 1988. *Disturbing the Nest: Family Change and Decline in Modern Societies.* New York: Aldine De Gruyter.

———. 1996. *Life without Father: Compelling New Evidence That Fatherhood and Marriage Are Indispensable for the Good of Children and Society.* New York: Free Press.

———. 1998. "Life without Father." In *Lost Fathers: The Politics of Fatherlessness in America,* edited by Cynthia R. Daniels, 33–50. New York: St. Martin's.

———. 1999. "Challenging the Culture of Fatherlessness." In *The Fatherhood Movement: A Call to Action,* edited by Wade F. Horn, David Blankenhorn, and Mitchell B. Pearlstein, 17–24. New York: Lexington Books.

Pronger, Brian. 1990. "Gay Jocks: A Phenomenology of Gay Men in Athletics." In *Sport, Men, and the Gender Order: Critical Feminist Perspectives,* edited by Michael A. Messner and Donald F. Sabo, 141–52. Champaign, Ill.: Human Kinetics Books.

———. 2000. "Homosexuality and Sport: Who's Winning?" In *Masculinities, Gender Relations, and Sport,* edited by Jim McKay, Michael A. Messner, and Don Sabo, 222–44. Thousand Oaks, Calif.: Sage Publications.

Quicke, Andrew, and Karen Robinson. 2000. "Keeping the Promise of the Moral Majority? A Historical/Critical Comparison of the Promise Keepers and the Christian Coalition, 1989–98." In *The Promise Keepers: Essays on Masculinity and Christianity,* edited by Dane S. Claussen, 7–19. Jefferson, N.C.: McFarland.

Rainwater, Lee, and William L. Yancey. 1967. *The Moynihan Report and the Politics of Controversy.* Cambridge, Mass.: M.I.T. Press.

Rhodes, Eric Bryant. 2000. "Fatherhood Matters." *American Prospect,* Mar. 13, 48–52

Roberts, Dorothy. 1998. "The Absent Black Father." In *Lost Fathers: The Politics of Fatherlessness in America,* edited by Cynthia R. Daniels, 145–62. New York: St. Martin's.

Robinson, Sally. 2000. *Marked Men: White Masculinity in Crisis.* New York: Columbia University Press.

Rotundo, E. Anthony. 1993. *American Manhood: Transformations in Masculinity from the Revolution to the Modern Era.* New York: Basic Books.

Schneider, David M. 1968. *American Kinship.* Englewood Cliffs, N.J.: Prentice-Hall.

Schneider, David M., and Smith, Raymond T. 1978. *Class Differences in American Kinship.* Ann Arbor: University of Michigan Press.

Schwalbe, Michael. 1996. *Unlocking the Iron Cage: The Men's Movement, Gender Politics, and American Culture.* New York: Oxford University Press.

Segal, Lynne. 1990. *Slow Motion: Changing Masculinities, Changing Men.* New Brunswick, N.J.: Rutgers University Press.

Shore, Chris, and Susan Wright, eds. 1997. *Anthropology of Policy: Critical Perspectives on Governance and Power.* London: Routledge.

Silverstein, Louise B., and Carl F. Auerbach. 1999. "Deconstructing the Essential Father." *American Psychologist* 54 (6): 397–407.

Stacey, Judith. 1996. *In the Name of the Family: Rethinking Family Values in the Postmodern Age.* Boston: Beacon.

———. 1998. "Dada-ism in the 1990's: Getting Past Baby Talk about Fatherlessness." In *Lost Fathers: The Politics of Fatherlessness in America,* edited by Cynthia R. Daniels, 51–84. New York: St. Martin's.

———. 2001. "Family Values Forever." *Nation,* July 9, 26–30.

Staples, Robert. 1982. *Black Masculinity: The Black Male's Role in American Society.* San Francisco: Black Scholar.

———. 1998. "Stereotypes of Black Male Sexuality: The Facts behind the Myths." In *Men's Lives,* 4th ed., edited by Michael Kimmel and Michael Messner, 466–71. Boston: Allyn and Bacon.

Staples, Robert, and Leanor Boulin Johnson. 1993. *Black Families at the Crossroads: Challenges and Prospects.* San Francisco: Jossey-Bass.

Stoltenberg, John. 1999. "Christianity, Feminism, and the Manhood Crisis." In *Standing on the Promises: The Promise Keepers and the Revival of Manhood,* edited by Dane S. Claussen, 89–110. Cleveland, Ohio: Pilgrim.

Tasker, Fiona L., and Susan Golombok. 1997. *Growing up in a Lesbian Family: Effects on Child Development.* New York: Guilford.

Tocqueville, Alexis de. [1835] 1990. *Democracy in America.* Reprint, New York: Vintage Books.

U.S. House. 2002. *The Responsible Fatherhood Act of 2000.* 106th Cong., 2d session, H.R. 4671.

Walk, Stephan. 2000. "Moms, Sisters, and Ladies: Women Student Trainers in Men's Intercollegiate Sport." In *Masculinities, Gender Relations, and Sport,* edited by Jim McKay, Michael A. Messner, and Don Sabo, 31–46. Thousand Oaks, Calif.: Sage Publications.

Walton, Hanes, Jr. 1995. "Public Policy Responses to the Million Man March." *Black Scholar* 25 (4): 17–22.

Weeks, Jeffrey. 1985. *Sexuality and Its Discontents.* New York: Routledge.

Weiss, Jessica. 2000. *To Have and to Hold: Marriage, the Baby Boom, and Social Change.* Chicago: University of Chicago Press.

Welter, Barbara. 1966. "The Cult of True Womanhood, 1820–1860." *American Quarterly* (Summer): 151–74.

Whitehead, Barbara Dafoe. 1993. "Dan Quayle Was Right." *Atlantic Monthly,* April 1993, 47–84.

Williams, Fiona. 1998. "Troubled Masculinities in Social Policy Discourses: Fatherhood." In *Men, Gender Divisions, and Welfare,* edited by Jenny Popay, Jeff Hearn, and Jeanette Edwards, 63–97. London: Routledge.

Williams, Gwyneth, and Rhys Williams. 1995. "'All We Want Is Equality': Rhetorical Framing in the Father's Rights Movement." In *Images of Issues: Typifying Contemporary Social Problems,* edited by Joel Best, 191–212. New York: Aldine de Gruyter.

Wilson, William J. 1987. *The Truly Disadvantaged: The Inner City, the Underclass, and Public Policy.* Chicago: University of Chicago Press.

———. 1996. *When Work Disappears: The World of the New Urban Poor.* New York: Vintage Books.

Yacovone, Donald. 1990. "Abolitionists and the 'Language of Fraternal Love.'" In *Meanings for Manhood: Constructions of Masculinity in Victorian America,* edited by Mark C. Carnes and Clyde Griffen, 85–95. Chicago: University of Chicago Press.

Zinmeister, Karl. 1996. "Is Marriage Necessary for Good Fatherhood? A Fatherhood Today Symposium Discussion." *Fatherhood Today* 2 (1): 7–8.

INDEX

ANNA GAVANAS received her B.A. from Göteborg University in Sweden and her Ph.D. in social anthropology from Stockholm University. She has taught at Swedish universities and lectured widely in the United States and Europe on masculinity, the family, marriage, and sexual politics. While working on this book, she was part of the cross-disciplinary project "Fathers and the State," based at Stockholm University's Center for Comparative Gender Studies. In 2001 and 2002, she held a post-doctoral fellowship at the State University of New York in Stony Brook and is currently lecturing at Stockholm University and working on a comparative social politics project based at Leeds University.

The University of Illinois Press
is a founding member of the
Association of American University Presses.

Composed in 9/13 ITC Stone Serif
with ITC Stone Sans display
by Type One, LLC
for the University of Illinois Press
Manufactured by Thomson-Shore, Inc.

University of Illinois Press
1325 South Oak Street
Champaign, IL 61820-6903
www.press.uillinois.edu